Lincoln Public Library

May 1978

920
Hapgood

WITHDRAWN

The Hapgoods

Three Earnest Brothers

The Hapgoods

Three Earnest Brothers

Michael D. Marcaccio

University Press of Virginia

Charlottesville

920
HAPGOOD
Marcaccio,M.

May 1978

THE UNIVERSITY PRESS OF VIRGINIA
Copyright © 1977 by the Rector and Visitors
of the University of Virginia

First published 1977

Library of Congress Cataloging in Publication Data

Marcaccio, Michael D 1946–
   The Hapgoods.

   A revision of the author's thesis, University of Virginia.
   Bibliography: p.
   Includes index.
   1. Hapgood, Norman, 1868–1937. 2. Hapgood, Hutchins, 1869–1944. 3. Hapgood, William Powers. 4. Social reformers—United States—Biography. 5. Intellectuals—United States—Biography. I. Title.
   HN64.M32   1977   301.24'2'0922 [B]   77-5102   ISBN 0-8139-0693-8

Printed in the United States of America

To the memory of my mother
and
to my father

Contents

Preface ix
1. The Alton Years 1
2. From Harvard to the *Commercial Advertiser* 18
3. Literature and Journalism: The Drama 32
4. Journalism: Immigrants, Toughs, and Criminals 50
5. *Collier's:* The Early Years 73
6. The Journalism of Controversy 87
7. Wilson Partisan 116
8. From Labor to Emotional Crisis 141
9. The Columbia Conserve Company 165
10. Final Years 189
11. Conclusion 208

Notes 225
Selected Bibliography 240
Index 256

Preface

Why do a book on the Hapgood brothers? None was of absolutely first-rate importance; they were not pivotal figures in American history. They were nevertheless significant. Norman Hapgood was unquestionably an influential editor during the Progressive Era, and Hutchins, a fixture of prewar Greenwich Village and Provincetown, authored two noteworthy books. William, probably the least important of the three, directed an unusual venture in industrial democracy. One is also nudged toward a book on the Hapgoods by the relatively little scholarly attention they have received. Despite Norman Hapgood's stature, the only scholarly piece devoted entirely to him that this writer has been able to find is a sketch in the *Dictionary of American Biography*. Hutchins has not received much more than an able introduction to a reprint of one of his books. William's career at the Columbia Conserve Company has been analyzed in a dissertation.

Uneven coverage surely encourages some effort, but it does not necessarily sanction an attempt to examine all three at once. I began research on all three Hapgoods, as opposed to working on just one of them, because I felt that three would be better than one, but I also found that each of the Hapgoods, especially Hutchins, was far more understandable after one was familiar with his brothers. Too often biographers have virtually ignored their subject's siblings. That the Hapgoods spent most of their adult lives apart from one another in some respects highlights their similarities.

The Hapgoods furnish an interesting story. Through the range of their activities, Norman, Hutchins, and William Hapgood participated in much of the social and intellectual ferment of their time. Certainly, it is remarkable that a family produced three such prominent individuals. Nor were the Hapgoods' attainments limited to the three brothers. Their father was a strong character and, included among the wives of his three sons were a significant writer, a stage producer, and a leading translator of Russian. A family that contained such diverse personalities as Norman and Hutchins Hapgood, Charles and Emilie Bigelow Hapgood, William and Neith Boyce Hapgood was certainly rich in the human element. The Hapgoods were one of the more gifted and important American families of the last part of the nineteenth century and the early part of the twentieth, the sort that a eugenicist might have pointed to as a worthy example.

Although a biography probably delimits itself more easily than other types of historical study, there is still great opportunity to exercise selectivity. Throughout this study emphasis will be given to only certain aspects of the Hapgoods' careers. Norman Hapgood is a case in point. Although he often wrote about trusts and labor, his thought on these topics was too derivative, too characteristic of other progressives, to be of much consequence. His experience as a critic during a significant period in the history of American journalistic drama criticism and his service as a progressive editor, especially his development as a political activist, were particularly important. Similarly, more weight will be given to neglected episodes of his life. This accounts for some of the disparity between the coverage of the *Town Topics* and Ballinger affairs, for example. The treatment of Hutchins will concentrate on his evolution as a writer and his emotional turbulence.

I would like to express my appreciation to Professor Joseph F. Kett, who supervised this study as a dissertation and offered valuable criticisms when I tried to revise it into a book; Professor William H. Harbaugh, a reader when it was in the dissertation stage, and James P. McPherson, a fellow graduate student at the University of Virginia, who neither supervised, nor criticized, nor read, but did first suggest one of the Hapgood brothers as a possible dissertation topic. Professor Aileen S. Kraditor made many perceptive, useful, and appreciated suggestions.

I wish to express my appreciation to the many helpful librari-

Preface

ans I encountered while doing this study, particularly those at the Library of Congress; the Beinecke Rare Book and Manuscript Library, Yale University; the Lilly Library, Indiana University; and the School of Law Library, University of Louisville. I am grateful to Professor Charles Hapgood for permission to quote from unpublished material by his parents, Hutchins and Neith Boyce Hapgood, and his grandfather, Charles Hutchins Hapgood, in the Hutchins and Neith Boyce Hapgood Papers, Beinecke Rare Book and Manuscript Library, Hutchins's letters in the Mabel Dodge Luhan, Alfred Stieglitz, and Carl Van Vechten Papers, all in the Beinecke Rare Book and Manuscript Library, and the Lincoln Steffens Papers, Columbia University Libraries, and Neith's letters in the Mabel Dodge Luhan Papers, Beinecke Rare Book and Manuscript Library. I would like to thank David Hapgood for giving me permission to quote Norman Hapgood's letters in the Hutchins and Neith Boyce Hapgood Papers, Beinecke Rare Book and Manuscript Library, the Louis D. Brandeis Papers, School of Law Library, University of Louisville, the Breckinridge Long Papers, and the A. J. McKelway, William Allen White, and Woodrow Wilson Papers in the Library of Congress.

I would also like to thank the following: Columbia University Libraries for permission to quote the Hutchins Hapgood letters in the Lincoln Steffens Papers; Donald Gallup as Literary Trustee for Carl Van Vechten for permission to quote a letter by Hutchins Hapgood in the Carl Van Vechten Papers, Beinecke Rare Book and Manuscript Library; Florence McGill for permission to quote a John Cowles letter in the possession of Miriam DeWitt; Barta Monro for permission to quote William P. Hapgood and Powers Hapgood letters in the Powers Hapgood Papers, Lilly Library, the Columbia Conserve Company Papers in the Lilly Library, the William Hapgood letters in the Hutchins and Neith Boyce Hapgood Papers, Beinecke Rare Book and Manuscript Library, the Louis D. Brandeis Papers, School of Law Library, University of Louisville, and the Mary Hapgood letter in the Hutchins and Neith Boyce Hapgood Papers, Beinecke Rare Book and Manuscript Library; Georgia O'Keeffe for permission to quote from some of the Hutchins Hapgood letters in the Alfred Stieglitz Papers, Beinecke Rare Book and Manuscript Library; George Rublee II for permission to quote from a letter of George Rublee in the Louis D. Brandeis Papers, School of Law Library, University of Louisville; the School of Law Library, University of Louisville, for permission to quote from the Louis D. Brandeis Papers; Joseph Solomon for permission to quote from a letter by Leo Stein in the Hutchins and Neith Boyce Hapgood Papers, Beinecke Rare Book and Manuscript Library, and to use a photograph of Neith Boyce Hapgood by Carl Van Vechten in the possession of Miriam DeWitt; Mark Sullivan, Jr., for permission to quote Mark Sullivan letters in the Theodore Roosevelt and Finley Peter Dunne Papers in the Library of Congress and in the Louis D. Brandeis Papers, School of Law Library, University of Louisville; Patricia Waller for permission to quote a Howard D. Wheeler letter in the A. J. McKelway Papers, Library of Congress; Yale University as Assignee by Agreement with John Evans as Legatee under the Will of Mabel Dodge Luhan for permission to quote an unpublished letter by Mabel Dodge Luhan in the Hutchins and Neith Boyce Hapgood Papers, Beinecke Rare Book and Manuscript Library, and Yale University Library for permission to quote from a William Kent letter in the William Kent Family Papers.

I would also like to thank Hutchins Hapgood's surviving children, Miriam DeWitt, Beatrix Faust, and Professor Hapgood, and Norman's daughter, Elizabeth Backman, for allowing me to examine manuscripts in their possession and for discussing their parents and uncles with me. Elizabeth Backman, Miriam DeWitt, and Barta Monro also furnished useful photographs. I would also like to acknowledge the work of Mrs. Dody Giletti who typed the manuscript. Anyone seeking somewhat fuller documentation or a more detailed bibliography, particularly of the writings of Norman, Hutchins, and William P. Hapgood, might consult my 1972 dissertation.

CHAPTER 1

The Alton Years

I

CHARLES HUTCHINS HAPGOOD, determined and in his late thirties, had moved his family from Saint Louis to Alton, Illinois. This trip was not a heroic trek across gruelling stretches of plains and desert but a twenty-mile jaunt over a route well serviced by railroads and boats. The ease of the journey was deceptive. A businessman fallen on hard times, Hapgood was at a crossroads. Alton would most likely be his last chance to reestablish himself financially.

While he uprooted and moved to Alton, this somewhat melancholy figure undoubtedly reflected on his life. He was born in good circumstances at Petersham, a comfortable and intimate Massachusetts community, in 1836. The only son of a successful banker-politician and the grandson of a prominent merchant-politician, he could trace his ancestry to Shadrach Hapgood, who came to America in 1676. Charles Hapgood enrolled at Brown University in 1853. During his years there Presidents Wayland and Sears substantially liberalized the curriculum and lowered degree requirements. Hapgood joined Alpha Delta Phi, the college's oldest Greek-letter social fraternity. Several of the Brown students of that day went on to notable careers. Richard Olney and John Hay served as secretaries of state, and Hapgood's classmates included William A. Rogers, later a noted mathematician and scientist, and Alexander Thompson Britton, later an attorney, businessman, and authority on land laws. Hapgood, however, was very unhappy at Brown. He found its religious atmosphere oppressive.

After graduating in 1857, he studied law in an office for a year, then spent a year at the Harvard Law School. Anxious to leave New England, he went to Chicago, where several of his friends were and where he thought there would be more opportunity. Hapgood's legal career ended within five years, when a William Young persuaded him to go into partnership in the plow business. This venture was quite successful, and Hapgood was able to invest with a cousin in a second enterprise, a dry goods store. In 1867 Hapgood married Fanny Louise Powers, a vivacious woman with dark, curly hair, the daughter of a leading physician. While in Chicago, they had three sons: Norman in 1868, Hutchins in 1869, and William Powers in 1872. Norman's birth must have been memorable indeed—he weighed fourteen pounds and "the support of his mother's womb was broken down." Unfortunately, Hapgood's wholesale store was a casualty of the great Chicago fire of 1871, and within a year he moved the plow business to Saint Louis.[1]

He had been in Saint Louis only two years when fire destroyed his plow company, in which he had invested all his assets. Again the crackle of flames had mocked his Spartan efforts. He would later remark that "the Climax of my evil star was the burning of the St. Louis Factory." It was a tribute to his ability that two shrewd entrepreneurs were willing to take him as a partner in an undertaking in Alton. Hapgood had to work exceptionally hard to build up his concern. Norman ingenuously explained, "We have been playing Whist in the evening for some time. Mamma and Willie generally play against Harry [Hutchins] and I, as Papa is too tired to play excepting once in a while." By 1880 Charles Hapgood was employing several times more men than the average Illinois manufacturer of farm implements. After a few lean years the Hapgood Plow Company became a thumping success.[2]

The manufacture of agricultural implements was a major Illinois industry throughout the last three decades of the nineteenth century. Plow manufacturing entailed a moderate capital outlay and did not require a large plant. After the development of the soft-center steel plow in the late 1860s, technological innovation was minimal. In fact, Charles W. Marsh claimed in 1910 that the early soft-center steel plows "were about as effective as those now on the market." Although the industry became increasingly concentrated, it remained well adapted to the

The Alton Years

wherewithal of the small entrepreneur while Hapgood was active. The Hapgood Plow Company, noted for its riding and Hancock disc plows, sold chiefly to farmers in Kansas, Nebraska, and the Dakotas.[3]

Charles Hapgood bought out his partners and was a leading Alton businessman. By 1889, perhaps earlier, he was a member of the prestigious board of directors of the Alton Board of Trade. The red-brick factory on Henry Street beside the railroad tracks became a local fixture.

II

Alton, a hilly town nestled beside the Mississippi, had been a participant in the eye-gouging rough-and-tumble contest for railroads. Although it had once been a commercial rival of Saint Louis, by the 1870s Alton no longer retained such ambitions. Nevertheless, it did have good railroad connections, an interesting New England heritage, and a sizable number of Irish and some Germans. It had also been the scene of two historic events: the murder of the antislavery editor Elijah P. Lovejoy and the final Lincoln-Douglas debate.

Charles Hapgood's business triumphs secured a comfortable life for his children. His three sons enjoyed not only the characteristic pleasures of life in the small-town America of that time but also some activities that only the most affluent of their neighbors could afford. Spacious yards at both the Hapgoods' first residence and at their later, more prosperous one at 628 East Fifteenth Street became the stage for much of the young Hapgoods' activities. "We have such nice grounds to play in and so many pets to play with," Norman informed an aunt in 1878. Mack, the family horse, Hero, the dog, and the many cats—six at one time—were undoubtedly significant personalities to the Hapgood children. Since Norman was only a year older than Hutchins, they were playmates. Baseball, fights with the local boys, billiards, sledding, and swimming occupied much of their time. The stocky Hutchins was a better athlete than Norman, although Norman was a little less frightened by horses. Norman declared, "Harry can swim the best of the three, but Will and I float and dive and he dont." Age and ill health segregated "Billy" from his brothers. After his business was flourishing, Charles Hapgood sent his wife and children to summer in the East, usually at Rye Beach, New Hampshire, and often in the company of the Robert Todd Lincolns.[4] A daughter, Ruth, was born in 1880. She died of diphtheria when she was almost ten.

As the Hapgoods grew older, girls played a more prominent part in their lives. The recollections of both Norman and Hutchins—there is no reason to believe that William felt differently—attested to their high regard for the girls of Alton, whose sweetness and charm relieved the drab Alton scene. Norman, who did not exult in combative sports and was a bit of a prig—he found the boys vulgar—especially sought female companionship. He did more than his share of dancing, coed buggy-riding, and rowing. Hutchins's emotional problems made for a more cautious and fumbling approach to girls, but he, too, enjoyed their company by his early teens.

III

Charles Hapgood was the major influence on his young sons. Sober, industrious, and valuing honesty and perseverance, he was a man of commanding character who inspired awe in his sons. It is already obvious that he was an exceptional businessman. He later recalled suggestively, "It has been my good fortune to have during most of my business career much better financial credit than Capital justifies." He was a fierce moralist who took great pains to use his sons' youth for their moral training and at times seemed to be conducting a boot camp of morality. He bought his sons a billiard table and introduced them to wine, not to develop in them a taste for these pleasures, but "to inoculate" them against severe infections in later life. During his early days in Alton he often worried about providing for his children. After he had achieved financial security, he feared that wealth would corrupt them and make them soft.

The Alton Years

Charles Hapgood later concluded that the Chicago and Saint Louis fires "were the greatest blessings of my life." Had he remained in either of those large cities, his sons would not have been raised so simply. Norman, recalling with pride that his father had paid him fifteen dollars a week for office work, observed, "He would have thought it a sin to pay me more than I was worth." [5]

Charles Hapgood dropped his Unitarianism early in life. An agnostic, he had no use for preachers, refused to send his sons to Sunday school, and removed any fear of Hell from them. His lack of religion was less intellectual than temperamental, a reflection of his pessimism about the human situation. Hapgood imparted his agnosticism to his sons more through force of character than through argument, and his sons accepted his irreligion as they accepted his adherence to discipline and honesty. Keeping a hard, Puritan-like morality because the world was hard, he forcefully preached the chaste gospel of "self-denying skepticism" to his sons and provided muscular example to them.[6]

Charles Hapgood never suffered in Alton because of his irreligion. In fact, the Hapgoods have revealed only one instance of being discriminated against, and this was not in Alton. Charles Hapgood tried to get Norman into Phillips Exeter Academy. Mr. Hapgood became uncharacteristically outspoken about his lack of religion, and the Phillips Exeter official suggested that Norman go elsewhere. The lack of persecution was more indicative of Hapgood's discretion than of the town's liberality. Almost always diffident about his agnosticism, he was no propagandist. That his children possessed the truth was enough. A good example of his almost tiptoeing prudence about the religious issue was his handling of his children's Sunday recreation. Norman and Hutchins were forbidden to play baseball, billiards, or any other games that would displease those who passed by the Hapgood house on their way to church. Later he relented and allowed his sons to play the noisiest and most conspicuous games on Sundays.

Hapgood's morality, which was strict, conventional, and sincere, undoubtedly shielded him from the community's censure. His aloofness was a good defense against disapproval. Although an imperialistic atheism was not well received in the small-town Midwest of the late nineteenth century, mere lack of church membership was no special cause for alarm, for "less than half the adult population were formal church members." Hapgood's conduct was typical of many who deviated from the beliefs of the small town. As Lewis Atherton has written, "Such families generally dared not flaunt their heresies in the face of local society, especially since they relied on local people for their livelihood, but they did maintain a measure of individuality." [7]

Hapgood was a flinty character. In a photograph taken late in life, Charles Hapgood, a man with piercing blue eyes, looked prosperous, confident, experienced in the ways of the world, and strong willed. If one did not know better, one might expect him to be a robber baron. Preoccupied with business and his sons' moral education, he believed that the arts, especially their lighter forms, were superfluous. To say all this is not to claim that he was flat. Indeed, his letters and diary suggest a more complex individual than the Charles Hapgood who appeared in the autobiographies of his two oldest sons. The elder Hapgood had a sense of humor, an affection for mountains, chess, and baseball, and, at least before his marriage, an eye for pretty women. His diary and "Reminiscences" were clear, straightforward, perceptive, and revealed a man who could jest about his seasickness, meet the possibility of an Indian attack with the same stoicism with which he would confront business problems, and after discussing his legal education conclude, "It took mighty little law to enable a fellow to gain admission to the Bar in 1859." Impressed with the seriousness of parenthood, he probably appeared harsher to his sons than he actually was. As he later wrote, "I always give my children a dose of wormwood to antidote sweets." He protected his sons from what he regarded as the town's superstitions and grew more tolerant with age. Certainly he did bend his principles in later years to accommodate his feelings for his sons. He retired from business when he imagined that he could provide for his family comfortably,

The Alton Years

and during his brief retirement—William's business venture forced him back to the business wars—he alternated summers at Mount Desert, Maine, with winters in Rome. Charles Hapgood tempered moral fixity with moral flexibility, love of virtue with love of children.[8]

IV

There is no reason to suspect that young Norman suffered from major emotional maladjustment. He believed his childhood relatively normal for a boy of his day, unusual largely for his father's irreligion and especially strong character. Norman remembered what he thought were miracles and his first senses of sin. Humiliation by an Irish tough was an experience which "has returned to haunt me as often as any single episode in my life."[9]

Norman was very compatible with his father, dedicated his autobiography to him, and concluded, "I cannot wish for anybody a better father than I had." Norman felt that his father's most important gifts to him, besides a general honesty and integrity, were agnosticism and thrift. Temperamentally nonreligious, Norman considered agnosticism's impact on his life an unmitigated good. It hindered him only once—the Phillips Exeter Academy incident—and, retrospectively, he was glad that he had not attended that institution. Irreligion provided an intellectual cornucopia: "The enthusiasm in the family, the arguments, the free search for ideas, the lack of fear, had a value beyond my praise." Dissent from religious orthodoxy was the beginning of his intellectual curiosity, he maintained. His father's teachings about money stuck with him; a belief in thrift became a basic feeling.[10]

Norman internalized his father's values more than Hutchins did and probably more than William. Charles Hapgood suspected that Norman was his most promising son, and, at least until the Harvard years, Norman was surely stabler and a better student than Hutchins, and much healthier than William.

V

Hutchins's reminiscences were quite different from Norman's. Conceding "that the greater part of my boyish life must have been joyous," he portrayed his youth unflatteringly. Indeed, Hutchins stood in shrieking defiance of what Page Smith has called "the idyllic picture of town and boy." [11]

Intensely self-absorbed until he was six, Hutchins felt that his early years were grievous. Companionship could cool his burning self-preoccupation, but his extrasensitive nature precluded easy familiarity. Most of his friends were social misfits or outcasts. He found this type of person, whether a German gardener or an epileptic, approachable. Possessing a country-style serving of libido, Hutchins sought all experience, even pain. He recalled, "I loved to fight. I loved everything violently physical. Nothing was soft about me but my soul." His father was impressed by Hutchins's ability to withstand pain.[12]

Sexual problems complicated Hutchins's malaise. As a result of a "tight foreskin" his "sexual nature . . . became active very early, as early as seven or eight years [old]." Guilt feelings burst forth. His agony "might have been alleviated by a society not held in the grip of a destructive Puritanism," he wrote later. "If I had known, before I knew hardly anything, that I was not a peculiarly unnatural and sinful being, it would have spared me intense suffering and years of ill-health." Ironically, one goal of Victorian reticence was the prevention of masturbation.[13]

Hutchins Hapgood put great stock in his childhood. Much of his later debauchery and his "viciousness," he speculated in his autobiography, *A Victorian in the Modern World,*

can be completely explained I think by the circumstances of my early life. A trivial circumstance was my tight foreskin; but a far deeper cause was that I found a social environment unadapted to the felicitous unfolding of my nature. . . . I was I think naturally virtuous, kindly, and social; but through no fault of anyone, my harmless creative impulses were not developed by circumstance.[14]

Although Hutchins undoubtedly was anguished, his sexual emphasis must be viewed with caution. He admitted that when

The Alton Years

he was eight, he had already been a problem in school for two years and was "apparently incapable of learning anything at all." [15] In view of his later intellectual accomplishments, his lack of achievement probably indicated a severe personality problem antedating his sexual awakening.

Hutchins's discussion, in his autobiography, of the bearing of his early sex life upon his character was curious. At one point he made a full-throated claim for the importance of his sexual difficulties:

My painful love of solitude, . . . my sensibilities, my religious instincts, and . . . all the intense though vague excitement of my youth . . . would have been impossible, at least would have assumed quite another shape, had it not been for my sexual nature. . . . If a slight surgical operation had been performed [on his foreskin], it is not impossible that the whole course of my life would have been changed.[16]

Yet just before this statement he had argued that his "natural passion for solitude, or perhaps for the cosmic, . . . [and] the character of my sexual life . . . [were] probably not related in the chain of cause and effect but equally a manifestation of my deeper self." Later in his autobiography he called his foreskin difficulty "trivial" and blamed the conflict between his nature and society.[17] He vacillated because he was using the foreskin problem to display vividly the repressive aspects of society, a display he was anxious to make. What could be more stupid or cruel than letting this young boy suffer because of something that was quickly and completely remediable? Sexual taboos stopped him not only from getting help but from being cured. He struck a blow against society in general and against its sexual mores in particular. Overdramatization bred part of his autobiography's muddleheadedness about the influence of his early sex life.

Whether society should be greatly blamed for his emotional dislocations, which probably were evident by the time he was six, is debatable. When he blandly sighed that the trials of his youth were "no fault of anyone," he was less than persuasive. There definitely was someone, who, from the logic of his analysis, should have been censured. Hutchins Hapgood argued that certain imaginative outlets, such as religion, fairy tales, and dancing, could have alleviated his condition. These were denied him, not by society, but by his father. Throughout his autobiography Hutchins did not display his usual bluntness when discussing his father. Hutchins did criticize him, but often in muffled tones instead of loud ones. Although on the whole Hutchins was favorable to his father, he sensed that Charles Hapgood was often at the root of his difficulties.

Hutchins treated his relationship with his father too glibly in one further instance. During Hutchins's youth his father believed that Hutchins had little promise. Hutchins asserted that the consequent absence of some paternal pressures allowed him a nice freedom. One has only to recall his dreams about a contemptuous "Presence," and "an external invisible Reproach," and his lifelong inferiority complex, which seemed related to his father's early lack of confidence in him, to doubt such an amiable solution.[18]

Although Norman and Hutchins were close companions, there was an undercurrent of resentment on Hutchins's part. Hutchins, breathless with emotion and averse to discipline, was piqued by Norman's self-possession. Hutchins saw himself as an outcast, a compulsive outlaw, who frequently broke rules, more often absentmindedly than intentionally. Norman, seemingly well adjusted to the dictates of his parents and of society, often made sure that Hutchins stayed in line. Norman became to Hutchins a concrete, proximate embodiment of his father's values. Hutchins thought Norman a cardboard figure, well constructed to fit smoothly with the system. Norman was undoubtedly the more conventional, but he also had difficulty with the school system, graduating only eighth in a high school class of fifteen. Young Norman's increasing cultural and literary interests also cast doubt on Hutchins's unidimensional portrait.

Hutchins was sounder as a teenager than as a child. Happily, "I began to be more at ease. My periods of depression and fear grew less. This was due partly to a slackening of the physical cause, and also I think to the growth in me of the love of general ideas." His parents began to appreciate his potential.[19]

VI

William, unlike his brothers, did not leave an autobiography, but his brothers have written enough about him to permit a few observations. Youth, poor health, and different interests kept him from sharing the comradeship of his older brothers. William was so sickly that it was feared he would not live to manhood. His parents, especially his mother, sheltered him and were more tolerant of his misdemeanors than they were of his brothers'. Not especially interested in violent sports, William preferred to raise chickens. Not unexpectedly, his brothers charged that William was overprotected and eagerly formed alliances to harass their younger brother. Hutchins recalled, "How Norman and I used to plague Billy because of the chickens. Whenever they had one for a meal, Norman & I shouted as we saw them on the table 'Chickee, Chickee, Chickee' & clucked or crowed and maintained that Mother had chicken so often so that Billy Could get rich." Hutchins must have felt crushed between his brothers. Norman obeyed without difficulty; William defied without punishment. Hutchins contended that William developed his great self-confidence during youth.[20]

VII

The Hapgood brothers were formally educated by the Alton public schools. Norman and Hutchins disliked them, and neither boy did very well nor learned very much. Their significant intellectual development took place at home. Their father provided them with books and took a liberal attitude toward their reading. The company of Everett W. Pattison, a prominent Missouri lawyer, and Dr. William A. Haskell, the humane family physician and later a business associate of the Hapgoods, provided the whole family with stimulating conversation. Occasionally, notables such as the politician Schuyler Colfax and John Fiske, the philosopher and historian, a cousin, visited.

All of this was important, but their mother furnished the Hapgood boys with their chief intellectual sustenance. Fanny

Hapgood was a cheerful person, "completely old-fashioned," "perfectly unselfish," a hard-working, uncomplaining companion to her husband during his trying years. A granddaughter remembered her as a small, friendly woman, who wore her hair in a bun and was fond of Italian silver jewelry, which often "clinked" as she moved about. Fanny loved gardening and delighted in the intricacies of shopping for food. During the Chicago fire she had hurriedly packed valuables into sheets, pillowcases, and bedspreads for evacuation from the house so effectively that her husband wrote admiringly, "About the only transferable things of value she overlooked were the Billiard Balls." [21]

Fanny Hapgood carried the characteristic cultural baggage of a woman of her status—skill in music, painting, and French. That she took upon herself the education of her children was no surprise—culture was considered to be largely the province of women in the nineteenth-century Middle West. Her success was remarkable. Her love for Shakespeare helped her greatly. Norman, Hutchins, and William warmly recalled their mother reading Shakespeare to them in the parlor in the evening. As they grew older, the children had Shakespearean contests, with celery as a prize. Even their very young sister, Ruth, walked about the house spouting garbled Elizabethan verse. Of their education in Shakespeare, Hutchins believed, and Norman agreed, "the value . . . can hardly be overestimated." Fanny Hapgood was no doubt responsible for both Norman and Hutchins's lifelong interest in the theater. Hutchins also found Shakespeare therapeutic, one of the few imaginative outlets available to him.[22]

One other person performed commendable intellectual service for the Hapgoods in Alton. Although Norman had expressed interest in attending college, he was not prepared when he graduated from high school. His father hired a private tutor, a Miss Ferguson. She taught Norman for three years, Hutchins for two, and William for one. Norman found this recent college graduate a strange sight, "the first young person I had met who actually liked to study." The arrangement between teacher and student was flexible. They met for an hour or two a day. The

Charles Hapgood c. 1910. (Courtesy of Elizabeth Backman.)

Fanny Hapgood c. 1870. (Courtesy of Elizabeth Backman.)

rest of the time was spent in independent work. All three brothers took noteworthy intellectual strides under her guidance. Hutchins brought a newfound seriousness to his work and also a desire for the change of atmosphere that college would bring.[23]

VIII

Did anything in the Hapgood brothers' Alton years foreshadow their later political outlook? Their youthful experience does not lend itself to an easy determinism on this point. Hutchins Hapgood observed that his father was "the first man I ever heard talk sympathetically about socialism, the ultimate advent of which he predicted and would have welcomed." One suspects that Charles Hapgood uttered these sentiments in moments of frustration, and Hutchins admitted that his father articulated these opinions "very mildly." As Hutchins correctly perceived, his father's political legacy to his sons was largely a distrust of wealth.[24] Certainly the Puritan suspicion of riches, a fostering of nonmonetary values, religious skepticism, and a receptiveness to ideas form a more credible background to the sons' later political activities than an occasional flicker of radicalism in a father who was not especially interested in politics. Hutchins's and Norman's references to their father's political heterodoxy, or rather to occasionally expressed heterodox beliefs, ring of something that took on much importance only in retrospect. There is no evidence that they held serious reformist or radical opinions when they entered Harvard. Although they left Alton with nothing that compelled them to be on the political left, they subscribed to certain opinions and had an openness that at least kept alive the option of a career on the left.

IX

The Hapgood family, defined broadly, had a significant impact on Norman, Hutchins, and William. Despite the general rarity of a college degree, the family had traditionallly esteemed education and culture and had college graduates in several generations. Charles and Fanny Hapgood encouraged their sons' intellectual development, but other relatives, including a grandmother and a couple of aunts, also helped. Indeed, the active cultural concern of the family was undoubtedly of greater importance to the creation of a stimulating environment than the irreligion Norman Hapgood made such claims for. Even if they had been raised as Unitarians, the young Hapgoods' intellectual development would probably have been about the same.

Not only their father but their forebears on both sides of the family provided Norman, Hutchins, and William with examples of success. Growing up in an atmosphere where the men had a tradition of accomplishment could hardly fail to build the children's confidence in tackling a variety of problems. Seldom employing physical punishment, Charles Hapgood refused to discipline his children unless he was certain that they had intentionally committed a wrong. Charles and Fanny Hapgood relied on the children's internalization of their values and guilt feelings to bring compliance. Although these practices might have had drawbacks, they probably encouraged a sense of responsibility in the Hapgood boys. The family had a long tradition of noblesse oblige. Several Hapgoods had engaged in public service, and Seth, Charles's father, died after helping a widow with her business affairs.

Emotional ties appear to have been deep. One might note the great love of Charles for his father and Fanny's intense grief at the loss of her daughter. The Hapgood family coalesced during times of tragedy. It was well known that Ruth's death alleviated the tension between Fanny and her mother-in-law and sister-in-law. The family cohered less in the sense of living together than in emotional ties and in vigorously aiding its members to rise in the world. Seth Hapgood had not prevented Charles from moving to Chicago—though he undoubtedly preferred that his son stay in New England. Charles, in turn, never limited his sons to Alton. The wealth and connections of the family were undoubtedly very important ingredients in the success of the Hapgood brothers. Charles and Fanny Hapgood were able to offer

Norman Hapgood c. 1877. (Courtesy of Elizabeth Backman.)

Hutchins Hapgood c. 1890. (Courtesy of Elizabeth Backman.)

William P. Hapgood c. 1882. (Courtesy of Elizabeth Backman.)

their sons a number of options, and none of their children had to drop out of school to help support the family. Although many families had as much or more money and advantages than the Hapgoods, the children of few equalled or surpassed the attainments of Norman, Hutchins, and William Hapgood.

CHAPTER 2

From Harvard to the *Commercial Advertiser*

I

THE HARVARD YEARS were momentous for the Hapgoods. While under the guidance of a private tutor, Norman, Hutchins, and William had exhibited a sharpened intellectual awareness, but in retrospect this awakening seems a mere prelude to the flowering of their Harvard days. Whatever cultural resources could be mustered in Alton—and Charles and Fanny Hapgood were eager that their sons should enjoy the best—could not compare with the variety and richness of those awaiting them in Cambridge. After they had been to Harvard, Alton appeared too small and too barren to satisfy their new tastes and aspirations.

Perhaps the most conspicuous feature of the Harvard of the 1880s and 1890s was the elective system implemented by President Charles W. Eliot. Although the elective system was regarded as radical in many circles, it was partly responsible for the three Hapgood boys' entering Harvard. Charles Hapgood had granted Norman a free choice of colleges; that is, he could go anywhere but to Brown, which Mr. Hapgood still disliked. Norman, struck by the variety of courses available at Harvard, decided to prepare for admission, and enrolled in the fall of 1886 as a freshman. Hutchins, influenced by his brother's favorable experience, entered Harvard in the fall of 1889 as a sophomore—he had spent one miserable year at the University of Michigan. In 1890 William joined his brothers at Harvard.

Harvard offered much more than a flexible curriculum. It had a fine faculty, at once scholarly and inspiring to many undergraduates. William James was one of the most brilliant of the teachers, and both Norman and Hutchins (William did not leave any accounts of these years) were much influenced by him. To Norman, James remained "the foremost philosopher of his time" and "the most important psychologist in American his-

From Harvard to the Commercial Advertiser

tory." Norman was captivated by James's delightful unpretentiousness; and, more significantly, James's pluralism, his scrambling approach to reality, became a permanent and essential part of Norman's beliefs. Hutchins, also an admirer of James, though less so than Norman, was intrigued by James's concept of the "stream of thought." Of course, other faculty members and administrators impressed the Hapgoods. Philip Littell recalled that in Josiah Royce's course in logic, Norman "looked amused. You would have guessed he found the detection of fallacy about the most amusing game he had ever played, and you would have been right. In those days he liked logic quite as well as baseball." President Eliot, who struck Norman Hapgood as a giant of almost the same magnitude as James, became a lifelong friend. Norman particularly remembered George Santayana, then an instructor; Professors Ferdinand Bocher, under whom he studied French literature; Francis J. Child, who taught a course on Shakespeare that pleased others less than it did Hapgood; and Charles Eliot Norton, who exasperated him. Hutchins was particularly fond of Santayana and C. C. Everett.[1]

Norman declared in 1930, "If there could be a place intellectually more attractive than Harvard University toward the end of the Nineteenth Century, my imagination does not give it form." Both Norman and Hutchins realized that it was not the particulars of their studies as much as the atmosphere of questioning, doubt, and searching that made Harvard so electric to its more concerned students. Most professors did not merely offer their material, but presented it in a way that vividly impressed their students. The Hapgoods felt the exhilaration of being on a freewheeling intellectual treasure hunt with the finest guides and the best companions, in the most hospitable place, and for the most worthy prizes.[2]

II

Classwork, no matter how stimulating, was only a part of the Harvard student's life. Indeed, Harvard required much less course-related study than a comparable institution would today.

At least in the circles in which Norman and Hutchins roamed, this did not result in a determination to yield the least possible effort to intellectual demands. Activities outside the classroom broadened and complemented the Hapgoods' formal intellectual pursuits. Theatergoing was a favorite extracurricular pleasure. Another was companionship with the students at the Harvard Annex (later Radcliffe College).

Informal contact with other Harvard students and some of the younger faculty members was even more important to the Hapgoods' development. Norman was particularly close to his classmate Louis H. Dow, later professor of French at Dartmouth College. Norman and Hutchins were very good friends of Robert Morss Lovett and knew just about all the Harvard students with strong literary interests, including William Vaughn Moody, Robert Herrick, Mark A. De Wolfe Howe, Philip Littell, and Justus Sheffield. Since there was at least one Hapgood at Harvard from the fall of 1866, when Norman entered, until the spring of 1894, when William graduated, the brothers were able to draw from a large pool of acquaintants and multiply each other's friendships. After the death of their daughter, Ruth, in 1890, Charles and Fanny Hapgood moved from Alton to Cambridge. They stayed for about a year and a half, were prominent in Cambridge, and enriched their sons' social life. The two older Hapgood brothers established warm relations with faculty members Santayana and George P. Baker, subsequently famous for his work in the Yale drama department. Many of these associations with students and teachers lasted a lifetime, and some later proved useful.

Although they shunned the more socially oriented club life, Norman and Hutchins were active in the Mermaid Club and the Laodicean Club. The Mermaid Club was a small, informal group devoted to the theater. Among the other members were Baker, Santayana, Herrick, Henry Taylor Parker, Jefferson B. Fletcher, Howe, and George Rice Carpenter. Unlike the Mermaid Club the Laodicean Club was an expression not of a particular interest but of a mood, an attitude, a style. This notable organization was an embodiment of "Harvard indifference" pushed to farce. Impressed by the reputed apathy of the Christian Church in ancient Laodicea, the club served bland refreshments, and under the watchful eyes of its pope, Santayana, members such as the Hapgoods, Lovett, and Arthur S. Hayes exercised the arts of noncommittal expression to a perfection that would have been the envy of many a Gilded Age politician. Lest the very belief in indifference smash the carefully built wall of insouciance, Robert Morss Lovett recalled, "it was the rule that if at any meeting a quorum should be present the club should *ipso facto* cease to exist. As a result, the second meeting was the last." [3]

III

The *Harvard Monthly* was the focus of Norman's extracurricular energies. It frequently published pieces by him, and at times he was an editor and editor in chief. Although Hutchins never held an official position with the *Monthly,* he wrote a few articles and was intimately associated with many of its editors and writers. William served as a business manager for a time, but it is uncertain whether he shared his brothers' literary enthusiasms. The *Monthly* suggested Norman and Hutchins Hapgood's intellectual milieu at Harvard.

The *Monthly,* which had been founded in 1885 largely under the guidance of Alanson Bigelow Houghton, its first editor in chief, announced in its first issue, "We purpose to publish a magazine which shall contain the best literary work done here at Harvard, and represent the strongest and soberest undergraduate thought." Hoping to tap the increased interest in English composition at Harvard, it sought work not only from undergraduates but from students in other parts of the university, faculty, and alumni.[4]

The *Monthly* was preoccupied with literary matters, but it devoted increasing attention to educational, especially to Harvard educational, issues. Although it was proud of Harvard, it did not hesitate to suggest and criticize, and sought to mediate between students, faculty, alumni, and administrators. In keeping with the outlook of its contributors, concern for social problems was displayed only occasionally, often by a passing awareness of the settlement movement.

In his autobiography Norman Hapgood declared, "I have no hesitation in saying there has never been in America an undergraduate publication to approach it." This was the recollection of an old partisan, but there was some merit to his claim. Among those associated with the *Monthly* of that time were Moody and Lovett (whom Hapgood had recruited), Baker, Santayana, Bernard Berenson, Bliss Carman, Herrick, Howe, Trumbull Stickney, and Owen Wister. Of course, individuals who later became famous did not necessarily produce outstanding work earlier in their careers. For example, Moody's college verses, which the *Monthly* so eagerly published, were among his worst.[5] Whether the *Monthly* was nearly so good as Hapgood believed was less important than that it had the allegiance and helped shape the outlook of many of the alert minds of the day.

It directed its pitch at "the serious men." Thomas W. Lamont recalled that the editors used to meet in the editor in chief's room and discuss profound subjects and munch Baker's sweet chocolate. Lamont observed, "During the first few months I dared say hardly a word: I felt that I was sitting unworthily in a group of great, wise, and witty men." Leslie W. Hopkinson recalled that when Hapgood was editor "we dreaded above all things to say or write anything that might strike him as banal." The *Monthly* considered the *Harvard Advocate,* its chief rival, contemptible, and the *Crimson,* inferior. Norman reminisced to the playwright Percy MacKaye, "We felt that for anybody worthy of the *Monthly* to be on the *Advocate* would be a sin against literature." [6]

An editorial in 1888 spoke the *Monthly*'s mind unblushingly. The editorial argued that three classes of students existed at Harvard. To the first type matters of the intellect seemed alien and even threatening. The second group comprised those of moderate aspirations and attainments, the famous " 'C' men." The last and best were those who studied intensely, for long hours, and on schedule. Their determination was commendable, but "their work is relatively blind, and is, therefore, impotent for culture." Although these classes encompassed virtually all Harvard men, there was a saving remnant who

form the barrier to the ever-rising tide of ignorance and materialism, rising alike in the college and in the nation. Their courses are chosen that they may gain in breadth of thought and mental training; their work is done well, because they are fond of it and are loath to do anything unworthily. But their work does not absorb all their intellectual vigor. They read broadly and thoughtfully; they strive to know the best that the arts can give them. . . . More than all else, their work and their lives are dominated by an ideal. And this ideal we call culture —the ideal that seeks ever for knowledge, but recognizes only such knowledge as is true, as is broad, as is human, as is vital.[7]

This was the goal of the *Monthly:* to combine the "grind's" sheer drive and, perhaps, some of the style and flair of the " 'C' man," and yet to improve this hybrid with a discriminating seriousness and breadth found nowhere else. This perspective created some problems. Hutchins quipped that Lovett "was the only one of the brilliant young men I knew at Harvard who had an humble spirit." The *Monthly*'s pretensions were not always well received in other quarters of the Harvard community, and in asking for more contributions, the *Monthly* found it necessary to deny that it "lived in an atmosphere of thin literary priggishness."[8]

Harvard refined Norman and Hutchins Hapgood's outlook. If their father's strong moralistic impulse had made them earnest in a general way, his two oldest sons increasingly added literary and cultural embellishments. Despite Norman's analytical bent and his desire not to be caught displaying a sophomore's emotions, his *Harvard Monthly* articles, indeed, his association with that magazine, often suggested great enthusiasm seeking a commitment, a commitment, that is, consonant with good taste. Norman was deeply impressed by the Harvard concern for culture, which in turn was influenced by the English critic Matthew Arnold. Arnold's ascription of high importance to the role of the intellectual and the critic particularly appealed to him. In the concern for standing for the best against a vulgar society, Norman found a challenge that satisfied his need for constant testing, both internal and external. Although Hutchins shared some of his brother's seriousness, he was more inclined to give his earnestness a romantic cast. Despite the much-talked-about Laodicean atmosphere, Harvard was, after all, a hotbed of mugwumpery; and many on the faculty, including William James and Charles Eliot Norton, showed a noticeable moral concern in their teaching. Blake Nevius has correctly contended that a highly developed sense of "moral earnestness" lurked beneath Harvard indifference.[9]

IV

The Hapgoods' years at Harvard were happy, active, and productive. Norman and Hutchins excelled academically. Norman made Phi Beta Kappa and the O. K. Literary Club and graduated with honors in modern literature and honorable mention in English, English composition, French, and philosophy. Hutchins also made Phi Beta Kappa and O. K., graduated with honors in French and philosophy, and presented a commencement part. Norman proved his loyalty to the *Monthly*'s cult of breadth by belonging to La Conférence Française, the Deutscher Verein, the English Club, the Philosophical Club, and the Natural History Society. Hutchins, participating less in organizations than Norman, belonged to the Browning Club. All of this was in addition to the Hapgoods' memberships in the Laodicean and Mermaid clubs. William did not graduate Phi Beta Kappa, but he did earn the very difficult second-year honors in mathematics. He also distinguished himself in a way his brothers had not; the once sickly William became an athlete of some note. He was an outstanding sailor and a substitute, but a letterman, on the very successful Harvard baseball team of 1894. Despite all the honors and activities, the two older brothers lacked a clear vocation. William, who went to work for the wholesale grocery Franklin MacVeagh and Company, in Chicago, was the only Hapgood to go directly into the line of work in which he was to spend a significant part of his life.

Norman and Hutchins experienced false starts before they entered journalism.

Norman desired a literary career, but he feared that it would be unremunerative, and he was reluctant to be dependent on his parents. A trip to Europe after his junior year toughened his resolve to escape the business career waiting for him in Alton. Inspired by the works of Mérimée and Henry James, he told his father during his senior year that he would not join the Hapgood Plow Company after graduation. Norman must have dreaded life in Alton, which could only have seemed horribly constricting, the very antithesis of Harvard. Looking back on his youth, Fred Waters, the hero of one of Hapgood's short stories, probably echoed Norman's emotions: "There were other simple country folk, male and female, who attracted me then, but who have passed entirely from my life. I have grown so far beyond them that I can scarcely understand, when I go home, how I could ever have been so wrapped up in them; though when I don't see them, when I merely call up the times as they were, ten years ago, the dream all comes back." [10]

Norman's decision to enroll in the Harvard Law School was a solution to, or rather a postponement of, his dilemma. Charles Hapgood, who had been restless in his youth, sympathized with Norman's troubles, and perhaps hoped that law school would be a convenient halfway house to the Hapgood Plow Company for his son. Norman's reluctance to enter the world beyond Cambridge was not unusual. Barrett Wendell thought such a disposition common and rooted in the often excessive self-criticism of the more serious Harvard undergraduates. Norman aired his fears in "Social Stages," a fictional statement of a young man's beliefs and feelings at twenty-one and twenty-five. At twenty-one the young fellow had been sensitive, uneasy, moralistic, individualistic, and distrustful of society's orientation toward success and insistent practicality. At twenty-five he was a man of affairs, well in tune with society, and wore comfortably the standardized garments of optimism and self-confidence.[11] Norman Hapgood surely worried that he might mimic his twenty-five-year-old, but he was probably more concerned that failure to conform to a society of twenty-five-year-olds would subject him to constant pressures and result in a growing alienation.

Outwardly, Norman's career at the Law School was successful. He was an editor of the *Harvard Law Review* and graduated cum laude with an A.M. (given for exceptional work) besides the LL.B. Despite some stimulating courses, especially James Bradley Thayer's on evidence, Hapgood's interest in the law waned and his thoughts turned increasingly to literature. When he left law school, the old crisis returned. Indeed, the photograph of the graduating class showed Norman sitting, hands on his knee, looking to his right with preoccupation, perhaps of the world ahead. After law school he worked for the law firm of Williams, Holt and Wheeler in Chicago and pursued his literary interests in his spare time and occasionally on the job. This proved an unsatisfactory arrangement. When in 1894 he wrote of Harvard as "where the mind's light is the purest in America," it was not merely a reaffirmation of his love for Harvard but a cry of despair from Chicago. He induced a member of the firm with connections in the publishing business to help him get into journalism and was offered a job on the *Chicago Evening Post* at "five dollars a week as a general assignment reporter, and with no hesitation I seized the offer." His father was disappointed, but journalism seemed a more fit vehicle for his son's aspirations; Norman reported from the *Chicago Evening Post*, "I like it thus far much better than I did the law." [12]

Hutchins's emotional condition improved at Harvard. In Alton he had believed that he was a renegade, but at Harvard he found that his supposed deviance was really a healthy and artistic sensitivity, which had increased his fitness for Harvard life. This reinterpretation of his early life, heavily influenced by romanticism, was one of the most important developments of his college years. It contributed to his emotional stability in the short run and influenced his journalism, but in the long run it helped to make him indecisive in confronting his personality problems and tied him to preoccupations that would often prove futile. He could not forget his romantic vocabulary. Certified by personal experience, which was always so vital to him, many of these ideas would appear to be permanently valid.

After earning his A.B. in 1892, Hutchins thought of going to law school but instead attended the graduate school for a year. He took courses in modern literature and fine arts and was an assistant in forensics. Avowedly for educational reasons, but actually for medical ones, his father urged him to study in Germany. Hutchins sailed for Europe, and on board met the intense, young Arthur F. Bentley, later an eminent political scientist, who was also going to the University of Berlin. Traveling alone through France, Hapgood was awakened to the delights of breakfast and impressed by the French openness about sex. Hiking across Burgundy, he developed a taste for that province's wine and was relieved of his virginity by the wife of an innkeeper. In Switzerland he realized that "it was as if the two former periods of my life had combined, the sensuousness of the child, without the harassing ignorance, and the thoughtfulness of the student, combined with physical excitement." [13]

Reaching Berlin in time to enroll in the university, Hapgood studied sociology under Georg Simmel, disliked German physiological psychology, and departed for the University of Strassburg to hear Wilhelm Windelband on Hegel. At Berlin a life of calculated debauchery fascinated him more than his course work. He concentrated on German beer and the companionship of girls of a sort who were "simple, honest, domestic, and physical." [14]

Continuing ill health induced Hapgood to take a world tour, including visits to Japan, India, Egypt, Italy, and Holland, accompanied part of the way by Leo Stein—Gertrude's brother—and Fred Stein, their cousin. After he had completed his travels, he returned to Harvard as a graduate student and as an assistant in English and received his A.M. in 1897.

After Europe, Harvard was just not the same. But it was Hapgood who had changed. His European experiences with drink, sex, the lower classes, and stimulating friends—an unmistakable prologue to his life-style for the next half-century—made Harvard seem bland. One might ask why Hapgood first plunged into low life in Europe and not in Boston. Part of the answer was no doubt the absence of family supervision in Europe, but more importantly Hapgood was searching for style, not mere dissipation, and this was most available in Europe, not in Boston, with its lack of bohemian life in the 1890s. Although Norman's European travels had reinforced his allegiance to Harvard life, Hutchins's adventures made him itch to encounter life beyond the Yard. Hints of Hutchins's restlessness at Harvard can be discerned in a passage of an address presented at commencement in 1892 and later published in the *Monthly*. Speaking approvingly of both the child and the artist, he noted: "They both stand expectant, with all their mental pores open, eager for impressions, and beyond those impressions they do not care to go; they do not care for moral significance, for practical value. They do not care for future ends, for present experience is so entrancing that it is an end in itself." [15] This passage attacked not only overbearing practicality but overanalysis. This disquiet intensified in Berlin, where a language barrier, some uninspiring courses, and ready chances for debauchery made more formal education seem less important than it had in his undergraduate days.

Hutchins Hapgood taught in the summer session at the University of Chicago in 1897 and was to assume an instructorship at Harvard in the autumn, but a trip to New York ended his Harvard career. The city was so fascinating and Norman's work for the *New York Commercial Advertiser* seemed so promising that Hutchins quit Harvard and joined the staff. Teaching had proved only a little more enticing for him than the law had for Norman.

V

The *Chicago Evening Post,* the first paper that Norman Hapgood worked for, was not one of Chicago's most prosperous journals, but it was a cut above the average American daily. Finley Peter Dunne, who later played a crucial role in Hapgood's career, was the chief editorial writer. Norman left the *Post* after a few months to take a position on the *Milwaukee Sentinel,* which he had secured through his Harvard friend George Rublee, the editor's son. Hapgood did well on the *Sentinel,* wrote some drama reviews, and managed to save enough money to stake a try at New York journalism.

New York was the hub of American journalism. The latest mechanical and technological improvements in newspaper publishing were quickly adopted by New York's frenetically competitive papers. New York's dailies were noted for their influence as well as for their size; the *Herald, Sun, Evening Post, World, Tribune,* and *Times* were powers in their own right.

It was often difficult to enter New York journalism. When the eager aspirants, showing the proper blend of awe, humility, determination, and sense of destiny, called at the editor's office to seek employment, they would probably run into what Charles Edward Russell met in the 1880s: a thoroughly unsentimental office boy "that regarded us with manifest contempt and then said, out of one side of his mouth, 'Well, whadda youse want?' " [16] Editors proved even less impressed.

The most common way to thaw this indifference, according to most givers of advice, was to submit a few articles to the editor. If they were good, one might get a tryout and eventually a regular position. Norman Hapgood was a close friend of George Rice Carpenter, who had been a young faculty member during Norman's Harvard days and was now teaching at Columbia. Through Carpenter's brother-in-law, Sherwood Seymour, business manager of the *New York Evening Post,* Hapgood was given a chance on that paper.

The *Evening Post,* one of the most prestigious journals in the United States, was probably the paper that young newspapermen with literary ambitions would most like to work for. Its reputation was awesome—young Frederic C. Howe, a Johns Hopkins Ph.D., was so impressed by the *Post*'s renown that he was too intimidated to ask for employment.[17]

The chief glory of the *Post* was its editor, Edwin L. Godkin, a "stern-looking graybeard" and "the only New York editor whom Harvard has honored with the title of LL.D." Godkin, editor of the weekly *Nation* as well as of the *Post,* wrote probably the most influential editorials in the land. Although both publications had relatively small circulations, Godkin's opinions were carefully watched by other journalists and opinion-makers. Godkin was also a political beacon to the two men Norman had most admired at Harvard, Charles W. Eliot and William James.[18]

During his service on the *Post*, Norman Hapgood gradually became a crack reporter. He began at space rates—that is, he was paid in direct proportion to the number of his columns the paper printed—but later was put on salary and made a regular. Although "by nature a good reporter of matters human and literary," he was slow to develop a knack for the more rough-and-tumble journalism, and more than six months passed between his amateurish, fumbling coverage of the collapse of the Ireland Building on August 8, 1895, and his fine handling of the Salvation Army controversy. Nevertheless, he early struck Lincoln Steffens, a very professional fellow reporter, as "a good writer," remarkable for "mental repose and thoroughness . . . with a freedom from limiting reverence." By the spring of 1896 Norman had added a lust for combat, a delight in the contest, to his other assets. According to several accounts, he became one of the best reporters on the *Post*.[19]

Success did not breed complacency. As Norman grew sure of his skills, he sought to experiment and to assume more responsibility, but Godkin, whose disregard for reporters was well known, thwarted him. Others on the staff were offended by Godkin's attitude. The city editor, H. J. Wright, "a lean, black-mustached Scot," and Steffens had been trying, largely unsuccessfully, to expand the *Post*'s coverage of police and crime news and the picturesque. Wright and Seymour quit and bought the *Commercial Advertiser*. Norman Hapgood, several others, and later Steffens jumped to the *Commercial*. When Oswald Garrison Villard joined the *Post* soon after Hapgood left, he found the editors "in a blue funk" although the *Post* regained its balance quickly.[20]

The *Commercial Advertiser*, New York's oldest daily, was in poor condition. It would gladly have traded a few years of its age for an increase in circulation. Although it lacked the *Post*'s prestige and sense of purpose, it was more malleable, less dominated by creaky traditions, and more responsive to innovative prodding. As city editor, Steffens set much of the *Commercial Advertiser*'s tone. City news was its staple. Special emphasis was given to the picturesque and to "literature"—meaning interpretation and philosophizing and escape from the lean, factual prose and interests of the reporter.

Regular reporters could not handle this type of assignment, Steffens believed. To get the right individuals, Steffens would as likely go to Morningside Heights as to Park Row, and more likely to Cambridge than to either. Professor Charles Copeland served as an unofficial recruiter on the Harvard campus, and George P. Baker sent Robert Dunn to Norman Hapgood. There were no large salaries and no guarantees of success, but considerable freedom and the chance of a good education. Among the young talents lured to the *Commercial* from Harvard were Hutchins Hapgood, Dunn, Guy Scull, Humphrey T. Nicolls, and Carl Hovey, later editor of *Cosmopolitan* and a Hollywood script writer. Dark, husky Pitts Duffield, a *Harvard Monthly* stalwart during the Hapgoods' years, and Philip Littell, a Harvard and *Milwaukee Sentinel* friend of Norman Hapgood, added more Cambridge flavor. Other volunteers were George Wharton and Walter Edwards from Columbia and Larkin Mead from Yale, and staff members included Frank M. Colby and Neith Boyce, an assistant to Steffens and later the wife of Hutchins Hapgood.

The *Commercial Advertiser* reflected the literary man's dislike for certain aspects of contemporary journalism—its rigidly prescribed style and interests, worship of a narrowly defined "beat," aversion to literature, and circulation consciousness. If the staff regarded most professional newspapermen as tough but uninspired, reporters on other papers thought the *Commercial* slapdash, amateurish, and literary. A rough city editor told Robert Dunn, who was looking for work, "Experience: Harvard and the *Commercial Advertiser*. That means that you can't write anything but literature." [21] Whatever the *Commercial*'s merits, Norman and Hutchins Hapgood first achieved some recognition during their service on it.

CHAPTER 3

Literature and Journalism: The Drama

I

NORMAN HAPGOOD HAD no intention of becoming an ordinary newspaperman. Aiming much higher, he hoped to combine journalism with a literary career and was more anxious to earn a literary reputation than to secure an eventual city editorship. As far as is known, Norman did not write poetry or drama, and his dislike of the novel is well documented.[1] He did write some short stories, but only at Harvard and immediately after leaving Harvard. For him, a literary career meant a critical career.

The magazine was the natural medium for the critical essay. Since it was difficult for an unknown to break into the better-paying, more prestigious magazines, Norman Hapgood's early articles appeared in such amateurish publications as the *New England Magazine* and *Bachelor of Arts*, in some of the more literary periodicals such as the *Chap-Book* and the *Yellow Book,* and most importantly in the *Contemporary Review*. Many of these essays were collected in his first book, *Literary Statesmen and Others: Essays on Men Seen from a Distance* (1897).

Norman was pleased with the shift from the law to journalism. The brooding left him. He became more confident of his ability to function in society and still maintain literary ambitions, to collect a paycheck and still be able to think. True, he did remark in 1897 that "it certainly is probable that the average man loses more individuality in the service of a daily journal than he would in a law office or a business house," but of course he was not "the average man."[2]

When Norman Hapgood assumed the dramatic editorship of the *New York Commercial Advertiser* in 1897, the theater became his chief concern for the next few years. Commenting on his interest in the drama during childhood and at Harvard, Hapgood thought "it was almost written in the stars that sooner or later I should become a professional critic." He wrote an unsigned column, "The Theatres," which appeared three or four times a week during the season and less frequently during the summer. Although his brother Hutchins and others occasionally contributed to this column, Norman Hapgood dominated it. He began a department, "Drama of the Month," in the *Bookman* in the fall of 1898 and also continued to write occasional pieces for other magazines. His *The Stage in America, 1897-1900* was largely a compilation of his articles and columns. Although he also wrote biographies of Lincoln (1899), Daniel Webster (1899), and Washington (1901) in these years, dramatic criticism was the primary means by which he sought to achieve literary standing.[3]

II

Norman Hapgood treated the theater seriously. His lifetime devotion was not a delight in the frivolous but a fascination for one of the sure and great manifestations of civilization. Much of the world's most powerful thought, Hapgood maintained, was most beautifully expressed in the drama. He did not particularly like novels, which he believed were too cluttered with detail to stand comparison with the lean, rich dramatic masterpieces. Not surprisingly in one who gave such weight to the drama, he thought the function of the theater was education, not amusement. He once argued that a well-run, endowed theater "in widespread and profound public service . . . would be a worthy rival of any university." [4]

Norman Hapgood believed that "there has really been no tragedy of the highest kind since *Faust.*" He loved the classics and believed Shakespeare's plays were the finest of the classics. Shakespeare, who represented the best in literature and culture, was the ultimate standard for the drama. Norman's conviction that "a tragedy cannot exist unless the author glorifies life, unless he puts magnified characters in ideal situations, working out exceptional plots" was Aristotelian to be sure, but certified by

Shakespearean practice. Norman's dislike for openly didactic plays, his beliefs that originality in plot was unimportant and that the greatest dramas relied on simplicity were surely based on his interpretation of Shakespeare. His longing for the verse tragedy led to an overestimation of the work of Stephen Phillips, but his classical emphasis usually sheltered him from the more transient breezes of the day.[5]

As a critic for a daily and a monthly, he had to meet deadlines and was expected to comment on what was being performed in the theater. To him the play itself was the most interesting part of a production. This concern distinguished him from some of the older journalistic critics, who focused on acting. He understandably gave much notice to American playwrighting, but anyone who had been weaned on the Elizabethans, indeed anyone of much discrimination, could find little to repay attention to the American drama. There were few good plays and no great ones. He applauded the more capable American dramatists and particularly liked the quasi-realistic plays of James A. Herne, such as *Shore Acres,* and the workmanlike efforts of William Gillette, such as *Secret Service* and *Sherlock Holmes.* Since established American playwrighting was so weak, Hapgood went to some lengths to encourage younger writers. He covered Edith Wharton's *Copy,* a one-act play given in a private home, and his review of Percy MacKaye's unpublished *Sylvia* "was the very first public critical notice of the young poet's dramatic work." [6]

The English theater was more promising. Norman Hapgood believed that contemporary British drama was "on a level higher than any it has reached more than two or three times before in its history." Although he was probably correct, he was never ecstatic about the English stage of the time. He enjoyed William Gilbert's work, but Gilbert had retired before Hapgood became a reviewer. Hapgood thought James M. Barrie the best of the active dramatists, but had mixed feelings about Arthur Wing Pinero and disliked Henry Arthur Jones. Hapgood was offended by George Bernard Shaw's didacticism, put off by his arrogance, and shocked by his belittling of Shakespeare. He rarely passed up a chance to pull at the Irishman's beard. Hapgood was not fond of the "problem play," so popular in England, and he liked the French well-made play even less. He found German playwrighting, notably that by the naturalist Gerhart Hauptmann and by Hermann Sudermann, much more encouraging than either England's or France's.[7]

Ibsen was the most important dramatist of the day. Although the Ibsen controversy was not as bitter in America as in England, where, among critics, William Archer led the supporters of Ibsen and Clement Scott the detractors, lines were drawn sharply. William Winter of the *Tribune* was the leading anti-Ibsen journalist in New York. To him, "Ibsenism" was "rank, deadly pessimism . . . a disease." Most of the other prestigious drama critics, such as J. Ranken Towse of the *Evening Post* and Edward A. Dithmar of the *Times,* disliked Ibsen's plays. Norman Hapgood, exposed to Ibsen at Harvard, considered him the greatest contemporary dramatist and campaigned for American productions of his works, but his judgment was that "dramatists of the future are likely to learn from his almost unrivalled exposition and his strange poetry, and let alone his attempt to prove that a silk purse may be made as readily from one substance as from another." Norman did not "believe that great art can be produced without great assumptions."[8] His classical concern for the educational function of the drama quickened his interest in Ibsen, but classical standards of excellence kept him from awarding Ibsen the highest laurels.

Considering himself more expert in the drama than in acting, he had, since his college days, sought the opinions of actors on acting. This was unorthodox, for in New York critics did not ordinarily associate closely with performers. J. Ranken Towse of the *Evening Post* tenaciously adhered to this tradition. Once Oswald Garrison Villard tricked him into meeting "the lovely Julia Marlowe." According to Villard, Towse "nearly wept at having the record of a lifetime spoiled." Norman Hapgood particularly esteemed the insights of Ellen Terry, the greatest Shakespearean actress of her day, and of Mrs. Fiske, the foremost American actress. Terry's critical abilities were well-known, and Mrs. Fiske could be stimulating. The hazard of such friendships was obvious: familiarity might blunt criticism. Hapgood contended that he had pretty much eluded this danger—

"I think my Puritanism saw me through." Except for a few reservations, it would be hard to disagree.[9] The ability to criticize those he was close to, to keep his analytical qualities to the front, were trademarks of his work in these years.

III

The Shakespearean and classical standards and the commitment to the educational function of the theater that Norman Hapgood had acquired at Harvard easily turned into hostility toward the contemporary stage. Occasionally, and with significant reservations, he would think a particular season worthwhile, but he was more inclined to speak of "the terribly low ebb of our stage." These years were not particularly distinguished ones for the American theater, but he did not consider the mediocrity of contemporary playwrighting disastrous. He remarked with exaggeration that "he who sees those [plays] which have survived the verdict of time sees greatness, and he who sees the plays of the year may, in a thousand visits to the theatre, see one work of art." [10] The American theater not only lacked genius, but it refused to pilfer intelligently the treasures of the past.

Norman Hapgood was a thoroughgoing critic of the stage's extreme interest in profits, which he thought reflected American society's preoccupation with money. A theatrical "success" meant a long-running, highly remunerative investment, he complained. Spectacle, press-agentry, the repressive star system, and the mindless pursuit of novelty were all manifestations of the commercialization of the American theater. The Syndicate, a group of managers who controlled the American stage, represented the lowest tendencies of the theater.[11] Norman Hapgood's disenchantment was not surprising; his father had imbued him with a distrust of excessive wealth. Defining culture largely in terms of small groups unobtrusively but wholeheartedly pursuing ideas, elitists sipping culture under the elms, the style of Norman's Harvard years was at odds with aggressive commercialism.

He was, moreover, critical of the theatrical audience. Never believing that the New York fans were knowledgeable, he insisted that "the road" was often a better test of a production's worth than New York. During the late nineteenth century, population growth, better transportation, and a decline in hostility to the theater contributed to the development of a "new audience" in London. A similar change was undoubtedly occurring in New York, but he did not welcome it. Most theatergoers were from the middle class and Norman felt that this class, the most loyal supporter of the overcommercialized theater, demanded spectacle and heavily moralistic drama. The result was that "children's day . . . is with us always." He concluded that its "taste in art is worse than the taste of those above it or of those below it." [12]

By "above" the middle class he meant not the wealthy but those who had superior education and discrimination. The aristocrats of the audience were "the submerged tenth—the tenth that is submerged in our theatrical system—the colleges, the arts and the kind of humanity generally that has heard of Marlowe and read Browning." The crowd, moved by the greatest art, even if it was touched by the masterpieces' more showy aspects, had a legitimate veto power: "Not everything which the public likes is good art, but nothing which the public dislikes is great art." [13] This authority was handy to deflate overly pretentious, overly involved dramas such as the problem play.

IV

Norman Hapgood demanded reform. He cheered theaters, usually foreign-language ones, that bucked the Broadway trend. He gave significant benefits a prominent place in his columns and, aided by his brother Hutchins, also gave unusual emphasis to the Yiddish and Italian theaters. Neither the benefits nor the Yiddish and Italian productions, however, were as important to Hapgood as Heinrich Conried's Irving Place Theater, which he called "Our Only High Class Theatre." Nowhere did Hapgood feel more at home. There were many reasons for his affection for Irving Place. Although it presented farces, it gloried in the classics and serious contemporary drama and was often the only New York theater where the work of Hauptmann and Sudermann could be seen. The Irving Place had not only good taste in the selection of plays but the good sense to change the bill frequently, largely neglect the star system, and avoid typecasting. Conried loved the classics, was a fine director, and knew how to run such a theater with a profit. In Hapgood's opinion Conried had "done more for dramatic art than any one else in America in our day." Hapgood thought that much of the Irving Place's success was based on its stable, earnest audience, for the Germans, unlike most other New Yorkers, recognized the cultural and educational importance of the theater.[14]

Norman demonstrated interest, but no great confidence, in the efforts of some of the more powerful managers, notably Charles Frohman, to improve the theater. An endowed theater was Hapgood's real hope for reform—"There is no road to the best but endowment." American and English concepts of government and of the theater forbade government subsidy, but he hoped that some millionaires would finance a modest effort. An endowed theater would be a home for the best drama, classic and contemporary, would encourage American playwrighting, and a stock-repertory system would improve acting. He desired something in the nature of an English Irving Place, thought Conried the best man to run such a venture, and was disappointed when Conried became the manager of the Metropolitan Opera Company.[15]

Norman Hapgood supported most attempts to establish an endowed theater, even though they often departed from his guidelines. Optimistic that a serious artistic theater would produce pervasive change, he wrote in 1899 that "one playhouse run in English as well as this [the Irving Place] is run in German could upset the prevailing standards," and in 1904, "We are ripe for such a change. Never have we been so ripe as now. Give us one theatre comparable to the best in Paris, Vienna, or Berlin, and the exclusive reign of standards now dominant on Broadway would meet a speedy end." [16] A true guerilla theater, it would challenge and, he hoped, subvert the commercialized American theater.

V

Norman Hapgood's relation to some of the more important New York critics tests his originality and suggests much of the style of his criticisms. American criticism was weak in virtually all fields, he maintained, and the drama was not an exception. During his freshman season he stated that his colleagues' work was "conventional, frozen, without ideas, and partizan. An observer can usually tell ahead, by the actors and the managers interested, what productions will be praised by most of the papers." He also charged that the critics of certain papers were subject to Syndicate influence.[17]

Many critics believed that something was profoundly wrong with the American theater. Winter of the *Tribune* and Towse of the *Evening Post*, perhaps the two most eminent New York critics, alleged that the theater was in decline. Winter, whose thin, intense, picturesque face and magnificent hair gave him nearly as striking an appearance as Mark Twain's, believed that theatrical decadence was largely a product of "the prevalence of Materialism, infecting all branches of thought, and of Commercialism, infecting all branches of action." Much of Winter's outlook was discernible in his statement "Ethical principles are more important than artistic principles." Rejecting the idea that a play should propagandize morality, he was affronted by plays that propagandized a morality offensive to him. Winter, who disliked Sudermann and detested Ibsen, led the opposition to much of the imported serious modern drama. Characters in contemporary dramas were increasingly becoming "delirious inebriates, sick harlots, humpbacked, spavined, pock-marked, splayfooted, scorbutic cranks, male and female." The *Bookman* quipped, "When Mr. Winter says 'tainted' we think of Ibsen. If he says 'putrid,' we are off like a shot in high hopes of finding something as workmanlike and clean as *The Second Mrs. Tanqueray*."[18]

Even more deeply than Winter, the Cambridge University–educated Towse was convinced that the theater was regressing. While Winter thought that decline had set in only in the 1890s, Towse, whose criticism was acting-oriented, believed that the Anglo-American stage had deteriorated after about 1825. He complained of "the degeneracy of the modern theatre in all matters of sheer artistry and histrionism. It is only in scenic accessories, and in the lighter and less permanent varieties of drama that it has made any notable advance." [19]

There were similarities between Winter, Towse, and Hapgood. Each considered the theater an educational institution, believed stock therapeutic, and was uneasy about contemporary conditions, especially about the commercialism of the stage. All opposed the Syndicate, but Hapgood was much less inclined to speak of decline.[20] Perhaps he thought the claims of the good old days exaggerated, but he was also much too young to swap stories about the past. He was only thirty-four when he left the *Commercial Advertiser;* Winter and Towse had been doing formal reviewing since the 1870s. The chasm that separated Hapgood from Winter and Towse was the work of Ibsen and some other serious European dramatists. Hapgood thought their plays beneficial, a cause for hope. Winter and Towse insisted that such work was part of the rot of the American stage, not a cause for rejoicing.

Hapgood's differences with Winter were sharper, partly because Winter tended to be shrill and mawkish. To him, Winter symbolized what was wrong with American criticism. Norman was disgusted by the tendency of some critics to reduce evaluation of a play to a series of moral judgments. Not only was such a process flabby and irrelevant, it was likely to be counterproductive. No one did this more prominently than Winter. He was incensed by Winter's close association with Augustin Daly, one of the most famous theater managers of the late nineteenth century, who was noted for his productions of Shakespeare and had a following among New York critics. Norman charged that Daly "has no more reverence for a great poet than a porkpacker." Winter, who collaborated with Daly on many Shakespearean productions, quarreled with Hapgood over a non-Daly production of *As You Like It* starring Julia Arthur. Winter claimed that Miss Arthur had wrongly and indecently distorted part of a line to read "my child's father" instead of "my father's child" (I.iii.12). Hapgood countered that Arthur's reading was correct and called Winter "one who has lived always in the pretty-pretty school of Shakespeare for infants" and "the regular agent of a manager who wishes a monopoly of Shakespeare in this town." [21]

How original were Norman Hapgood's ideas? His unfavorable opinion of the contemporary theater and his reformist outlook were common. In New York, Winter and Towse were leading spokesmen for dissatisfaction. Reformism was also popular. Indeed, as Robert Harlow Bradley has written, "The general American periodical from 1885 to 1915 was a voice for the dramatic dreams and proposals of the theatrical reformers." [22]

The endowed theater, in which Hapgood put so much faith, was an old idea, one that had great currency in both England and America. William Archer, from whom Hapgood probably got the notion and who did much to publicize it in the late 1880s and in the 1890s, was largely rehashing the arguments of the 1870s. In America the concept of an endowed theater won many friends. A New York theatrical magazine remarked in 1902 that it had "been long a cherished dream by all earnest lovers of the drama and of the art of acting." Norman's ideas on scenery, stock, and repertory conformed closely to general reformist thought. He joined Winter, Towse, and, to a lesser degree, Dithmar as a devotee of stock. His appreciation of the Irving Place Theater differed but slightly from the comments George Henry Lewes had made a quarter-century before about the German theaters.[23] Norman's emphasis on the classics and his belief in lasting rules for drama had been common to many literary critics in the Gilded Age.

He was imbued with the reformist ideology of his day. Of the major New York critics, Franklin Fyles of the *Sun* probably stood most outside this orthodoxy, though it would be hard to impute much originality to his ideas. Fyles, who was favorable to the Syndicate, skeptical of stock, and against an endowed theater (though later apparently hoping that the Syndicate would establish one) declared, "We are getting along very well under the prevailing conditions." [24] Originality is probably the wrong attribute to look for in a dramatic critic. A better test might be how well he encouraged the sounder work of the day, and Hapgood had a good record on this point. His enthusiasm for Ibsen, Hauptmann, and Sudermann exceeded that of most New York critics. So did his encouragement of the Irving Place, Yiddish, and Italian theaters. His interest in young playwrights and in presentations of the classics was commendable. Giving much attention to the critical works of Archer, Arthur Walkley, Max Beerbohm, and Shaw, he served as an intermediary for much of the progressive thought of his day. If his ideas were not unique, he managed to present them with discrimination. An irony hung over Hapgood's complaints about the American stage: devoid of conspicuous originality, he would probably have had little to contribute to a flourishing theater patronized by a discerning public. The integrity of his stand against inferior conditions was perhaps the most valuable aspect of his dramatic criticism.

VI

Norman Hapgood's criticisms were as notable for tone and style as for particulars. Three qualities marked his work. First, he was often described as "serious" or "earnest." The *Outlook* called him "one of the small body of serious critics of the theater." A book reviewer in the *Bookman* thought him "one of the very few dramatic critics in either England or America who are worthy of serious consideration." The London critic William Archer, who met him at a party, described him as a "young critic, a good fellow and frightfully in earnest."[25] Hapgood, apparently greatly influenced by Matthew Arnold's emphasis on the importance of criticism and on the critic's need for absolute integrity and disinterestedness, took his job seriously. Indeed, at the heart of his criticism of the American theater—his concern for the play as opposed to the acting, his support for the classics, stock, and repertory, and his dislike of the well-made play and for elaborate scenery—was a conviction that the theater simply was not acting in earnest, that it was not serious about itself.

Second, Hapgood's work reflected his analytical bent, a trait highlighted by his seriousness and his self-confessed lack of humor. Norman did not develop this quality while he was a critic —it was evident at Harvard and in his *Literary Statesmen,* a lean, virile book that fired epigrams as if from a revolver. Discussing his article on Gladstone, the *Bookman* remarked that he seemed "to be a critic by nature and breeding rather than a critic by pose." Percy MacKaye recalled a party at the Arena restaurant after the premiere of Moody's *Sappho and Phaon.* The mood was optimistic. "Only Norman Hapgood . . . uttered ominous morning-edition forebodings from his all-critic-fathoming mind. And Norman's acumen was amply confirmed." [26]

Hapgood's columns, written for the more intelligent theatergoers, were respected by some of the more serious followers of the theater. He was one of the few critics to be taken into Mrs. Fiske's confidence, and Mrs. Campbell, a British actress known for her talent, beauty, wit, and will, asserted, "In those days [1902] in New York Mr. Norman Hapgood was the dramatic critic upon whom the actors' minds centered." Even the American playwright Clyde Fitch, with whom he had uneven relations, paid an unintentional compliment when he explained to a critic that "Hapgood wrote at least three times as long on the Theater as you have without gaining *complete* confidence of sane people as you have done." [27] Hapgood was a standard of competence.

A final quality, perhaps spoken of more often than any other, was Norman Hapgood's independence.[28] He could criticize those whom he most respected and could chastise an inferior production. To appreciate the notice that his integrity attracted and to achieve a fuller awareness of his significance, it is necessary to place his career in the context of the New York criticism of the time.

VII

At the turn of the century, journalistic drama criticism was straining to develop a measure of professionalism. As S. R. Littlewood has remarked, "Dramatic criticism in London had undoubtedly become something like a small profession, though it still had to be eked out for the most part with other occupations." The major New York critics of the 1890s were better paid and often had served longer than their London counterparts. In the smaller American cities, however, newspapers frequently considered criticism unimportant and often assigned their least experienced, least valuable men—often fresh from the campus —to cover the stage. The job was usually part-time, with a high turnover, and the young critics generally tried to escape to more prestigious jobs as soon as possible. The development of the "new audience," the increased number of attractions as well as the desire of the papers to cater to a greater variety of reader interests, probably encouraged more stability and professionalism in New York, but even there some journals continued to believe that theatrical criticism was insignificant. By Norman Hapgood's day bribery seems to have passed. "Time was when favorable articles in certain journals were purchasable," one critic wrote in 1900, "but there is no such scandal now." [29]

The Syndicate, or Theatrical Trust, which dominated the American theater through control of booking, was often the acid test of a critic's independence. By the late nineteenth century local stock companies had been replaced by the "combination," which created a company for a play and disbanded it when the play had concluded its run. Since "the road" was still important, routing was crucial. After several unsuccessful attempts to bring some order to routing through circuits, the Syndicate appeared in 1896. It was a combination of six managers—Charles Frohman, Al Hayman, Abraham Erlanger, Marc Klaw, Samuel Nixon (Nirdlinger), and J. Fred Zimmerman—and was an understandable by-product of the economic changes in the American theater. The Syndicate did not, as an organization, own theaters, plays, or productions, although its members did.[30] It did not need to. Through skillful use of its booking power, it regulated access to most of the leading theaters.

The growth of the Syndicate went neither unnoticed nor unopposed. At first several stars fought the Syndicate, but most quickly reached agreements with it. Its chief antagonists were Mrs. Fiske and her husband, Harrison Grey Fiske, editor of the

New York Dramatic Mirror. Despite the efforts of the Fiskes and others, the Syndicate was not effectively threatened until a rival syndicate run by the Shubert brothers challenged the older trust after 1905.

Norman Hapgood battled the Trust. Conceding that the Syndicate had boosted the economic condition of the theater, he believed that it had lowered the quality of acting, shied away from serious drama, and made it difficult to produce the dramas of unknown native playwrights. Such charges were familiar anti-Syndicate arguments. Although Norman was solidly against the Trust, he was careful not to be blindly anti-Syndicate. He reprimanded Harrison Grey Fiske for unfair remarks about the Syndicate and denounced the anti-Semitism of James Metcalfe, *Life's* anti-Trust critic. Hapgood was no friend of David Belasco, who contested the Syndicate for some time, for in Hapgood's eyes Belasco was no better.[31]

Hapgood contended that the Syndicate exercised a good deal of control over theatrical news. "In their desire to influence the press, the members of the Syndicate are only like other managers," he explained. "In their ability to do it, they are unrivalled." Furthermore, "their influence on any New York newspaper of the first class, even the *Sun,* is probably not greater than Mr. Daly exercised on the *Tribune* and the *Times.*"[32] Daly's conduct did not justify the Syndicate's. Hapgood, who had opposed Daly's efforts, would continue to oppose the even more dangerous ones of the Trust.

The professional integrity of the New York critics was one of Norman's preoccupations. Never reluctant to point out those whose conduct he thought suspect, he accused the *Herald, Mail and Express, Telegraph,* and *Sun* of being Syndicate organs. The means of Syndicate influence were varied. It was able to distribute news—the *Herald* particularly benefited from this—and to remunerate critics for professional services. Hapgood, who thought that critics should not write plays because of a conflict of interest, needled Fyles because some of his plays had been produced by the Trust. The Syndicate could also use its advertising power. Hapgood made allusions to bribery, but he claimed that it rarely took place. The real danger, more roundabout than all of these, was "in its essence like the deference which is always given to the very powerful." [33]

Norman Hapgood's charges had much validity. The behavior of Dithmar, Winter, and Fyles was not always on the highest level. Some of the lesser critics were probably worse. Surely Norman's attempt to establish some kind of ethical standards was one of his most valuable services, even though he sometimes judged unfairly those who disagreed with him. He failed to realize that what he perceived as a lack of principle in other critics was sometimes a different interpretation of the functions of the critic, an interpretation sanctioned by the practice of the past generation. His contribution was not merely the chastisement of his colleagues' weaknesses. The Syndicate struck at him and his integrity was tested.

VIII

The Syndicate's advertising boycott of the *Commercial Advertiser* marked the peak of Norman Hapgood's controversy with the Trust, but, quite possibly, this was not the first trouble he had had with it. His friend Ellen Terry wrote George Bernard Shaw in January 1900, the same month in which Hapgood's article on the Syndicate was published, "A nice fellow (Norman Hapgood of New York) is being slated (by the D. Syndicate, I rather think!) for what he writes about the unfairness of the arrangement." The harassment may have been pressure on Hapgood's superiors. In any event, there can be no doubt of the major effort to intimidate or even eliminate his criticism. On October 3, 1901, eight Syndicate theaters and their allies stopped advertising in the *Commercial*. The next day seven more followed. Norman contended that the boycott was retaliation for "a review in which I said it [a Syndicate play] would not last over two weeks." Besides canceling advertisements, the Syndicate "has demanded his [Hapgood's] discharge . . . [and] has stopped sending tickets to the paper." Earlier in 1901 the *New York Dramatic Mirror* had reported rumors that the Syndicate would attack certain critics and, by intimidating them, bring the rest into line. Hapgood was not named, however. During the boycott a Syndicate organ boasted that the Trust had already stifled critics in Boston, Providence, Washington, and Detroit, and that Norman Hapgood would be another victim.[34]

The *Commercial Advertiser* was never strong financially, but according to Hapgood the editor in chief, H. J. Wright, "behaved with encouraging firmness, and I carried on the fight." A later account claimed that the loss of revenue was seventy-five dollars a day. On October 26 the advertisements of twelve theaters returned; on October 29 the remaining three came back. Hapgood had won. Not long after this episode Norman left the *Commercial Advertiser.* In his autobiography he claimed that he had resigned in 1902 because the quality of the theater was so low "that I found my ideas repeating themselves." According to Hapgood, the fight with the Syndicate merely "coincided" with his growing boredom. Although Norman's ennui, noticed by his father, may have preceded the Syndicate fight, it probably developed at about the same time.[35]

There are additional grounds for questioning Norman's story. He correctly observed that he did not leave until the battle had been won. It is probably true that Wright did not press him because of the loss of revenue, but Hapgood, who was being helped financially by his father, may have been embarrassed by the increased financial burden on the paper. One version of the conflict claimed that he even "offered to resign, for he does not depend on his salary."[36] If this is true, it would indicate that the financial pressure was less direct than he suggested.

Shortly after the controversy an article in the *Chicago Post* claimed that the review that was the immediate cause of the incident—although the underlying cause was the Syndicate's long-time desire to get Hapgood—had been written not by him but by the musical editor. Furthermore, the comment that had allegedly upset the Syndicate was that Klaw and Erlanger's musical *Liberty Belles* was "suggestive," an opinion shared by no other New York critic. The Trust, realizing that it was after the wrong man and aware of the amount of negative comments its action had occasioned, apologized.[37] If this story is correct, Norman's victory was less than total. He must have been mortified at defending a review attacking a production for indecency, especially when no other reviewer agreed. He had often criticized Winter for just such conduct.

The manner in which he fought the Syndicate was revealing. Norman Hapgood had been the target of advertising boycotts before; in response to unfavorable reviews Daly's and the Casino theaters had taken similar action. Hapgood met these two challenges by noting the withdrawal of advertising, deriding those responsible, and parading excerpts from other newspapers critical of the theater managers' actions.[38] He reacted differently to the Syndicate attack. He did not ridicule the managers and did not print the condemnatory words of other papers. In fact, there was no mention of the boycott in the *Commercial Advertiser*. Only the shrinkage of theatrical advertisements testified to trouble. This was curious behavior, contrary to previous conduct and contrary to the hard-hitting tenor of his criticism. Norman's instinct must have been to slug it out. Of course the Syndicate's boycott was more serious than Daly's or the Casino's. He may have felt that he could not be as aggressive in this difficulty without creating serious financial troubles for his paper. He compromised. He did not curb his independent criticism of various productions, but he did leash his reaction to the boycott.

Norman must have been aware of his dilemma. Able to battle with the smaller fry of the dramatic world, he could not criticize the giants with all the vigor that he wished. His departure from the *Commercial* was undoubtedly amicable, as he claimed, but this was partly because he took a broad view of his position. It was a dilemma of situation, not of personalities. Had the *Commercial Advertiser* been solider economically, he might have contested the boycott more openly. More importantly, most New York papers were unwilling to do much fighting about the drama. As Hapgood knew well, the New York press hardly made a noise about the boycott. He must have realized that this silence made it easy for the Syndicate to use such tactics against critics. Many newspapers regarded the theaters as a source of income and did not take their drama columns very seriously. Speculation that business considerations occasionally governed critical behavior was widespread.[39] Obviously, this was a situation the Trust or several of its members could exploit.

Not long after leaving the *Commercial* Norman recalled that he had been "glad to be out of journalism" and sure "that there was a necessary conflict between popularity and sincerity." This discontent was due to something more than his running out of ideas. After he quit the *Commercial,* he went to Italy. He spent his time "nosing about the gallaries of Rome and Florence" and "was . . . glad to be in beautiful towns, seeing beautiful pictures, talking with people of charm and education." [40] His moving to Italy was richly symbolic. Few things suggested a free pursuit of literary and artistic development more clearly than Italy. He had returned to the problem of reconciling journalism and literature, or rather he had taken a new stand on that issue. In his early years as a newspaperman, he had been fairly confident that he could mix a literary with a journalistic career. That hope was gone, at least temporarily. Rather than yield his literary aspirations, he fled from active journalism. At Harvard, when he had feared entry into the real world, the student found refuge in European culture. He now found similar refuge in Europe itself.

CHAPTER 4

Journalism: Immigrants, Toughs, and Criminals

I

WHILE NORMAN HAPGOOD was writing dramatic criticism, Hutchins Hapgood was doing work important to his own career. In a sense the *New York Commercial Advertiser* had a more lasting impact on Hutchins than it did on his older brother, who after becoming the editor of *Collier's Weekly* in 1903 did not, with the exception of occasional discussions of the theater, do much with the drama for over two decades. Only with the publication of his *Why Janet Should Read Shakspere* in 1929 did Norman again take up that interest in a serious way. True, many values from the *Commercial* days remained with him and shaded his outlook and political beliefs, but the *Commercial Advertiser*'s legacy to Hutchins was more direct. He evolved a style of journalism that in some respects survived for a decade and a half. The years on the *Commercial* influenced most of his major writings.

Hutchins Hapgood, who, like Norman, could not be a conventional newspaperman, was initially very excited about the *Commercial*. Literate, anxious to encounter new experience, eager to write, strongly individualistic, and desirous of doing something more vital than grinding out conventional news, Hutchins met the criteria of city editor Lincoln Steffens: "I wanted fresh, young, enthusiastic writers who would see and make others see the life of the city. This meant individual styles." [1]

The *Commercial* no less than the old *Harvard Monthly* made a cult of style, as much in approach as in writing. It stressed not only doing certain things but doing them in a certain way. If the *Monthly*'s emphasis on the proper blending of intellectual values and charm helped to set up a contrast to a society inhospitable to them, the *Commercial*'s ideal gave assurance and justification to these bright young college men who could not and did not want to take their journalism straight.

The spirited people Steffens brought to the *Commercial Advertiser* "were," as he said in his autobiography, "writers, getting the news as material for poetry, plays, or fiction, and writing it as news for practice." [2] Norman Hapgood looked for a reconciliation of literature and journalism in a career as a critic. Others, more interested in creative writing, hoped their journalistic experience would lend force and direction to their work. Many desired to end vocational confusion and inject some drops of literature into practical life. Abraham Cahan, a noncollege man frustrated by the Yiddish press, came to delight in the flexibility of this journalistic experiment.

Larzer Ziff has perceptively noted that "of the staff Steffens gathered as a result of his appeal to university English professors to send him their most promising writers, not one ambitious novelist or poet achieved anything in belles-lettres." Not only did they fail in this regard, but hardly any of them achieved much in newspaper journalism. The importance of the *Commercial Advertiser* was not to newspaper journalism, for it would be hard to find a significant impact, but in the influence it had on those who worked for it. Cahan's training would help him greatly after his return to the Yiddish press; [3] Norman Hapgood absorbed a democratic theory of journalism that would contribute to his success at *Collier's Weekly;* Hutchins Hapgood developed a style of journalism that would play a large role in his work.

Reminiscences attest to the unusual intensity at the *Commercial.* Several factors seem to have accounted for this excitement. In these years American writers were often optimistic about their opportunities, and many on the *Commercial* believed they were close to the desired breakthrough. A new life-style—particularly if following a period of vocational uncertainty—and the joyousness of youth, a "Beat Yale" attitude, also contributed. Enthusiasm was more than a state of mind; it proclaimed the *Commercial* men's apartness from the hard-bitten, cynical, professional reporters they so disliked. If the *Commercial* paid poorly and if other newspapermen looked upon it as amateurish, so much the better. The future writers were reassured that they had not succumbed to standardized journalism.

The *Commercial Advertiser* had little regard for much conventional news. As was pointed out earlier, the *Commercial* experiment had been in part a reaction against the stiffness of the *New York Evening Post*. Steffens had stretched the *Evening Post*'s coverage of crime and other news, but he still felt restricted. At the *Commercial* his plans were more ambitious. He gave greatest attention to local news. This was no doubt in part expedient—it would have been hard to imagine the *Commercial* competing in coverage of national and international events. "My inspiration was a love of New York, just as it was," Steffens reminisced, "and my ambition was to have it reported so that New Yorkers might see, not merely read of it, as it was: rich and poor, wicked and good, ugly but beautiful, growing, great." In other words, the *Commercial*'s city was the exhilarating one of Dreiser, not the crushing 1930s Chicago of James T. Farrell. Richard Hofstadter has noted that one characteristic of late nineteenth-century American journalism was that it "*elevated* events, hitherto considered beneath reportorial attention, to the level of news occurrences by clever, emotionally colored reporting." [4] Extensive coverage of everyday city life was a fixture of the yellow journals, but the *Commercial* hoped to do it with greater depth, seriousness, and literary skill.

This slant was peculiarly suited to the *Commercial*'s young writers. It let them deal with what was most fascinating, but it also permitted them to challenge newspaper journalism's emphases on the beat and on the rapid collection and dissemination of news. Able to display their background, to sift the essential from the unessential, in short, to exhibit the fruits of their literary interests and training, they could become distinctive. By raising the doings and thoughts of immigrants, "characters," and people generally considered not very noteworthy to the level of quasi art, Steffens's reporters were often able to mix literature and active life, to maintain literary standards and still participate in society at large.

The *Commercial Advertiser* was in some respects a strange vehicle for the fulfillment of these aspirations. Before Seymour, Wright, and Steffens gained control, it had been conservative, anti-yellow press, pro-trust, and Republican. Maintaining a McKinley Republican position even after the takeover, it admired Theodore Roosevelt not so much for being a potential reformer as for being the great Republican vote-getter. Its editorial page was unexciting. The stories that captivated the young writers—people like Hutchins Hapgood, Neith Boyce, and Abraham Cahan—appeared, initially at least, in the Saturday supplement. The *Commercial* did not publish a Sunday edition. Before 1899, to pick a somewhat arbitrary date, if one saw a story titled "Chuck Isn't Blue," or "Between Two and Four A.M.," one knew it was Saturday. After 1899 this was less the case, for this type of writing was gradually scattered throughout the weekday editions.

II

Hutchins Hapgood began to work for the *Commercial Advertiser* in 1897 and Neith Boyce, who joined a little later, observed that "it was clear almost at once, that H. [Hutchins] couldn't do routine stuff, or anything that he wasn't interested in, he couldn't report a court trial, for instance." [5] Like Norman, he did not become an all-around reporter immediately; unlike his brother, Hutchins never qualified as a crack reporter. But the *Commercial* did not demand this sort of expertise. Hutchins Hapgood helped Norman with the drama column, did some standard reporting, but most importantly wrote feuilletons about immigrants, bums, characters, and the more commonplace New York life.

Hutchins Hapgood had matured emotionally to the point where newspaper work could be satisfying. The former loner craved human companionship. His stay in Germany had helped develop his social nature. He wrote in 1895, "I like strong vigorous animality better than anything else, and my greatest loathing at present is the complexity of intellectual effort." Claiming that "he went into newspaper work in order to come in contact

Hutchins Hapgood c. 1895. (Courtesy of Elizabeth Backman.)

William P. Hapgood c. 1892. (Courtesy of Elizabeth Backman.)

Norman Hapgood c. 1900. (Courtesy of Elizabeth Backman.)

with the rhythm of life from a new angle," Hapgood most often found "the rhythm of life" on the East Side and on the Bowery.[6]

III

Steffens had been fascinated by New York's immigrant Jews when he was on the *New York Evening Post*—"as infatuated as eastern boys were with the wild west." Fondness for Jews was fashionable for many intellectuals in the late nineteenth and early twentieth centuries. Steffens carried his concern for the East Side with him to the *Commercial.* Attention to the ghetto was "good journalism and good business," and no doubt the *Commercial,* plagued by low circulation, hoped to enlist readers on the East Side.[7] No one symbolized the *Commercial*'s ties to the ghetto more clearly than Abraham Cahan, who had already had an influential career in Yiddish journalism and was now a reporter for the *Commercial.*

Hutchins Hapgood, finding the East Side "by far the most interesting section of foreign New York," often wrote articles for the *Commercial* and for magazines about various aspects of its cultural life. He often reviewed the Yiddish stage for Norman Hapgood's column and noted that "the *C. A.* is a kind of household word" at those theaters. His wife, Neith, was the first to grasp that these articles could make a book. Although he had trouble finding a publisher, *The Spirit of the Ghetto* is today very highly regarded, often labeled a "minor classic." Ronald Sanders has called it "the richest description of the life of New York's Jewish quarter that had ever been written in English," and Moses Rischin has termed it "the first authentic study by an outsider of the inner life of an American immigrant community, devoid of stereotype or sentimentality, sympathetic yet sober and realistic, intimate yet judicious and restrained."[8]

Cahan accompanied Hapgood on several of his visits to the quarter, introduced him to many intellectuals, and educated him about the ghetto. Hapgood's emphasis on the struggle between American, Jewish, and socialist influences, his familiarity with a range of Jewish intellectuals, as well as his acquaintance with

Cahan's published works justify Rischin's statement that Cahan was Hapgood's "silent collaborator without whose knowledgeable aid and intervention the work would doubtless not even have been attempted." But Rischin's assertion that *The Spirit of the Ghetto* "appears as much the work of Cahan as it was of Hapgood" is not supported by sufficient evidence. In *The Spirit of the Ghetto* Hapgood dealt with topics that his training and interests could best cope with: poetry, short stories, essays, and the theater. For example, his writings on the Yiddish theater were not very different from his work on the German and Italian theaters or on vaudeville.[9]

Hapgood stated well the approach of *The Spirit of the Ghetto* in the preface:

> The Jewish quarter of New York is generally supposed to be a place of poverty, dirt, ignorance and immorality—the seat of the sweat-shop, the tenement house, where "red-lights" sparkle at night, where the people are queer and repulsive. Well-to-do persons visit the "Ghetto" merely from motives of curiosity or philanthropy; writers treat it "sociologically," as of a place in crying need of improvement.
>
> That the Ghetto has an unpleasant aspect is as true as it is trite. But the unpleasant aspect is not the subject of the following sketches. I was led to spend much time in certain poor resorts of Yiddish New York not through motives either philanthropic or sociological, but simply by virtue of the charm I felt in men and things there.[10]

This passage reveals several premises of *The Spirit of the Ghetto:* a desire to challenge some prevailing stereotypes, to avoid patronizing or merely issuing a reformer's call to action. Hutchins's interest in the ghetto, as in many other things, was based essentially on liking, but he was not blindly partisan. Appreciative detachment was one of the most notable assets of this dignified and sensitive book. Jacob Epstein's brilliantly evocative sketches perfectly complemented Hapgood's prose. Hapgood, who had early thought the reformer's role thin, "perhaps useful but undeveloping work," refused to claim, as Charles Edward Russell did, "Good times, bad times—what difference to the Lung Block?"[11] After reading *The Spirit of the Ghetto,* which was not reformist, one does not want to knock down tenements, pass laws, or incarcerate someone. In this sense it was dissimilar to

Jacob Riis's *How the Other Half Lives* or Steffens's *The Shame of the Cities*. The reader wishes to think, perhaps go to a Yiddish theater, or walk down Canal Street if he has the opportunity.

Several factors accounted for Hapgood's detachment, a quality remarkable not only because much subsequently written about the ghetto was innocent of this trait but because it was absent from several of Hapgood's other efforts. Hapgood was alienated from the Jewish intellectuals he encountered on the East Side. He was not fond of the socialists, whom he found rigid, narrow, and unacquainted with the complexities of America. He pointed out the weaknesses of the ghetto intellectuals in certain types of poetry and "plastic art," and noticed a lack of "smoothness." [12] One reason for his aloofness was that he was an intellectual evaluating other intellectuals. This was not true, by and large, of the rest of his books. Hapgood, as his autobiography would show, was sharpest, most discerning, when assessing other writers and thinkers.

Hapgood thought the three determinative forces at work on the East Side were Jewish, American, and socialist. His first chapter, surely heavily influenced by Cahan, was attentive to the clash between old and new, and undoubtedly the traditional touched him most deeply. Hapgood sympathized most with the " 'submerged' " scholars and rabbis who were committed to a mode of intellectual life that was dying.[13] Indeed, there was a sense of melancholy throughout *The Spirit of the Ghetto*. The Yiddish theater, Jacob Adler and Jacob Gordin had said—and Hapgood apparently agreed—will soon vanish. The Yiddish literary sketches, which he admired and did much to publicize, were declining because of what he thought was the inevitable withering of socialism in America.

The ghetto was beginning to crumble under the onslaught of Americanization. Hapgood predicted the quick triumph of Americanism over socialism, but he was less sure about the degree to which the Jews would become assimilated, although he hoped they would retain some of their best characteristics.

The New York Ghetto is constantly changing. It shifts from one part of town to another, and the time is not so very far distant when it will cease altogether. . . . The picturesqueness it now possesses will disappear. Perhaps, however, by that time an art will have been developed which will preserve for future generations the character of the present life; which may thus have historical value, and artistic beauty in addition.[14]

In 1909, in a new preface to *The Spirit of the Ghetto,* Hapgood noted changes in the East Side and predicted that in time his book would be "an historical monument," not a work of contemporary relevance. A few years later he observed. "The picturesque combination of Russian realism in literature, revolutionary instinct in social and political thought, Jewish traditions, and American conditions, which produced so many intense and expressive personalities holding forth in the cafés of Grand and Canal streets, has faded away into paler forms." [15]

IV

The Griffou Push, an informal group often meeting in the Hotel Griffou, was a more important influence than Cahan and the East Side in shaping Hapgood's work. The three major figures of the Push were Josiah Flynt Willard, Alfred Hodder, and Hutchins Hapgood, but many others, especially, Arthur Bartlett Maurice, editor of the *Bookman,* often participated. Hapgood, Willard, and Hodder roomed together, and even after Hapgood married in 1899 they continued their companionship. At one time Willard and Hodder, Hapgood recalled, were "my two most intimate friends," and Hapgood and Willard planned to collaborate on a book.[16]

Hapgood had met Willard, a short, pale figure with thin, cynical lips, in Berlin. A nephew of Frances Willard, he early suffered from wanderlust. He ran away from home several times, was sentenced to a boys' reformatory, escaped, and spent a good deal of his life tramping. At the time he joined Hapgood and Hodder he was turning his tours "on the road" into literary capital. The enigmatic Willard (he wrote under the name of Josiah Flynt) came to be regarded, in the words of Van Wyck

Brooks, as "a master of the tramp-world, as Audubon was of the world of birds or Charles Godfrey Leland of the world of gypsies." [17]

Hodder's career, though not as vivid as Willard's, was unusual. Hapgood had known the idealistic, boyish-looking Hodder at Harvard: Josiah Royce, he recalled, had said "that Hodder was as an undergraduate the most promising student of philosophy who had ever gone through the university, but that his usefulness as a philosopher might be sadly damaged, if not entirely destroyed, by his romantic temperament." Hodder had taken his doctorate at Harvard, taught at Bryn Mawr, participated in reform politics, and helped William Travers Jerome in his campaign for district attorney in 1901 and, after his election, became his private secretary.[18]

Hapgood, Willard, and Hodder drank hard and played hard. Hapgood claimed that Willard believed "it was indecent to go to bed early." Neith Hapgood somewhat dryly remembered their "rather juvenile exploits," and thought them "a sort of gang, devoted to night-life and free pleasures." Hutchins's bohemian adventures were in a sense a throwback. Melville Stone had said that in the 1870s "every competent journalist was expected to be a drunkard." In the early twentieth century it was alleged that the day of the heavily imbibing newspaperman had passed, that modern journalism was too demanding, too professional, to tolerate such nonchalance.[19] The wild life had become a sensitive issue for those who defended the professional status of American journalism. Precisely at the time Willard and Hapgood were expanding into new journalistic fields, they were indulging in the old life-style.

Hutchins Hapgood had more than a good time with his two companions. The Push was not frivolous; "these bohemians insisted upon having ideas mixed up with their dissipations." When Hapgood remarked that Americans were often too intense and too energetic to be perfect bohemians, his comments were no doubt partly autobiographical. Both Willard and Hodder affected Hapgood's journalism for the next decade. Willard emphasized observation and firsthand experience and traveled throughout trampdom as "Chicago Cigarette." He castigated those who had studied only incarcerated tramps and criminals, and criminologists who, he felt, conceived theories and then found examples to fit them. He termed his research "scientific in so far as it deals with the subject on its own ground and in its peculiar conditions and environment." Willard, Hodder remarked, "knew his vagrant in the open." [20]

Willard's studies of tramps were wracked by ambiguity. Hapgood perceptively observed of Willard that "much of his writing included a moral condemnation of the material that held his imagination." The conflict in Willard's work was between fascination and value. Absorbed by tramps and tramping, he had a hard time justifying the grip tramping had on him both as a way of life and as a literary subject. Perhaps this was clearest in *The Little Brother: A Story of Tramp Life* (1900), a novel. Although not the best of Willard's books, it was peculiarly revealing. Eight-year-old Benny ran away from his schoolmistress sister and became a tramp, a "Prushun," a sort of assistant, to West Virginia Blackie, his "jocker," or master. Willard skillfully portrayed the rival pulls of civilization and trampdom on Benny, a discord Willard himself felt, and Benny was in some respects the young Willard. Willard could not resolve the struggle, so he had Benny killed in an accident and closed the book with a thoroughly melodramatic encounter which disclosed that Benny's sister was actually his mother and West Virginia Blackie his father. Blackie had tricked Benny's mother into believing they were legally married and then deserted her. In his nonfiction Willard's answers were often as unsatisfying. One minute he was delicately studying essentially harmless tramps; the next, he labeled them a national threat that must be severely repressed. Willard for a time used his knowledge against his comrades by becoming a special railroad investigator. He was seldom sober during his last three years.[21] More than a glimmer of the maladjustment causing his alcoholism was evident in his earlier writings.

Willard and Hodder were interested in reform and helped to shape Hapgood's outlook on politics. Louis Filler has argued that Willard "might be considered more than any other man as legitimately the first muckraker or magazine reformer." Willard might not have appreciated the designation, and certainly would not have sought it. He never achieved the audience or recognition that Steffens did in good measure because he did not fit well into progressivism. There was too much fatalism, too much recognition of evil in this dark, brooding figure. Willard explained: "My position is more pessimistic than that of a number of the Under World critics. I can't imagine a large city in this country so reformed, no matter who should bring about its regeneration, that in it I could not gamble, find illegal resorts and guns, hear of good 'touches,' and occasionally run across a crooked official." [22]

Although Willard did some investigative work and Hodder was associated with Jerome, both were aware of the weaknesses of reform movements. Above all, Willard and Hodder detected paradox, verging in Willard on moral anarchism. As West Virginia Blackie said in words Willard at least partially believed but was reluctant to express directly in his writings. "The world's just as crooked as I am—every damn bit!" Hodder detected irony in the actions of reformers.

> For all practical purposes . . . the puritan idealist and the "practical politician" are confederates in a game to defraud the public. The puritan plays for the credit of striving on all occasions in public, in season and out of season, for the recognition of his code; the practical politician plays frankly for money. The two play into each other's hands, with never a wink to betray them, and the public pays.[23]

Hodder's judgment was more optimistic than Willard's: "However little natural gift or liking it [Tammany] may have for the administrative lie, it has accepted its existence, it has built upon it; its whole vast edifice is overthrown when that is overthrown." Hodder, the Harvard metaphysician, expected to cripple Tammany with a syllogism. Hodder and Willard in "The Great Idea," a chapter of their *Powers That Prey*, intentionally pushed their criticism of reformers to farce. Ruderick MeKlowd, a shrewd head crook, supported a reform administration in Cornville, became the chief of detectives, made a fortune, and left. Such was the impotence of narrow-minded reformers. The outlook on the *Commercial Advertiser*, where Steffens contended with some exaggeration that "most of my men so disliked reformers that they could not write fairly about anything they said or did," coincided to a degree with the insights of Willard and Hodder.[24]

Journeys to the underside of life, a desire to have direct experience, an interest in criminals, the demonstration that fraternizing in saloons was not only compatible with, but vital to, some kinds of creative work, a standoffishness toward respectable morality, and a skepticism about most reformers—these were Willard's legacies to Hapgood. Willard did a little writing for the *Commercial,* but his studies had a more investigative quality than the *Commercial*'s sketches of common life, and he was more absorbed in the lives of his subjects. Hapgood found that the often complementary influences of the *Commercial* and Willard satisfied some of his literary and psychological needs as well as confirmed some of his ideas. Hapgood gradually developed different topics from Willard's and always brought to his writing a different background, intellect, and temperament from the authority on tramps.

V

In the last years of the nineteenth century and in the first decade of the twentieth, Hutchins Hapgood spent a good deal of time on the Bowery socializing and writing about "characters." To regulars in several hangouts he must have been a familiar figure. Five feet seven inches tall, Hapgood had blue eyes that as he grew older would take on the appearance of "bloodhound" eyes. He parted his brown hair at the middle; his "face [was] roughly chiselled, forehead not too high, balanced by a strong mouth and chin, ears small and set close to the head, a short strong neck." His deep bass voice probably attracted some notice. Many years later Norman Hapgood reported that his young son, Ten Eyck (David), had "asked him what was [the] distant rumbling sound. I said I thought it sounded like a locomotive. 'What!' he cried scornfully. 'You think a train make so much noise like that? Like Hunkle Bunch?' "[25] In these Bowery haunts, frequented by an assortment of customers and furnished without distinction, Hapgood drank cheap beer and whiskey. Sometimes in the company of a professional pickpocket, Hapgood passed as a taciturn Chicago confidence man, but Hapgood's blood must have been racing. Although many present were bleary-eyed after a hard day's work or a hard night's drinking—or both—Hapgood's mind was tingling with excitement as he came into contact with an often rich mine of anecdote, chanced across a usable quotation or a potential article. Most important, however, was the closeness to colorful personalities, the human contact. Hutchins Hapgood's Bowery excursions were more than an idealization of the saloon down the street or a delight in companionship. They helped formulate his outlook on life.

Hapgood, particularly struck by the nobility of the Bowery tough or bum, noted that "there is an instinctive feeling of sympathy between the aristocrat and the tough. Both are primarily simple and human." The ungarnished delighted Hapgood, who argued in *Types from City Streets* (1910) that "the very lowest people, like the very highest, in the social scale, come very close to the facts of life. They are, through poverty, through toughness, through crime, brought up hard against the 'limit.'" Indeed, he found a striking and straightforward earnestness in his Bowery bums. The tough and the aristocrat are

both unhesitating and authoritative in matters of relative value; for the aristocrat has learned that the simple things are the best and most significant; while the tough has known no other. They both, therefore, express only the best. The middle-class person, on the other hand, striving constantly to rise, to get where he is not, is comparatively vulgar, graceless, and unformed. He is admirable in a moral sense, but his words lack literature, for they are confused and pointless, overabundant and reveal a lack of conviction as to what is the "real thing." How can he know, in his Cook's-tour-like voyage through life, what the necessary and fundamental things are? [26]

The anti-middle-class feeling, the dislike for the parvenu in this passage recalls the similar feeling at Harvard in the 1890s and Norman's chastisement of the bourgeois theater audiences. Hutchins was largely adapting the antiphilistine sentiment of the

Harvard days not to the drama but to Bowery figures. That Norman's anti-middle-class sentiment would virtually disappear during his years as editor of *Collier's Weekly*, while Hutchins's persisted, indicates the extent to which Hutchins continued to deal essentially with cultural values in contrast to Norman, who became increasingly occupied with politics.

Hutchins Hapgood also inverted a characteristic American conception. American democracy had often been tied to social mobility, but, at least in the case of the bum, Hapgood saw democratic worth springing from lack of movement. Ellery Sedgwick noted of a saloon habituated by criminals, "It was a model of a well-ordered society," but tradition appealed to Hapgood less as order than as integration. Hutchins who spent much of his life wracked by emotional crises, wrote in 1894, "If we can only build up a form of civilization where mind and body go lustily hand in hand and play each other no scurvy tricks we shall realize the Utopia." Chuck Connors, the Bowery personality, was at peace with himself. Hapgood noticed that "Chuck knew his world exactly. Not approximately, but exactly. He therefore had a sure criterion of judgment." One of the things that most pleased Hapgood about the ghetto was the cohesiveness of "the orthodox Jewish culture." [27]

The selection of the bum and the aristocrat was significant in one other sense. When Hapgood noted that the middle class's "words lack literature," he was referring not only to the texture of their speech but to its ultimate value; Hapgood used the term *literature* normatively. Uninterested in the middle class, he never wrote much about them and used the term vaguely and pejoratively. His tendency to neglect the bourgeoisie as a subject distinguished him from Theodore Dreiser and Frank Norris, who often wrote about people on the rise.

A tough was by definition "an artist in words." Chuck Connors, the mayor of Chinatown, he remembered was "not only a philosopher, but also had the taste of an artist." Employing Matthew Arnold's dictum that literature was a "criticism of life," Hapgood found the more acute perceptions of the Bowery tough to be literature.[28] His work on Bowery characters differed from his East Side sketches. The word *poet* in *The Spirit of the*

Ghetto meant one who wrote poetry. On the Bowery the words *poet, artist,* and *philosopher* denoted those who had the ability to express a truth in a generalized form, at once able to grasp some reality and move beyond it. Hapgood greeted his Bowery characters frankly, with few conscious intellectual barriers, and on a direct emotional plane. Partly because of this his work on the Bowery never reached the sustained heights of *The Spirit of the Ghetto,* but it showed his hand more openly.

The tendency to see art among the lowly, to discuss outcasts in the language of culture, was a trademark of Hapgood's work. Many characters claimed cultural distinction. Shorty, a tramp, told Willard, "There's diff'rent kinds o' beggars; some gits there, 'n' some does n't. Them what gits there I call arteests, 'n' them what does n't I call ban'crupts." Even such as Tom Sharkey, pugilist, claimed literary taste.

> "Do you like Shakespeare?"
> "Sure," he [Sharkey] said.
> "What play of his do you like?"
> "Don't remember the name."
> "Was it 'Hamlet'?"
> "No, the other one." [29]

Hapgood's speaking of bartenders, bums, and athletes as poets, artists, or philosophers lent a certain charm to his writing. He recalled that Norman had praised "the Hegelian twist that I gave even to the meaning of a leg-show." Who, after all, could forget a comparison of Cy Young, baseball pitcher, to Diogenes? The juxtaposition of a character from low life with cultural concerns often produced an interesting epigram, and Hapgood ever since his Harvard days was an enthusiast of the epigram. Connors, speaking of his production in a vaudeville theater, declared, "Dere ain't no plot in me play, fer it's de real t'ing. Dere ain't no plot in life, is dere?" [30]

It was a useful device, but it would be wrong to see Hutchins Hapgood's preoccupation with these figures as manipulative in the sense that he saw them merely as literary treasures. He once wrote of himself that he "emotionally, rather than intellectually, understood 'any old thing,'" and he had a strong democratic impulse. To call a tough a poet or philosopher reconciled Hapgood's pleasure in outcasts with cultural imperatives. He would have appreciated Shakespeare and Chuck Connors separately, but this partial synthesis made his enjoyment of each greater. Hutchins of course did not confuse a tough with Goethe, but he did like to believe that there were similarities. He found not *Faust* or *Hamlet* on the Bowery but "the strange gift of expression, the power, in a few words, of composing a spiritual picture; always, of course, fragmentarily—a suggestion, a hint, but with the life of art in it." [31]

Hapgood's work about the Bowery contrasted to that of Edward Townsend, Stephen Crane, and Jacob Riis. Townsend's fictional " 'Chimmie' Fadden" stories, which were very popular at the turn of the century, and their imitators were essentially superficial, lacked the tragic element, and emphasized comic situation, not deep characterization. Crane was much more aware of the cruelty and violence of the slum than Hapgood and was less inclined to sentimentalize. One might note an article Crane wrote on tramps in 1894. Appealing to the reader's sense of smell and vividly using color, it debunked the glamor of trampdom. The characters in Crane's *Maggie: A Girl of the Streets*, are not of the sort to be found in Hapgood's writings. Indeed, Neith Hapgood, unlike her husband, held a negative and ominous view of the Bowery.[32]

The contrast to Riis, an avid reformer, was striking. Conscious of playing for large stakes and eager to hasten reform, Riis was often urgent, sometimes strident. "Those who would fight for the poor must fight the poor to do it" were words unlikely to be spoken by Hutchins Hapgood. Riis was preoccupied with the tenement and particularly with its impact on children; Hapgood rarely wrote about people in their homes and seldom discussed children. This suggested the extent to which Hapgood was a frequenter of saloons and public places of amusement rather than one who spent his days in the slums. Riis thought whatever beauty came out of the slum rare and mute. *Out of Mulberry Street: Stories of Tenement Life* (1898), perhaps Riis's only book that frequently acknowledged the existence of virtue in the tenements, was fiction, and as David M. Fine has explained, Riis was in part responding to the sentimental conventions of slum fiction.[33] In most of these stories virtue paraded only at Christmastime—an indication that it was exceptional. In contrast, Hapgood considered the beauty of the slum-dwellers expressive, positive rather than passive. Riis, unlike Hapgood, did not realize that the poor could make epigrams.

Hapgood felt that Bowery life was more real. He wrote Mabel Dodge some years later, "If you sometime will go down to the Bowery and see the Booze victims—you will see another way in which God manifests himself. God doesn't manifest himself at all in Walter Lippman [*sic*]." Part of Hapgood's democratic philosophy was an intense interest in personality and a need for human contact. Harvard and Germany had combined learning and socializing. He at one time described himself "as a temperamental sociologist," that is, a student of temperament. Later he claimed that "the true democrat has an almost religious respect for personality." [34] This had always been implicit in his writing.

Hapgood's merging of democratic and cultural interests integrated his work. It partially helped him, unlike Willard, to accept his subjects with few strings attached. His studies of the Bowery thus did not vacillate as much as Willard's works. Although his use of "artist," "poet," and "philosopher" lent grace to his sketches, he began to overemploy such terminology and to lose effect, to become predictable. There was also a muffled note of patronization—Hapgood was never as demanding of his Bowery chums as of intellectuals. One senses that he felt less threatened by those he met on the Bowery. His concern for discovering whether a character was an artist tended to blur distinctions. Although he discussed bohemians, bums, and aristocrats, he was not really concerned about how they reacted upon one another. It is sometimes hard to accept his happy similarities. His works do not discuss how Jews reacted to the Bowery, or vice versa, or antagonism between various of his outsider groups. Hapgood was looking for expressive temperament or poetry or, in other words, basically something that would move him. When he called a tough an artist, he was saying that the tough made an artistic impact on him. He was more involved with his own response than with intergroup reactions.

VI

Inclined to give psychological explanations for his interest in outcasts, Hapgood claimed that associating with outsiders helped soothe his inferiority complex. In his autobiography he explained, "I have . . . always liked maimed and pathetic things. People 'who are not worth while' have always appealed to me. This is due largely, I think, to my experiences as a boy." He felt that the life-style of the saloons gave him not only physical but spiritual pleasure.[35]

Although temperamental peculiarities did play a significant part in his preoccupation, they are an incomplete explanation. His sympathy was selective. He did not seem particularly fond of the Irish in the Alton of his boyhood, nor was he upset when an Irish "gorilla" harassed a Chinese man on the Bowery. In his autobiography he contended that an incident during his world tour as a youth, in which Indian boys and girls bowed before him and a friend as representatives of the Anglo-Saxons, left him "deeply humiliated, ashamed of being in a position which had nothing to do with myself." An article written a few years after the event told a different story. He explained that the "two ordinary young Anglo-Saxons . . . would have felt ashamed of their undue eminence *were it not for the proud consciousness that they stood, for the moment, as the symbol of their race.*" [36]

Historical and cultural circumstances as well as emotional peculiarities accounted for Hapgood's fascination with outcasts. Slumming was fashionable at that time; people like Connors, who had a great following among journalists, arranged tours, often bogus ones, of the underworld. Like almost every other American fad, it became a business. In *Peter Whiffle* Carl Van Vechten satirized a vogue among many writers when he had Whiffle exclaim, "I found my heroine the other day, a little Jewish girl, who works in a sweat-shop. She had one blue eye and one black one. She has a club-foot, a hare-lip, and she is a hunch-back. I nearly cried for joy when I discovered her." Christopher Lasch has demonstrated that his "new radicals" were attracted to immigrants and outcasts, partly because they felt the outsiders led more satisfying lives and partly to employ them as critics of society. Hutchins's concern for outcasts, the belief that suffering was often ennobling, that the simple was more real, were legacies of romanticism. The poetry of Wordsworth, which Hapgood had admired immensely at Harvard, had often emphasized the common and the actual, and, as Harold Kolb has suggested, served as a link to realism for some American writers. Indeed, Hapgood, who often wrote about subjects favored by the more realistic writers, usually brought a romantic perspective to his work.[37] Other factors also influenced his work. Cahan and the *Commercial Advertiser* prodded him toward an examination of the East Side and Willard and the *Commercial* encouraged his exploration of the Bowery and his contacts with criminals.

VII

Hapgood, gradually finding his intellectual pursuits at odds with newspaper work, snapped, "Early reporting is sometimes crude literature. Late reporting is not crude and it is not literature." This remark resulted from his service on the *Commercial*. In an article appearing in *Types from City Streets* but published before 1906, Hapgood called the *Commercial* experiment "An Interesting Failure" and argued that the old spirit had lasted only a year and a half; then the *Commercial* "became . . . a perfectly conventional, conservative, dull, and commonplace sheet." He attributed the fall to Steffens, who he alleged grew stale and preoccupied with his own writing, and to suppression by Wright, the editor in chief. Hapgood, consistently frustrated by his low pay, once referred to his job as "a humiliating position" and tried to get a consular post or work for Hearst. He apparently resigned in 1900, although he actually did not do so until 1903.[38] After he left the *Commercial,* Hapgood and Neith, whom he married in June 1899, and their young son, Boyce, went to Italy. The similarity to Norman Hapgood was striking. Both had found their service on the *Commercial* ultimately frustrating and both believed that a stay in Italy would provide relief. Their disillusion was just one conspicuous example of the difficulty each had making peace with the journalistic world, a rough indication that their standards were never entirely those of workaday journalism.

Hutchins Hapgood sailed to Italy with more specific plans than had Norman; once there he labored on manuscripts of books and completed *The Autobiography of a Thief.* Neith also wrote, and their few months in Italy seem to have been delightful. She recorded one conversation: "Hutch confessed his desire for an affair with a fascinating Russian woman of the world. And I said that if a woman had to have more than one child she ought at least to have the privilege of selecting a different father for each. We had an amusing time." [39]

The death of Neith's father forced them to return to the United States. Through Finley Peter Dunne, Hutchins got a job on the *New York Morning Telegraph.* Primarily a racing sheet, it hired twice as many reporters as were normally required to insure enough sober ones to do the day's work. Although he enjoyed some of the frivolity, "the deeper currents of journalism had a much greater appeal," and he left after about a year. In late December 1904 he joined the *Chicago Evening Post.* Finding the salary too small and means of supplementing his income in that city scant, he tried New York and then Chicago again. In 1906 he sailed to Europe for a two-year stay. He had hoped to "give up all journalistic nonsense, all my half-hearted attempts to fit into the machinery of modern life, live cheaply & sit down & try to do a few things in really good form, cultivate the really contemplative mood, and brood over my Past and the Universe and see if I can't extract a little permanent expression out of it." [40]

VIII

Hapgood's works during the early years of the century were, besides *The Spirit of the Ghetto, The Autobiography of a Thief;* an unpublished manuscript on Frank Butler, a fellow reporter on the *New York Morning Telegraph;* and "A Marionette," or "The Story of a Singing Soubrette." *The Autobiography of a Thief,* published in 1903, was the prototype of half a dozen other works:

"Marionette," the biography of Butler, "David," *The Spirit of Labor* (1907), *An Anarchist Woman* (1909), and "Cristine."[41]

The Autobiography of a Thief, the story of an ex-pickpocket identified as Jim, actually Jim Caulfield, was indebted to Willard, who had introduced Caulfield to Hapgood. The concern with the criminal class, particularly pickpockets, the manner of research —interviews in saloons—bore the Willard imprint. *The Autobiography of a Thief* was essentially an "as told to" book. He interviewed Jim over several months about his career as a pickpocket and his life in prison, organized his story, and published it with introductory and concluding comments. Hapgood split the royalties with Caulfield—an indication of the joint nature of the enterprise. In this book, unlike some others of this type, Hapgood stayed in the background. It was perhaps the best integrated of his efforts in this genre because the subject was less complex, because Jim was unusually vivid, and because his rise and fall as a criminal were a good framework. Particularly revealing about the mores of the underworld, *The Autobiography of a Thief* deserves to rank as a significant and interesting specimen of the memoirs of criminals, a literary subgenre that has existed in America at least since the nineteenth century and is popular even today. Hapgood's optimism about Jim's future was noticeable. "I am convinced that Jim is strictly on the level, and will remain so. The only thing yet lacking to make his reform sure is a job." Jim used his royalties to buy cocaine and to purchase fancy clothes to improve his effectiveness as a pickpocket.[42]

Hapgood developed a literary method out of his books and journalism. His approach was based on the newspaper interview, but he contended that it also resembled Defoe's in *Moll Flanders* and *Robinson Crusoe.* The subject had to be "expressive," and Hapgood's protagonists were more articulate than the run of their friends. One convict had exhorted Jim to "talk United States and not be springing whole leaves out of a dictionary." Yet it was necessary to be more than individually revealing.

The expressive individual should not only be interesting in himself, but should also represent a class. If he be thoroughly identified with some social *milieu,* his story cannot be well told without involving that *milieu.* In the process of touching his life, the ideals and habits of his class would be shown. A section of life would thus be portrayed and a human story told at the same time.[43]

The autobiographical mode catered to Hapgood's fascination with personality. He was more at ease dealing with individuals than with groups. Although he claimed that his method could be used on all social levels, the best results were achieved with "low life" and "plain people," who were the most authentic. Living people were more interesting, truer than imagined characters. Hapgood, warning that he was not doling out a recipe for literature, that one had to have the proper "temperament" to exploit the opportunities, reasoned that Connors was "ready-made art. All that was needed was to put the fragments already formed into a whole. To do it required nothing but patience, taste, and love for the material." He concluded that "done right [it] would have been as good and permanent a piece of literature as the Memoirs of Benvenuto Cellini." [44]

Hapgood believed his technique capable of revitalizing American literature, which, too concerned with romance, sentimentality, and fantasy, had lost touch with real life. His human document was peculiarly characteristic of the America of the muckraker era, when there was a pervasive interest in the factual and the real. Ray Stannard Baker spoke for many writers when he asked. "Why bother with fictional characters and plots when the world was full of far more marvellous stories that were true: and characters so powerful, so fresh, so new, that they stepped into the narratives under their own power?" [45]

Hapgood's identification of the actual with literature had embarrassing consequences. During the First World War, when the Provincetown Players produced *Enemies,* a duologue by Neith Boyce and Hutchins Hapgood based on their marital relations, Hutchins and Neith played the roles of He and She. Hutchins, who forgot his lines even though he had written them, was surprised that he had to read from the text to complete his performance.[46] It is not difficult to account for his blunder. He had so approximated the real, the usual, that it had little uniqueness, little individuality. This was only one of the problems his work would have.

CHAPTER 5

Collier's: The Early Years

I

WHEN NORMAN HAPGOOD returned to New York from Italy, he did not pursue the "more varied literary work" that he had planned after leaving the *Commercial Advertiser*. While in Rome he had received a cablegram from Robert J. Collier offering him the editorship of *Collier's Weekly* at $25,000 a year.[1] He sailed to New York, talked over the proposal with Collier, and quickly accepted. If Hapgood's sojourn in Italy after quitting the *Commercial Advertiser* was a retreat from the frustrations of dramatic criticism, his leaving Rome to work at *Collier's* at Thirteenth Street, near the bustle of the docks, was a return to the compromises of journalism.

It would be hard to understand Hapgood's decision merely in terms of his experience as a drama critic. He had been, after all, hard to please, profoundly disturbed by the quality of the contemporary American stage, an upholder of *Harvard Monthly* standards in a world that had little use for them. Changing ambitions influenced his decision to return to journalism. Skeptical of his talents as a creative writer and disappointed by his attempt to combine criticism and journalism through dramatic reviewing, Hapgood sought a literary life free from the demands of everyday journalism. Some evidence suggests that he found this less stimulating than he had expected, that he had become too much the working journalist. More important, his self-estimation certainly made him susceptible to an attractive opportunity in journalism. He concluded in 1903, "The truth is, undoubtedly, that for the highest literary talent books and plays are the most telling weapons, but for the man of action, intelligence, force, and elasticity, without exceptional gifts, journalism is more nourishing."[2]

Hapgood's dramatic criticism was only one, though surely the most important, aspect of his work during the preceding five years. The *Commercial Advertiser* had had many ties to magazine journalism. The staff buzzed with interest in magazines. As Hutchins Hapgood recalled, "How often we talked about what we would do with our own monthly!" [3] The Saturday supplement was for many a springboard to periodical work, and among the writers who earned reputations in popular magazines—some before, some during, and some after their service on the *Commercial*—were Lincoln Steffens, Neith Boyce, Bliss Carman, Josiah Flynt Willard, Hutchins Hapgood, Edwin Lefèvre, and Harvey J. O'Higgins.

Most significantly, the *Commercial Advertiser* gave Norman Hapgood a new perspective on the press. Revolting against the starchiness of the *Evening Post*, the *Commercial* writers had learned to appreciate the old *New York Sun* and the yellows. Norman shared much of this outlook. Although not an admirer of the yellows, he recognized their value and chastised the respectable papers in good *Commercial Advertiser* fashion: "They are dead. They think like college professors. They carry on a tradition unsuited to our people. They bore us. Yellow journalism is changing this. It is doing a work of destruction." [4] Anxious to infuse the press with liveliness, Hapgood was understandably interested in journalism of the *Collier's* sort.

II

The story of *Collier's Weekly* was inseparable from the story of Peter F. Collier. Collier, an Irish immigrant who had arrived in the United States with twenty-five cents, eventually became a book salesman specializing in Catholic Bibles. Once, while Collier was trying to make a sale, a customer gave him an idea. " 'No, me boy,' an old woman said to him, 'I would like yer Bible, but I have no dollar. If ye want to lave it here, I will give ye tin cents, and ye can come back some ither time and get the rist.' " After attempting unsuccessfully to interest his employer in selling books on installment, Collier went on his own, adopted the installment plan, and later published books himself. Although in the late nineteenth century many publishers looked down on this kind of business, Collier made a fortune. By the time of his death in 1909 he had sold, either by agents or through the mail, fifty-two million books, mostly low-priced editions.[5]

A stocky man with a thick head, a resolute chin, thin, challenging lips that would have seemed ominous were it not for his expansive good nature, and small, quick eyes, Collier might have been mistaken for a successful Tammany politician or one of the legendary New York bartenders of the time. He was an avid hunter and poloist, and his son noted in 1903, "He still hunts three and sometimes four days a week, breaking ribs and collar-bones with cheerful regularity and keeps young accordingly." Peter F. Collier took an active interest in social life and often made the society pages. A devout Catholic, he was an emotional man and very sentimental and generous. He did not publish books that had even a touch of immorality, and he made a practice of continuing to do business with those who had helped him on his way up. Having known poverty, he followed a relatively enlightened labor policy. He also kept his old horses in graceful retirement and bought a house for the old Irishwoman who had inspired him with the installment idea.[6]

III

Collier founded a magazine, *Once a Week,* in 1888 (called *Collier's Weekly* after 1896) as a throw-in to be sold with his books. He took relatively little interest in the magazine, especially during the years that Hapgood was associated with it; his son, Robert, more than anyone else, was responsible for the rise of *Collier's Weekly*. Robert Collier was its "creator." This thin-lipped, thin-browed, blue-eyed Irishman shared many traits with his father, including an enjoyment of the outdoors and a fondness for luxury. Robert Collier, who had attended Georgetown, Harvard, and Oxford, wanted to improve *Collier's Weekly*. After he took over the *Weekly* in 1898, it showed quick and sure progress.

Collier's covered the Spanish-American War particularly effectively, and during 1898 advertising linage increased by more than two and one-half times. Between 1897 and 1906 annual advertising rocketed from under $6 thousand to over $1 million. Circulation leaped from under fifty thousand in January 1898 to two hundred and fifty thousand by the end of 1900. By 1902 P. F. Collier and Son was printing three hundred thousand copies of the magazine and one hundred thousand books a week.[7]

Robert Collier was much more inclined to consider the *Weekly* an independent entity and to invest money and effort in it than was his father. Young Collier exhibited a fine knack for hitting popular taste. One of the most obvious qualities of *Collier's Weekly* from the Spanish-American War through at least the next decade and a half was its visual appeal. A large magazine, measuring 10½ by 14¾ inches, *Collier's* effectively exploited its size. It made profitable use of two-page, center-spread pictures. Barely five feet two inches tall, Jimmy Hare, the *Collier's* ace in news pictures, was equally adept at photographing battles, the Wright brothers' early airplane flights, and New York City from an unstable balloon, and became "probably the most famous war photographer in the world." Illustration was given high priority at *Collier's*. The work of such artists as Frederic Remington, Charles Dana Gibson, Jessie Willcox Smith, E. W. Kemble, A. B. Frost, Maxfield Parrish, and F. X. Leyendecker appeared in the *Weekly*. *Collier's* was also noted for its war correspondents. Richard Harding Davis and Frederick Palmer were perhaps the best, but there were many others. One of the *Collier's* writers only mildly exaggerated when he claimed, "Wherever there is an army in the field, and clash of arms and bullets and the thousand tragedies of war, there, too, is a man from *Collier's*." [8] The interest of *Collier's* extended not merely to war but to spectacle in general. It gave major coverage to royal visits, coronations, and world's fairs.

Fiction was one of the *Weekly*'s more popular features. Although emphasis on fiction declined after *Collier's* became preoccupied with politics, it still played a significant role in the *Collier's* of the Progressive Era, and the short stories and serials had undoubtedly boosted the *Weekly*'s circulation and reputation early in the century. The highest prices were paid for pieces by such writers as Arthur Conan Doyle, Rudyard Kipling, and Richard Harding Davis.[9] *Collier's* also developed a series of features, departments such as Walter Camp's on sports and special numbers on automobiles, outdoor life, and fiction. The appeal was always varied. *Collier's* appealed to those who liked to look at interesting photographs or Gibson girls or to read the latest adventure of Sherlock Holmes or the work of Richard Harding Davis, and, increasingly under Hapgood's editorship, it catered to those more concerned with politics.

Robert Collier was surely one of the more gifted magazine publishers and editors in perhaps the greatest era of American magazines. Both Hapgood and Mark Sullivan, his closest associates during most of his best years, regarded his talents very highly. Without Collier, who had a gift for what Hapgood called "the varied, human, bustling side" of magazine work, the *Weekly* would not have become such a widely read and influential organ.[10] Collier had a promoter's sense of publicity, and the *Weekly*'s shrewd self-exploitation reflected his talents. When he signed Charles Dana Gibson to a $100,000 contract to do 100 drawings, Collier was canny enough to realize that the fee was as newsworthy as the fact that Gibson was to work for *Collier's* (in addition to *Life*).

Much of the *Weekly*'s success was due to money. Collier, like his father, was a spender, but young Collier was more inclined to spend on the *Weekly*. Robert Collier admitted, "I have been accused by authors of seeking 'big names,' and by publishers of 'inflating prices.' My reply is that I want the best for *Collier's* readers and am willing to pay for it." Collier was more a bold than an innovative publisher and editor and did not make significant original contributions to American magazine journalism of the sort that S. S. McClure did. He was not as shrewd a judge of talent as McClure. Although Collier wanted "the best," the best was usually the established or someone or something recommended to him by another. It would be hard to imagine Collier reading an article on the French sewer system and becoming interested enough to contact the writer, Ida M. Tarbell, as McClure did. The *Collier's* record in fiction, while good, was probably inferior to that of *McClure's*. But Collier was never satisfied with mere popularity; his ideal was not that of the *Saturday Evening Post*. "I want a large circulation to bring advertising," he explained. "I want advertising to bring revenue; I want revenue to make the *Weekly* that much better." Collier's liberal spending did some good. The short-story contests resulted in the *Weekly's* paying a minimum of five cents a word for fiction, a rate that raised the price of fiction throughout the periodical market.[11]

IV

By the close of 1902 *Collier's Weekly* was popular and flourishing, but not influential. President Theodore Roosevelt, who kept a sharp eye on magazines, was so little aware of the *Weekly* that at the end of 1903 he confused Robert Collier with his father. Hapgood described the situation pithily: "Nobody of my acquaintance read the magazine, or even knew its name." Collier had interested his friend Finley Peter Dunne in becoming editor, but after some service Dunne quit. Collier was upset and complained to Dunne that "I took you as the point of departure in laying all my new plans." Dunne recommended Norman Hapgood to Collier.[12]

Collier wanted Hapgood "to strike a note that would create a reputation."[13] With such a goal, Hapgood's work as a dramatic and literary critic and as a biographer was an asset, and the fact that he had not done much editorial writing was not a severe liability. Indeed, his dramatic criticism was in some respects quite good preparation for his career as an editor. He had managed his own department probably with greater freedom than he would have enjoyed had he been doing political writing. Qualities that had got him into many disputes as a critic—combativeness, independence, and sometimes hypercriticalness—were at a premium in the new magazine journalism. Hapgood's disdain for some aspects of American cultural life lent credence to the claim that he was upgrading the *Weekly*, that he was, to use Chuck Connors's expression, 'de real t'ing."

When Hapgood became its editor, *Collier's Weekly* was already a successful paper with a character. His role was thus not that of a McClure, who founded a publication, or of an Edward Bok, who substantially transformed another. Collier had hired Hapgood chiefly to enhance the editorial pages. There he was to lend tone to the magazine. Hapgood in his first few years seems to have concentrated on the editorials, but Collier surely consulted him about a variety of matters. As *Collier's* became more political, Hapgood's power increased and he became an editor in the broader meaning of the word.

The layout of the editorials, which Hapgood was to make famous, had been devised for Dunne. Two pleasant pages of short, usually one-paragraph, editorials appeared toward the front of the magazine throughout Hapgood's years; longer editorials were sometimes used, and for a time the pages were expanded to three. The editorials were most frequently about politics, but usually included some on the drama, literature, or less serious subjects. Nonpolitical topics enabled Hapgood to discuss genuine interests, but also gave a lighter quality to the pages and advertised his range. An editor capable of leaping from Tammany to *Othello* undoubtedly pleased Collier, who craved an aura of culture. The motley, though carefully planned, pages were aptly described by *Hearst's International* some years later when Hapgood was doing similar work for it. It called one of his efforts "Hapgood on Socialism, Ladies, and Nonsense." [14]

Hapgood did not write all the editorials. Collier wrote some and so did Mark Sullivan after he joined *Collier's*. Among the others who contributed were Samuel Hopkins Adams, Will Bradley, C. P. Connolly, John M. Oskison, Leonard Hatch, Frederick Palmer, and William Kent.

Brief, tight editorials became Norman Hapgood's trademark. One indication of his skill and reputation was that he subsequently did similar work for three other magazines. The brief editorial form was influenced by Arthur Brisbane, Hearst's right-hand man. Norman brought an intense seriousness to his work. His stance was independent and critical, although he never was as ready to find fault as an editor as he had been as a drama critic. Suffering from a lack of humor—his best was usually sarcastic—he made some attempt to lighten the content, and, especially in his later years with *Collier's,* partially succeeded through the use of confessedly nonserious topics. He gradually realized the advantages of discussions of strawberry shortcake and baseball.

V

Hapgood's development as a progressive editor was preconditioned by his development as a progressive. Although some progressives claimed that dramatic incidents turned them into reformers, his life furnished no equivalent of Jane Addams's experiences in East London or at a Spanish bullfight. Nor did Hapgood contend that he had violently overthrown his old beliefs. Although he later doubted some of the values he had learned during his formal education, there was none of the estrangement of Lincoln Steffens, Frederic C. Howe, or Ray Stannard Baker. The gradual development of Hapgood's progressivism was partly a reflection of the analytical quality of his mind. Arthur H. Gleason once quipped, "He would love to be more radical than his clean, honest thinking will permit him." [15] The smooth evolution was also a tribute to the tenacity of the old values, the extent to which new beliefs often covered, rather than replaced, old ones.

The two most important early political influences on Norman Hapgood were his father and Harvard. From his father he probably got little in the way of specific creed, but did receive some important principles. Charles Hapgood's moralism and wariness of wealth became a permanent part of his son's makeup. His father's integrity and probity provided a model by which Norman often judged political figures. Harvard added an aesthetic justification to his thoughts about wealth. The relativism he absorbed in Cambridge gave him a certain flexibility, but its impact on his reform thought was not apparent until later. Indeed, much of Hapgood's relativism was often little more than a pretext for doing things he wanted to do and for not doing things he did not want to do. At the Harvard of the early 1890s mugwumpery and relativism were not in opposition; they usually operated in different fields or complemented one another. A Laodicean was more likely than not a mugwump.

Hapgood had been closely associated with two of the mugwumps' grandest institutions, Harvard and the *New York Evening Post*. His later mild contempt for mugwumpery was essentially a critique from one raised within. He early snickered at Gilded Age politicians, described himself as "a republican on silver, a democrat on tariff, satisfied with neither party on civil service," and enthusiastically backed Grover Cleveland in 1888 and 1892. Hapgood recalled that when he left Harvard, "I was careful and respectable. I was more affected by taste and less by moral tendency. In politics I was a snob." He cheered Cleveland's use of troops in the Pullman strike and voted for Palmer in 1896—a position consistent with the *Evening Post*'s, which supported McKinley out of expediency, but liked Palmer best. Most progressives, as George E. Mowry has noted, came from conservative backgrounds.[16]

Hapgood's disdain for party loyalty, his interest in English statesmanship, and his faith in disinterested service and noblesse oblige demonstrated the mugwump influence. He asked in 1903, "Why does Tammany, for instance, so often win? Why did it win the other day in the teeth of all reason? Because there are so many people who, although willing to inflict virtue upon others, do not relish it themselves." Although he eventually developed a more sophisticated analysis of urban politics, he never exhibited the grasp of Herbert Croly or Jane Addams. Throughout his first few years as editor of *Collier's Weekly*, he was most happy supporting fighters against graft, such as Joseph Folk and William Travers Jerome.[17] It was mildly ironic that Hapgood, who had ridiculed the tendency of American dramatic critics to indulge in moral judgments, was so moralistic in his discussion of politics. If his mugwump background imbued him with a vigorous opposition to corruption and with a strong desire to see principle, not self-interest, dominate politics—all links to progressivism—it also gave him some specific ideological ties, such as antitrust and low-tariff views.

Richard Hofstadter has pointed out that a mugwump had to overcome certain obstacles before he could become a progressive. Most important he had to develop a greater faith in democracy, temper his belief in laissez-faire, and seek wider public support. The key to Hapgood's evolution certainly was his increasingly democratic outlook. His relativism would undermine laissez-faire once it could be found to stand in the way of democracy. As a journalist he would to an extent have to reach a wider following. It is hard to tell how much of a democrat Norman was at Harvard. Robert Morss Lovett had been impressed by his midwesternness, and it seems likely that Hapgood was more democratic than his writings of the early and mid-nineties indicated, yet he always stopped short of a fundamentally democratic statement, as if he feared that a Laodicean might be spying on him. By 1898 he explained, "In the United States when our educated young men get their degrees they have a distant view of the conditions before them; but the deeper they live the more they accept the principles which guide the democratic tendencies of the time." Newly optimistic about American politics, he believed it was becoming better because it was becoming more moral.[18]

Hapgood's biography of Abraham Lincoln was particularly revealing. An annoyed reviewer criticized his too frequent quoting of the Lincoln wit.[19] Hapgood was no doubt partly compensating for his own lack of humor and partly trying to make his popular biography popular, but his fascination with Lincoln's wit was much more. Wit was one expression of a feel for language. For Hapgood the Lincoln wit reconciled the aristocratic stress on style with democracy. After reading Hapgood's biography, one might imagine that had Lincoln been born later and in more favorable circumstances, he could have been an editor of the *Harvard Monthly*.

If Lincoln suggested a synthesis between democracy and culture, Hapgood's critique of the *New York Evening Post* type of journalism, discussed earlier, signaled his most thoroughly democratic assertion, his most important deviation from the mugwump tradition, and it represented a wide bridge into progressivism. Precisely when Hapgood was writing dramatic criticism that was most at ease speaking to "the submerged tenth," he was absorbing a democratic theory of journalism. Hapgood was able, from at least his *Commercial Advertiser* days onward, to separate his views on literature and drama from his views on politics. He entertained few illusions about the ability of the average citizen to hold sophisticated opinions on cultural matters, but he did have, especially in the Progressive Era, faith in the capacity of the public to reach the right political decisions. He warned the readers of *Collier's:*

> I dislike reviewing, because on literary topics the public interest and my own are much further apart than they are in politics, economics, moralizing, and things in general; and what is the sense of talking to a person who is not listening? The trouble with writing to a large public about literature is that it is almost necessary to talk about the subject, instead of the way the subject is handled, which makes it literature. The small public has all the criticism it needs, so what is the use of writing criticism at all? [20]

VI

Any portrait of Norman Hapgood during his years with *Collier's* would be incomplete without reference to his life-style. In 1896 he married Emilie Bigelow of Chicago. She was attractive, but her dark, blue, intelligent eyes and aristocratic features more vividly suggested strength of character than beauty. Norman perhaps spoke paragraphs when he remarked, "I disagree about Emilie and Mrs. Toy and think they would have fun together. Both like to expand." One suspects that Emilie could be more persuasive with a mocking laugh or a gesture than Norman could be with elaborate analysis. Hutchins Hapgood remembered her as "largely selfish and egotistic" and "often lying in a chaise longue looking picturesque and impressive." He thought her a social climber and contended that his brother became "her slave." [21]

Emilie Hapgood had a deep interest in the theatre and became a well-known producer of amateur and professional theatricals. One account, mentioning her contributions to the theatre, recalled: "There was in her spirit a kind of magnificent blindness to the small or incidental or even practical; a strange, bold mysticism, a sort of baroque richness of soul; and a faith which, once aroused, was like a child's or mad saint's." Her production of three of Ridgely Torrence's plays has been hailed as the first Broadway performance of "realistic drama of Negro folk-life, with Negroes as major characters." Emilie seems to have had some interest in Negroes and during the First World War organized a private relief effort for black soldiers. The Hapgoods had one daughter, Ruth. Norman and Emilie Hapgood were divorced in Paris during the spring of 1915. Why their marriage collapsed is uncertain, although there was vague reference to her mental condition.[22] Interestingly, Norman Hapgood did not mention his first wife in his autobiography.

The Hapgoods lived comfortably during Norman's editorship of *Collier's Weekly*. He earned many times what he had as a critic. His winter residence, on East Seventy-Third Street in New York City, was praised by an architectural magazine. For most of these years he also owned a fashionable summer home in New Hampshire. "The estate is far and away the most charming in Cornish," one reporter concluded. Both homes were heavily influenced by Italian architecture, as if to serve as a reminder of the aesthetic life he had once wished to lead. The two residences revealed Hapgood's appreciation of good living and a willingness to spend money to achieve it, but always what he sought was in good taste. Both houses were distinguished by a wonderful simplicity. He was occasionally bothered by some of the demands made upon him as an editor, particularly those of the elder Collier to attend affairs of his flashy social set.[23] Hapgood seems, however, to have regarded these as minor impediments to work which he thoroughly enjoyed.

VII

The *Weekly's* relations with President Theodore Roosevelt provide some insight into its performance during the early days of Hapgood's editorship. *Collier's* had been generally favorable to the president during the early years of his first administration. Although the *Weekly* had claimed that John Hay was often responsible for Roosevelt's diplomatic successes and that Roosevelt took himself too seriously, there was no notable friction until the 1904 presidential election.

A shift occurred when Roosevelt, writing to Peter F. Collier, referred to "two or three points where I think your editorial writers have done me grave injustice to my harm." Shortly thereafter Roosevelt complained that the *Weekly* was "neutral." Robert Collier replied, "So far as was consistent with an independent attitude, we have upheld the Administration on nearly every issue." He conceded that Hapgood was "inclined to be captious now and then on every subject," but denied that *Collier's* was hostile to the president and pointed to its sharp critique of Judge Alton B. Parker's gold telegram as evidence of good faith. Roosevelt replied that Collier's defense was "manly" but still expressed doubts.[24]

Hapgood's criticism of Roosevelt's racial policy, the chief difficulty between him and Roosevelt throughout most of 1904, had triggered this dispute. He had accused the president of stirring up racial tension and had warned him that, had he not been so able in other areas and had the Democrats not nominated such a weak candidate, Roosevelt's record on race would have been "the overshadowing issue." Hapgood never showed much concern for the Negro. Convinced, like many of his generation, that radical Reconstruction had been a terrible mistake, he hoped that the Fourteenth and Fifteenth Amendments would not be enforced. The South should be left to deal with its own problems, and the Negro should be content with the Booker T. Washington gospel of work, he maintained. Roosevelt thought he occupied a middle ground between Norman Hapgood and Oswald Garrison Villard, between *Collier's Weekly* and the *New York Evening Post*.[25]

Late in the campaign another issue flared, this one of a sort more responsible in the long run than views on race for creating difficulties between Roosevelt and Hapgood. Hapgood and Robert Collier had come across information that Roosevelt was working against the Democratic candidate for governor of Missouri, Joseph W. Folk. Hapgood, one of Folk's most enthusiastic admirers, wanted to launch an all-out attack on the president, but Collier stopped him and corresponded with the president, who did not want to be pressed on this question because of its potential weight with independent voters. Although Collier accepted Roosevelt's confidential explanations and the material was not used against him, Hapgood remained dissatisfied. Antagonism became severe a year and a half later, when Hapgood again challenged Roosevelt's veracity. Hapgood and the president engaged in a heated argument over whether Roosevelt had changed his story about the extent of his cooperation with a publication associated with *Town Topics,* the scandal sheet.

The president, convinced that he had got the better of these exchanges, enjoyed boasting to Henry Cabot Lodge: "It is only rarely that one can get at a conceited and insincere jack of the advanced mugwump type, because usually it doesn't pay to shoot at him; but this particular time I did take solid satisfaction out of hanging even so small a hide on the fence." For his part Hapgood referred to Roosevelt's "usual bunco." [26]

The *Weekly*'s relations with Theodore Roosevelt from 1904 to 1906 revealed many of the qualities of Hapgood's work. He maintained a tough independence. Indeed, in some respects the controversies of 1904 to 1906 marked the coming of age of *Collier's* as an independent journal. That Roosevelt was nettled by *Collier's* suggested that the *Weekly* was beginning to exist politically. Despite the sharpness of the controversy, despite considerable provocation, Hapgood was still favorable to the president. Highly valuing principle in politics, he refused to become a bitter antagonist out of pique. His dealings with Roosevelt also displayed some of Hapgood's narrowness, his racial bias, and the large claim that mugwumpery had on him. His commentary on the 1904 election, while certainly independent, was hardly perceptive. One who had thought so highly of John Sharp Williams for the Democratic nomination—at least until the convention—still had a long way to go to be near the vanguard of progressivism.

CHAPTER 6

The Journalism of Controversy

I

NORMAN HAPGOOD BECAME a muckraker gradually. During his first years of the *Weekly* he was more a commentator on, than a participant in, the literature of exposure. Intellectually and temperamentally averse to the wilder muckrakers and preoccupied with distinguishing worthy from unworthy work, he most admired the writers of *McClure's:* Ida M. Tarbell, Ray Stannard Baker, and Lincoln Steffens. McClure's well-known emphasis on accuracy appealed to Hapgood. "Trust-busting and frenzied reform, carried on with a violent and giddy disregard of truth," he warned, "is likely to break itself and fall to pieces against the hard sense of the pillars of society." Hapgood got into several arguments with the effervescent Thomas W. Lawson over such questions, and an editorial censuring David Graham Phillips, one of the more sensational muckrakers, upset that journalist.[1]

Hapgood's dislike of overstatement often made *Collier's* cautious. The *Indianapolis Star* remarked, "If you see it in *Collier's,* you never know whether it will be retracted or not." Mr. Dooley once parodied Hapgood: " 'Th' Homeeric Legend an' Graft; Its Cause an' Effect; Are They th' Same? Yes and No,' be Norman Slapgood." Upton Sinclair was less good-natured. He complained that Hapgood "spent his editorial time balancing like a tight-rope walker on the narrow thread of truth, occupying himself like a medieval schoolman with finding the precise mathematical or metaphysical dead centre between the contending forces of conservatism and radicalism." [2] Although this quality refelcted Hapgood's outlook, at least during his first few years on the *Weekly,* it was also good public relations. A nicely timed vacillation here and there probably did much to convince readers of the *Weekly's* integrity and believability.

This moderation was open to the charge of opportunism, a desire to soothe advertisers and avoid antagonizing the public. Sinclair claimed that Robert Collier and Hapgood stood by while Peter F. Collier suppressed an article of Sinclair's, a critique of Steffens's work on urban corruption. Supposedly, "Pat" Collier had found Sinclair too radical. A second controversy involved an article that Sinclair had submitted to *Collier's* denouncing conditions in Chicago's meatpacking houses. After accepting it and giving it advance publicity, *Collier's* substantially edited the piece and placed alongside it a few excerpts favorable to Sinclair's viewpoint from the London *Lancet,* a prestigious medical journal, and an article by Major L. L. Seaman. Seaman's article, commissioned by *Collier's,* called for a few reforms and argued that "there is no tainted meat sold from Chicago stockyards." *Collier's* concluded: "This incident will serve as an example of the policy mapped out for the conduct of this paper. We shall be guided no more by the hundreds of thousands of readers who love virulence toward great corporations than we shall be by the preferences of these corporations." [3] Sinclair was furious. He claimed that *Collier's* had treated him poorly, that it refused to publish his letter of protest, and that Seaman's article was a cover-up of the Beef Trust. His explanation of the *Weekly*'s conduct was that Hapgood "had backed the horse of gold, the horse that came to his office loaded with full-page advertisements of packing-house products." [4]

Sinclair's first accusation, that Peter F. Collier suppressed an article by him, seems plausible. The details conformed well to the division of authority within *Collier's* at the time of the incident, 1903. Hapgood's subsequent denial of the charge does not necessarily contradict Sinclair's story. Hapgood may not have known of Collier's decision, or, if he knew, he may have forgotten about it. The second charge is more important. *Collier's* surely treated Sinclair roughly, but the *Weekly* did publish his letter of protest. Although Seaman asked a few good questions about the Sinclair article, he had not refuted it. Seaman simply refused to deal with many of Sinclair's arguments, and his conclusion was complacent. No less an authority than President Roosevelt bellowed, "I do not think very highly of Collier's

Weekly, but I am surprised that even they should have employed such a fakir as Dr. Seaman." [5]

In his autobiography Hapgood denied Sinclair's allegations but mentioned a proposed serialization of *The Jungle* rather than the specific issues involved. One historian has condemned this as a "dignified refusal to answer Sinclair's charges directly." Perhaps, but a more plausible explanation of his treatment of the subject is that much of his autobiography was written in Europe and in general suffered from a lack of research. It does not seem likely that Hapgood and *Collier's,* strong supporters of pure food legislation, were doing the bidding of the meat trust when they sustained Seaman. Nor is there substantial evidence to back Louis Filler's contention that *Collier's* checked its pure food crusading "until after Sinclair had managed to push *The Jungle* past the boycott of fear and special interest." [6]

The most reliable explanation of the Sinclair-Seaman affair is that it was a logical if exaggerated result of Hapgood's preference for a cool, methodical, balanced literature of exposure. His eagerness to be "objective" overcame his critical judgment, and he accepted shoddy work. This episode was important in another respect. It established the distance Hapgood had to go to be a muckraker. Although he always considered himself removed from the wild-eyed radicals, he was not so concerned to refute Sinclair in 1907 or 1908 as he had been in 1905. The reason for the change was his growing participation in the literature of exposure.

II

The *Town Topics* affair, perhaps not a full-fledged muckraking venture, took place at about the same time as the patent medicine crusade. *Town Topics* was a peculiar magazine. Specializing in society news and scandal, it was widely read, "but one never saw anyone reading it." *Town Topics* always had a rather strange relationship with its readers. One of its former writers, Burgess Johnson, recalled that it "catered to a set with whom the pursuit and maintenance of a place in the 'social' news was a vocation.

Many of them would rather be the butt of a paragraph of malicious gossip than not be mentioned at all. Many even sent in sensational items about themselves." [7]

William d'Alton Mann, who had a taste for mutton, champagne, dollar cigars, and gossip, ran *Town Topics*. Far from holding a low opinion of himself, he alleged that his work possessed redeeming social value, that his real purpose was not pandering, but acute social commentary. Thinking that his revelations had a purgative effect on the Four Hundred, he regarded himself as what George Washington Plunkitt might have termed a practical sociologist.

An item in *Town Topics* on Alice Roosevelt, the president's daughter, brought retaliation from *Collier's*. The criticism of Miss Roosevelt was not the sharpest Mann had ever made—*Town Topics* sometimes made veiled allegations of adultery against various members of society—but it did have a disturbing quality, a "leering" quality, Hapgood later termed it. Robert Collier was upset enough to ask Hapgood to write an editorial unfavorable to Colonel Mann and *Town Topics*. Collier felt that the resulting piece needed fire so he, in passion, added that Mann's "standing among the people is somewhat worse than that of an ordinary forger, horse-thief, or second-story man." These were the kind of words that invite libel suits, and *Collier's* did not bother Mann or the scandal sheet again for some time.[8] Cooler heads had prevailed at the *Weekly*.

In the summer of 1905 *Collier's* began to harass Mann. The revived audacity of the *Weekly* resulted from reports in various New York papers producing damaging evidence against *Town Topics*, and, more important, the arrest of a *Town Topics* employee. Besides attacking Mann and *Town Topics*, *Collier's* conducted sorties against Judge Joseph Deuel for alleged association with the scandal sheet. In August 1905 Mann brought a pair of civil libel suits, which *Collier's* predicted would never be tried. In mid-September Judge Deuel filed a criminal libel suit and Hapgood was arrested. Mann also filed a criminal libel suit.

Altogether there were four libel suits. Mann's two $100,000 suits can be dismissed with little comment. They were never tried and were probably only token protests. Mann's criminal libel suit against both of the Colliers and Hapgood did at least get a hearing, raised a little controversy, but was not really important. It was soon overshadowed by Deuel's criminal libel suit against Hapgood and dropped. Deuel's suit is the one usually referred to as the *Town Topics* case. A dramatic trial that exercised a viselike grip on most of New York's front pages, it has been largely neglected by historians.

Judge Deuel's suit was based on an editorial of Hapgood's that had charged that Deuel "is part owner and one of the editors of a paper of which the occupation is printing scandal about people who are not cowardly enough to pay for silence." [9] Since truth is an absolute defense in a criminal libel suit, if Hapgood could prove that what he had written was true, he would be found not guilty. He would also be found innocent, even though his allegations could not be proved, if he could establish that he had made his remarks with good intentions and after suitable efforts at verification.

Hapgood was not the dominant figure at the trial. Since what he had said was in print, establishing his exact words was not a point of controversy, although their meaning caused some debate. Deuel and Mann logged the most time on the witness stand because Hapgood's attorneys relentlessly cross-examined them in an attempt to authenticate the *Collier's* charges. Indeed, late in the trial one of the defense attorneys quipped to Hapgood, "It's you that's being tried, isn't it?" [10] Robert Collier made elaborate preparations for the trial. He hired Edward M. Shepard and James W. Osborne, two of the ablest members of the New York bar, to represent Hapgood. Collier also spent lavishly on investigations of *Town Topics* and managed to lure two of its employees to *Collier's*. Robert Collier was in his glory; his alert face became a fixture at the trial. A center of attention, he found that the trial satisfied his fondness for the dramatic and the personal.

Hapgood's trial began in mid-January 1906. Within a few days it was apparent that Deuel and the cooler Mann were in for a rough time. *Collier's* demonstrated that Deuel's link to *Town Topics* was hardly casual, that he was serving as a sort of censor, pointing out the legally permissible to Mann. It was also established that Mann, without collateral, had obtained substantial loans from some of New York society's finest. Curiously, these transactions were often followed by rapid betterment of the creditor's treatment in *Town Topics*. Most interesting, perhaps, was the story of *Fads and Fancies,* a limited edition book of nondescript biographical sketches of the wealthy, allegedly published in cooperation with *Town Topics*. Subjects of the authorized sketches often paid exorbitantly for a copy of this book—sometimes thousands of dollars. The subscription agent had used threats of retribution from *Town Topics* to pressure reluctant subscribers. Although Mann's tie with *Fads and Fancies* was never definitively documented, it was loudly suggested.

The trial climaxed when District Attorney William Travers Jerome—the district attorney prosecuted criminal libel suits—asked Hapgood on what he had based the allegedly libelous editorial. Hapgood replied that information from the district attorney's office had been a major source. After this admission—the strict-principled Hapgood had not even told his lawyers this from fear of violating the professional confidence of his friend Jerome—it was virtually certain that he would be found not guilty. Indeed, according to one account, the jury was even persuaded that his editorial was true.[11]

The trial had been unusually jocular. The claim of Mann and Deuel that their reputations had been impugned was, as Mark Twain observed, at least a little incongruous. Shepard, Osborne, and Jerome had wittily discomforted Deuel, Mann, and the Four Hundred. At one point in the trial the presiding judge had to turn from the assemblage to hide a hearty laugh. The foreman of the jury, a cartoonist, earned a few extra dollars by sketching the proceedings from the jury box for the Hearst press. The trial was a good show. The *New York American* assigned its drama critic, Alan Dale, as one of its correspondents. Dale, in a tongue-in-cheek review, proclaimed, "Quite on a par with Bernard Shaw's 'Man and Superman' was the delightful little intimate domestic society comedy by one Norman Hapgood, entitled 'Mann and Society-Man,' 'presented' in the Criminal Courts Building yesterday." Dale concluded that "it achieved the rarest of all combinations, for it was vulgar and funny at the same time." Even the magnificent Emilie Hapgood managed to participate. While the jury was deliberating, a policeman told Mrs. Hapgood that unseemly demonstrations would be frowned on. The aristocratic Emilie

surveyed the old man through her lorgnette for a moment, and then said:

"I don't just know what you mean about a demonstration. I'm sure I've no intention of making one."

"If you do," said Capt. Lynch sternly, "it will be in contempt of court, and we are sworn to put such persons out."

Mrs. Hapgood smiled upon the friends who had accompanied her to court, and then walked out of the room and remained in the corridors until the verdict was announced.[12]

III

The *Town Topics* case, more than a spectacle, had great impact on *Collier's* and had some interesting implications for American journalism. Probably no magazine of its time more successfully used judicial and quasi-judicial proceedings. *Collier's* prided itself on its legal acumen during the patent medicine fight and would play an important if unofficial role at the Ballinger-Pinchot hearings. In at least one case Collier was the plaintiff and won a $50,000 judgment (later set aside) against the Postum Cereal Company, "the largest . . . ever rendered in a libel case in New York County and probably in the United States." *Collier's* realized that suits were not always nuisances but sometimes could be turned to advantage. Although *Collier's* ran many potentially libelous articles during Hapgood's editorship, and was involved in much litigation, it seems not to have lost, but once, at least, it reached an accommodation out of court—with William J. "Fingy" Conners allegedly because of the unavailability of key personnel—an unconvincing excuse. Hapgood was proud of his ability in this line, and Mark Sullivan once offered *Collier's* expertise to Theodore Roosevelt, who was contemplating a suit. The *Town Topics* case, with Collier spending heavily—the whole affair cost the *Weekly* over $75,000—hiring outstanding attorneys and using special investigators, was the archetype of other ventures.[13]

Collier's was richly rewarded for the contest against *Town Topics*. During the peak of the trial the proceedings ruled most of New York's front pages. Such publicity was well worth $75,000. *Collier's* not only received wide exposure, but exposure of the most desirable kind. The scenario was wonderful: *Collier's*, with the applause of the American press, stood for decency and against filth, while Mann appeared as an impugner of reputations and a ruffian. Indeed, the conflict was so clearly drawn, and worth was so largely ascribed to the *Collier's* position, that more than one publisher probably asked his managing editor if he could not come up with something like that. Fighting scandal enhanced the moral stature of the *Weekly* in a way that Gibson girls and war correspondents could not. Conducted at the same time as the patent medicine fight, it changed *Collier's* from a mere popular organ to one of some weight in public affairs. Hapgood shared in the glory. The Author's Club of New York gave him "a formal reception"—only the third time in its history that it had honored a nonmember in that way.[14] Most significantly, he became a marked figure among American journalists.

Although Collier, Hapgood, and the *Weekly* all reaped a rich harvest from the *Town Topics* affair, their efficacy in maiming scandal journalism was disputable. According to Mann's biographer, *Town Topics* was hurt by the affair. Neither Mann nor Deuel enjoyed their time on the stand and both were subsequently tried, Mann for perjury, Deuel for improper conduct. Both were acquitted. On the other hand, the imminent collapse of *Town Topics*, which *Collier's* predicted, did not occur.[15] In fact, although *Collier's* survived *Town Topics*, the latter maintained its character as a scandal sheet longer than the former retained its reputation as a progressive magazine.

The attack on scandal journalism partially caricatured what it was fighting. Apparently no one bothered to ask why Robert Collier, who cut a social figure, had been reading *Town Topics* when he discovered the famous passage on Alice Roosevelt. Revelations about individuals named Morgan, Vanderbilt,

Whitney, and Huntington bore more than a casual relation to the size of the courtroom audience. Conspicuous was the "royal box," a "fetching coterie of society women in constant attendance throughout the trial." [16] Although they often gasped in unison at the foul dealings uncovered, none of these society beauties was recorded to have turned in her ticket to the proceedings, a ticket as treasured as an invitation to a select Newport social gathering. Actually, the assault on *Town Topics* appealed to many of the interests that Mann had. The trial transferred the spectacle from the cheap pages of a scandal sheet to the courtroom and to the pages of New York's leading dailies. Both Mann and the trial played to the public's curiosity about the Four Hundred; both Mann and his detractors claimed that they sought to improve the moral tone of society. Certain similarities have been noted, not because Mann and his critics were morally equal, but because only with such awareness is much of the incident understandable.

The paradoxical nature of the affair was perhaps most evident in press reaction. Virtually all the New York papers cheered the *Collier's* campaign. Such support, especially from entities like the *Sun* and the *American*, should have been enough to alert *Collier's* that the contest was more than a battle between believers and infidels. It was well known that many of the papers sneered at *Town Topics* but swiped its stories. Disclosure that people seemed to have purchased immunity from Mann was met with surprised horror, but the practice of keeping lists of individuals who were not to be criticized was widespread in American journalism.[17]

No one more directly challenged the press than District Attorney Jerome. He questioned the New York press's purity, wondered why the very papers hounding Judge Deuel had been quiet about another judge, one who had worked for certain economic interests, and charged that many of New York's papers exploited scandal. He concluded his diatribe by noting that "the papers are run from the counting room and in many instances are influenced by a corruption fund." The district attorney was denounced by the papers nearly unanimously. It remained for the *American*, a newspaper which weaned its readers on the scandalous and the lurid, to strike a pose of sanctimonious disbelief as only the Hearst press could. "Nobody knows better than Jerome that the newspapers of New York, with inconspicuous and trivial exceptions," it instructed, "are not subject to such an indictment as this." [18]

Hapgood, always interested in the effect of business considerations on journalism, defended some of Jerome's statements and criticized the papers for treating the district attorney as if he were mad. Although Hapgood was surely aware of the character of some of his journalistic support, he does not seem to have realized the extent to which an interest in scandal, rather than a desire to end scandal, contributed to the fanfare. Although he kept up the attack on *Town Topics,* within two years of his victory he was shaking his head that few people and hardly any newspapers had retained any interest.[19] Perhaps Hapgood grasped more than he acknowledged. Perhaps he was understandably reluctant to debunk a venture that had done so much for him and for the *Weekly* and that had been grand fun. A gap between acclaim and achievement would appear in several of the *Weekly*'s enterprises.

IV

Although its precise origins are unclear, the *Collier's* crusade against patent medicines was one of its most famous. It is known that Edward Bok, capable editor of the *Ladies' Home Journal,* referred an anti–patent medicine article by Mark Sullivan to Hapgood, who accepted it. Bok, according to his autobiography, had thought the article "too legalistic" for the *Journal's* readers; Sullivan had believed it too long, but Bok might have been more worried about legal complications than about either style or length. In any case, Bok and the *Ladies' Home Journal* were simply not heavyweight reformers.[20]

Until the attack on patent medicines, *Collier's,* often a critic of the literature of exposure, had carried a few muckraking articles, but none had created much public interest. Hapgood and the *Weekly* were open to the charge that they were too inexperienced and too unsympathetic to render competent judgment on muckrakers. As Louis Filler has argued, a campaign against patent medicines would have "all the virtues and none of the vices of muckraking." Although such a venture was not so safe as Filler alleged—Hapgood's subsequent experience at *Harper's Weekly* with George Creel's series would demonstrate the hazards of poorly done work—his essential point is convincing. The patent medicine business was so bizarre that one could use extreme language and yet be truthful. The *Weekly* remarked at the close of the campaign, "While there was always the intent and purpose to be strictly fair, it seemed necessary to put certain truths bluntly and even harshly at times—not because we liked to use such terms, but because accuracy could be expressed no other way." [21]

Although there had been assaults on patent medicines since the Jacksonian Era, and in the late nineteenth century such magazines as *Popular Science Monthly* and the *Ladies' Home Journal* had been prominent fighters against proprietary abuses, the industry was flourishing. Its "manufactured value" in 1904 was almost $75 million. The Progressive Era, with its reformist outlook and advances in science, witnessed a new questioning of these remedies.[22]

Hapgood fired the first big gun in the *Collier's* attack with an article, "Criminal Newspaper Alliances with Fraud and Poison," appearing in the July 8, 1905, issue. If one had to select a single piece of Hapgood's writing as a great contribution to muckraking, this would be it. It was a superb blend of fine purpose and shrewd showmanship, a union of public service and professionalism. The layout of the first two pages was brilliant. Wide margins, in which mottoes of some of the most prestigious newspapers were juxtaposed with some of the rawest proprietary frauds, surrounded the text. Such slogans as "If You See It in the Sun It's So" *(New York Sun)*, "All the News That's Fit to Print" *(New York Times)*, "First in Everything" *(St. Louis Post-Dispatch)*, and "It's All Here and It's All True" *(Philadelphia North-American)* looked cheap and revolting in the company of patent medicine advertisements. This highlighted one of the most important aspects of the undertaking. Complicity with patent medicines measured the reformism of various newspapers and individuals. Hapgood had early used this technique to embarrass William Jennings Bryan, who published proprietary medicine advertisements in the *Commoner.* Irking Bryan and discomforting a good many newspapers placed the *Weekly's* virtue in nice relief, and neither Hapgood nor *Collier's* was known to shun such exposure.

Hapgood blamed the press, legislators, and manufacturers for the patent medicine menace. Calling for journalistic reform and better laws and proclaiming that the *Weekly* would no longer accept proprietary advertisements, a move that had begun several months before, he also announced that a series exposing the evil would begin soon. Sustaining the drama, Hapgood refused to name the "prominent journalist" who was to author it.[23] He was, of course, husky Samuel Hopkins Adams, and his series, "The Great American Fraud," became one of the classics of muckraking.

Adams's series became the centerpiece around which were placed Hapgood's editorials, Adams's editorials, articles by other writers, and cartoons to form a genuine muckraking enterprise. *Collier's* was in the forefront in urging national legislation, yet the movement stalled until *The Jungle* by Upton Sinclair created a furor and "made a pure food law inevitable." The Pure Food and Drug Act had a checkered career. Although it stopped some of the grossest swindles and wounded a few of the smaller entrepreneurs, sales of patent medicines continued to rise, and an unfavorable Supreme Court decision in 1911 left the law less than completely effective. Part of the difficulty had been that the law was not well drawn. *Collier's,* superb at exposure, had too willingly deferred to Dr. Harvey W. Wiley, chief chemist in the Department of Agriculture, and others in framing the necessary legislation. Hapgood became aware of the growing strength of the industry and conceded in 1911 that although it had been "made groggy," "it is coming back." Adams commented on the problem for *Collier's* in 1912, and at *Harper's Weekly* Hapgood later supervised a series dealing with patent medicine frauds. The *Collier's* impact on general drug advertising proved short-lived. In the 1930s, for example, advertising of questionable patent medicines was widespread.[24]

The patent medicine fight was significant to the careers of both Hapgood and the *Weekly*. Although it did hint at being one of the less dangerous muckraking efforts, it was not without risk, and *Collier's*, which had conducted itself with aplomb, could proclaim that "out of all the two hundred and sixty-four concerns and individuals attacked, [there are] just two suits for libel [left] on the docket and two personal protests filed with us." Although, as Judson Grenier has pointed out, businessmen were often reluctant to sue even if the muckrakers' charges were false because they feared more publicity, the *Collier's* record was impressive. *Collier's*, Hapgood, and Adams have received well-deserved accolades for their anti–patent medicine efforts.[25] It is important to note that the patent medicine campaign was only the beginning, not the culmination, of muckraking at *Collier's*. The episode gave Hapgood valuable experience fighting the "interests." Although little could be said in defense of proprietary frauds, the manufacturers often fought tenaciously to protect their position. Hapgood could not avoid developing a deeper understanding of the difficulties of the muckraker's task. The addition of Mark Sullivan to the *Collier's* staff, a by-product of the controversy, was to prove important to the *Weekly*.

V

The patent medicine fight altered the advertising practices of the *Weekly*. Its stoppage of proprietary advertisements in 1905 was not unprecedented. Most notably, the *Ladies' Home Journal* had taken such a step in 1892 at the suggestion of John Adams Thayer, its advertising manager. *Collier's Weekly* had originally intended to exclude only patent medicines, but the flow of events pushed it into a more restrictive position. Readers asked why it did not prohibit advertisements for such products as whiskey and cigarettes. The *Weekly* replied unconvincingly that patent medicines were a different case because they created a demand for themselves, whereas advertising for whiskey or cigarettes merely distributed demand among various brands. *Collier's* repeated that it had no qualms about advertising beer or whiskey because they were not fraudulent, but in the fall of 1905 "purely to save personal explanation and remove all misunderstanding between our readers and ourselves," it refused advertisements for such articles. The *Weekly* announced a comprehensive policy.

"Collier's" will accept no advertisements of beer, whiskey, or alcoholic liquors; no advertisements of patent medicines; no medical advertisements or advertisements making claims to medicinal effect; no investment advertising promising extraordinary returns, such as stocks in mining, oil, and rubber companies. The editor reserves the right to exclude any advertisement which he considers extravagant in claim, or offensive to good taste.

Later *Collier's* dropped advertising for cigarettes, spurious correspondence schools, and other questionable products and services.[26]

Unmasking frauds such as investment swindles and loan sharking was a concern of *Collier's* throughout the remainder of Hapgood's editorship. J. M. Oskison and Samuel Hopkins Adams did particularly valuable work in this field. The Progressive Era was marked by increased solicitude for advertising ethics, and *Collier's* occupied a position of leadership in developing and popularizing this awareness. *Collier's* rejected a good deal of advertising. In the first year $77,000 worth was turned down, in the next over $80,000 and a total of about $213,000 over the first three years. The *Weekly* reported after the initial year of the new policy: "So great has been the response of other lines of business that the amount voluntarily thrown out will be more than equaled by new business, a remarkable and to us unexpected result, as we thought the place of patent medicines, whisky, and beer would be taken very slowly if at all." This was a sign of a flourishing magazine. It not only did good, but did it with a profit. Almost five years later Mark Sullivan concluded, "It is perfectly certain . . . that it was not in the long run a money losing act. The increased prestige and standing which came from our new advertising policy really resulted in the long run in more business and better business." [27]

VI

By the close of 1906 it was obvious that *Collier's* had changed greatly in a few years. Although it continued to review the literature of exposure, it increasingly commented from the perspective of an active and genuine participant. *Collier's* greeted Roosevelt's muckrake speech with hostility, and Roosevelt, for his part, believed the *Weekly*'s muckraking detrimental.[28] Although both Hapgood and Roosevelt stressed the necessity of judicious exposure, by the time of the muckrake speech Hapgood was to the left of the president on this issue. Roosevelt's criticisms hardly stopped the *Weekly;* most of its muckraking came after Roosevelt's speech. Another preoccupation during these years was journalistic ethics. This was the motif of the *Town Topics* affair, the struggle against patent medicines, and the change in advertising. It would remain a conspicuous trait of the *Weekly* through Hapgood's editorship.

How did the Laodicean Hapgood become a muckraker? First, even in his more frenzied moments, he never became so extreme a muckraker as Upton Sinclair. Part of the explanation lies in the spirit of the times. Other magazines were doing it or had done it. The writer Zona Gale remarked in the spring of 1904 that "one cannot even spend one's dime to pass the time of day in the elevated without, willy-nilly, supporting a cause." [29] *Collier's* came late to the movement. The decline of *McClure's* had left an opening that *Collier's* gradually filled.

Hapgood's moralism explained much of his immersion in the journalism of controversy. Greatly influenced by his father, Hapgood was most at home in a fight with loud ethical overtones. In the famous *Puck* cartoon "The Crusades," in which muckrakers were garbed as medieval crusaders, he was near the front wearing a cowl. Possibly the artist recognized the ethical flavor of Hapgood's work, though he may have been more concerned with placing the hawk-nosed Hapgood in profile. Even with raised visor, Hapgood would not have appeared as conspicuous in armor. Some of his occasionally fierce and self-righteous positions seemed to contradict his relativism. In part this was explained by opportunism, a desire to build a sturdy bridge to his audience; perhaps this was what Hutchins Hapgood meant when he asked "whether the old boyish feeling for the use of moral indignation did not linger in the man." In part it also reflected the extent to which movement often conquered doubt. The Laodicean had been a mugwump; he could also be a muckraker. One finds in Hapgood and *Collier's* what Harold Wilson has called "the real goal of *McClure's* muckraking"—an "intent to be a vital participant in the political process and an agent in decision-making." [30] Influenced by the writings of Matthew Arnold at college, Hapgood now applied Arnold's dedication to integrity and to the best to the fostering of political reform. Hapgood's earnestness, his desire to grapple with life's deep issues, which had once been channeled into literature and philosophy and then into dramatic criticism, now more readily found outlet in muckraking, in political activity.

VII

In none of its campaigns did *Collier's* do tougher fighting than in the conservation controversy during the Taft administration. The *Collier's* activity is hardly understandable without reference to a sequence of events. These incidents clustered so well about Hapgood's reaction to the Ballinger affair, and so much of the development of Hapgood and of the *Weekly* was apparent in them, that they merit examination.

Hapgood maintained a comfortable optimism throughout the campaign of 1908. Although he seemed to prefer Hughes for the presidency, Hapgood, like most progressives, was quite happy with Taft's nomination by the Republican party and, in the words of a close associate, favored Taft "without reserve." At *Collier's* only Sullivan had significant doubts. Some of the reasons for Hapgood's support are not hard to find. Although Roosevelt had left office on good terms with Hapgood, their relationship had been marked by friction. The three-hundred-pound Taft, if less colorful than the Rough Rider, seemed to guarantee an institutionalization of reform. Although the *Weekly* endorsed Taft over Bryan, the Democratic candidate, its editorials were less partisan than Hapgood's feelings. Hapgood, flaunting the *Collier's* fair-mindedness, neglected the significant differences between Taft and Bryan and failed to appreciate the narrowness of Taft's experience.[31]

One eventual conflict between Taft and the *Weekly* was previewed shortly before Taft took office, when he refused Robert Collier's request to challenge Speaker Joseph Cannon, a leading conservative. Taft claimed the Speaker's support was vital to his legislative program. *Collier's,* still a champion of Taft, became miffed at his lackluster performance on the tariff. Another incident that hurt Taft's standing with the *Weekly* was the recall of Charles R. Crane, a wealthy businessman of progressive sympathies, whom Hapgood and Sullivan greatly admired, as ambassador to China. Sullivan, by this time a power at *Collier's,* complained to Finley Peter Dunne, "I have not in years been so moved as I was at the sense of outrage that a man of Mr. Crane's character should be put in a position where he had to endure attempted humiliation at the hands of a vulgar little beast like [Philander C.] Knox." [32]

The Ballinger controversy broke against this background of budding suspicion. Hapgood, who had been converted to conservation by Gifford Pinchot, took a keen interest in the storm developing in the Interior Department in the summer of 1909. By late August a *Collier's* editorial argued that Secretary of the Interior Richard A. Ballinger should go, and by the close of September, Hapgood was convinced that Ballinger was "crooked." In August, he had warned, "Don't mix up Ballinger and the President," but by October 1909 *Collier's* was predicting that Taft would not be reelected.[33]

So far Hapgood and the *Weekly* had not done anything extraordinary. This changed when Hapgood decided to publish an article by Louis R. Glavis, a young ex-investigator for the General Land Office. The article had been brought to him by John Bass, a journalist. Hapgood, already firmly anti-Ballinger, "read it very carefully that night and decided it was absolutely accurate and absolutely just, and the next day accepted it." The carefully revised piece, called "The Whitewashing of Ballinger," appeared in the November 13 issue and charged that Ballinger had tried to validate "fraudulent" land claims. George E. Mowry has commented, "Sensational in tone, it so stirred up public opinion that a showdown in a congressional investigation seemed inevitable." In the December 18 issue the article "Can This Be Whitewashed Also?" went further than Glavis and linked Ballinger to the Guggenheims and to possible Standard Oil interests.[34]

Collier's was intimately, if unofficially, involved in the subsequent congressional hearings. There had been rumors that Ballinger, after being cleared by a rigged investigation, would sue the *Weekly* for $1,000,000. Actually Ballinger had wanted to sue *Collier's* soon after the Glavis article was published, but Taft persuaded him not to do so. Ballinger later toyed with the idea, but nothing came of it. Partly from fear of a libel suit, but, more important, to safeguard its credibility, *Collier's* decided to retain an attorney to represent Glavis in his capacity as a contributor at the hearings. It was Hapgood's idea—one of his most important acts in the whole affair—to hire Louis D. Brandeis.[35]

The hearings began in January 1920. After the publication of Glavis's article Hapgood increasingly characterized the controversy as a struggle between the system and "the Truth, which is on our side," or "between integrity and illegal privilege." Under Hapgood's generalship the *Weekly* mercilessly probed Ballinger's early career. Had the issues been less momentous, "the method in which we have pursued *Ballinger* would have been cruel and unjustifiable." The opponents of Ballinger were not the only ones to see events conspiratorially. Both Taft and Ballinger began to believe that their opponents had plotted against them. After Taft refused to drop Ballinger and instead supported him more vigorously, and as other aggravating incidents took place, notably the proposed hike in second-class postage rates for magazines, Taft received less than enthusiastic coverage in the *Weekly*. Although Hapgood continued to express hope that Taft might change for the better, these remarks were tinsel, concessions to display *Collier's* fairness and probably responses to business pressures. More indicative of the *Weekly's* sentiments was Sullivan's writing at the bottom of a letter, "Roosevelt will be President in 1913." [36]

During the hearings, from January to June 1910, Norman Hapgood played an important, if not a critical, role. Maintaining close communication with Louis Brandeis, Hapgood was the only one in touch with him when Brandeis discovered that Attorney General George Wickersham's report, on which Taft had allegedly based his decision against Glavis, actually was completed only after the president had rejected Glavis's contentions and then was predated. Both Brandeis and Hapgood thought that this disclosure had a profound impact on public opinion, and this lapse in the administration's case undoubtedly hurt it greatly. Although the committee, the majority loyal supporters of Taft, found for Ballinger, Glavis and Pinchot won a great victory with the public. Almost all the progressive magazines had supported Glavis and Pinchot in the Ballinger controversy, but Hapgood and the *Weekly*, by publishing the Glavis article and by retaining Brandeis, had been unusually conspicuous.[37]

VIII

The Ballinger affair was a decisive event in Hapgood's life. In the patent medicine crusade he had challenged an industry; now he conspicuously defied an administration. At the core of American politics, Hapgood had come a long way from the detached editorial writer of 1903 or 1904. The *Weekly's* evolving activism permitted it to play this role. It would be difficult to imagine the *Collier's* of 1903 or 1904 making such an opportunity out of such an issue. The *Weekly* would have lacked the interest, the expertise, and the confidence. Editors in general were more energetic and aggressive. Hamilton Holt of the *Independent* argued, "The modern editor does not sit in his easy-chair, writing essays and sorting over the manuscripts that are sent in by his contributors. He goes hunting for things." It has been noted that some progressives, because of their wide contacts, gave a certain cohesion to the progressive movement. Hapgood and other progressive editors were surely among the more important of these. Hapgood was on the lookout for ideas and articles, causes to fight and candidates to help; the reformers, desiring support and publicity, often found the local press hostile. In many instances mutually beneficial arrangements were worked out.[38] Brief editorials enabled him to call attention constantly to a range of developments, developments that might not have sustained full-length editorials.

Perhaps no year had been so significant to the *Weekly*'s maturing activism as 1908. Its position on the presidential election has been recounted, but senatorial and state elections provided a keener insight into the transformation of the *Weekly*. In 1908 *Collier's* criticized a series of conservative politicians, mostly United States senators, the "Senate undesirables," and worked diligently to have them replaced by progressive individuals. Besides general editorial coverage, Hapgood used articles by such journalists as C. P. Connolly and J. M. Oskison to undermine the "undesirables." The *Weekly* also intensified its attacks on Speaker Cannon, whom it had been pursuing since 1905. Indicative of the new mood was Robert Collier's interest in founding "an *Editorial Council of American Periodicals,* whose object should be the co-ordination of the scattered work now being done along humanitarian lines." Focusing the power of the press to bring about social reform, it was to be "a trust on the side of the angels." Not surprisingly, *Collier's* took over the financing of the People's Lobby when that organization was floundering.[39]

The decline of fiction and the shift in personnel were a good measure of the increasingly political slant of the *Weekly*. Charles Dana Gibson, Arthur Conan Doyle, and Richard Harding Davis starred for *Collier's* in the first half of the decade; Mark Sullivan, Samuel Hopkins Adams, Will Irwin, C. P. Connolly, and Arthur H. Gleason stood out in the second half. No one more clearly symbolized the new commitment than Sullivan. His column, "Comment on Congress," and the Washington bureau that he ran became headquarters for progressive attacks on Congress. Sullivan's power at the *Weekly* grew until he, Collier, and Hapgood formed a ruling trio. In his early editorial years Hapgood had interpreted the function of the *Weekly* as detachment and

The Journalism of Controversy

criticism. He now increasingly defined its purpose as the promotion of social change.

The new activism was not without drawbacks. Accuracy as well as readers might be lost. Robert J. Collier confessed that "there are many implications in our articles not covered by the Glavis report." Specifically, Ballinger's alleged ties to the Guggenheims were never clearly substantiated, nor were the attacks on Ballinger's early years done in the spirit of fair play. The *Weekly* did not establish that Ballinger "has busied himself actively and *illegally* to help these exploiters beat the present law." Because of its determined stand against Ballinger, *Collier's* lost circulation in the Northwest and some advertising revenue.[40] Most importantly, the new commitment sometimes placed adherence to groups or individuals ahead of independent journalism. This would become apparent a few years later, when Hapgood edited *Harper's Weekly*.

IX

The last years of Roosevelt's second administration and the first few of Taft's administration, marked the height of the *Weekly*'s power. Frank Luther Mott has concluded that "the paper's influence on national affairs doubtless exceeded for a time that of any other single publication." Mott has also remarked, "Few periodicals in America have exerted, over any decade, as strong and direct an influence on national affairs as that of *Collier's* during the Hapgood regime." The *Weekly*'s ascendancy has been generally recognized, not least by those who had been associated with it. It was the *Collier's* golden age. An assistant to Hapgood remembered that "literally scores of young people . . . drifted out of the office, looking to Hapgood as a source for guidance and inspiration." A. J. McKelway, a social reformer and journalist, recalled that the *Weekly* played a significant role in making him a progressive. An article in *La Follette's Weekly* in 1912 claimed that *Collier's* was "most nearly our great national magazine," and found that it was the second most progressive magazine in the country—second only to *La Follette's*.[41]

Part of the *Weekly*'s prestige was won by muckraking. Hapgood thought the fundamental explanation of the magazine's success was that "it combined a general popularity with an intellectual keenness and an aggressive stand on political questions." The assertion that much of its influence derived from the fact that it was popular was correct. Its circulation during Hapgood's editorship ranged between three hundred thousand and six hundred thousand. The *Weekly* also attracted the right kind of readers. By 1909 it claimed that it was read by one-fifth of the nation's physicians, one-sixth of its lawyers, and one-tenth of its other professionals. Hapgood's liking for midwestern progressivism helped to make the *Weekly* particularly popular in that region.[42] A capable spokesman for the American middle class during the Progressive Era because he shared many of its values, Hapgood was not an extremist, but he was moving leftward, as was the country. His caution and equivocation improved his believability. Sharing in much of the moralistic outlook of the middle class, he dressed his opinions in enough culture to appeal to the educated. Both Hapgood and the *Weekly* were adept at selling their crusades. *Collier's* always salted its concern for ethics with an awareness of its own interests. Never the type of magazine that would readily kill itself, it was an effective organ, one that was productive partly because it knew how to advertise itself, to communicate to its public what it was trying to do.

X

After the disillusionment with Taft, *Collier's* identified most with the Insurgents, who were made up chiefly of midwestern progressive Republicans, but Hapgood criticized them when they failed to vote for Canadian reciprocity and he supported Taft on that issue. He tersely lectured, "A special interest is a special interest; it is to be judged by its methods and its motives, not by the side it happens to be on." [43]

Hapgood wished that both parties would nominate progressive candidates in 1912. He hoped that Woodrow Wilson would be chosen by the Democrats and Roosevelt, Hughes, La Follette, or another progressive by the Republicans. Relations between Roosevelt and the *Weekly* had improved during Roosevelt's last years in office, and when T. R. left the presidency he was on nice terms with Collier, Sullivan, and even Hapgood. Roosevelt noted in 1908, "I have an entirely different feeling toward Collier's Weekly from the feeling I had four years ago." The feckless Taft was the perfect person to place the dynamic Roosevelt in the best light. After the Ballinger hearings, Hapgood dashed to London to inform Roosevelt of the latest developments and Hapgood's disappointment with the Insurgents over reciprocity boosted Roosevelt's stock. The vicious campaign against Champ Clark's candidacy for the Democratic presidential nomination was a good warning that in 1912 Hapgood was not in a mood to be detached. When the *Weekly* conceded that it had misrepresented Clark's position on immigration, it explained that it has been misled by "a bulletin sent out from the Woodrow Wilson headquarters." Despite their harassment of Clark, the Speaker, Arthur S. Link has observed, "could at least point to a more consistent progressive record than Wilson or any other Democratic candidate could claim." [44]

Since backing Taft in 1912 was out of the question, the choice was between Wilson and Roosevelt. It was a tough decision because Hapgood had vigorously supported each of their drives for the nominations. Brandeis's influence was important, possibly decisive. Since Hapgood had met Brandeis in 1906, he had developed an intense respect for the Boston lawyer as well as an intimate lifetime friendship. Both men had lean personal habits, shunned ostentation, and were wary of wealth. Although both had strong cultural interests, Hapgood's were probably deeper. Brandeis probably would have been satisfied with a nation of thrifty, small, independent entrepreneurs. Hapgood would have been pleased, but he would have been more likely to crave further cultural accomplishment. Brandeis, more than anyone else, had fit Hapgood's definition of the ideal muckraker —balanced, avoiding socialism yet ardently committed to reform, practical, relativistic, innovative, and specific. Brandeis's work for savings-bank life insurance, in the Boston gas controversy, in the Oregon and Illinois cases, and in the campaign against the New Haven Railroad's merger with the Boston and

Maine—all appealed greatly to Hapgood. Brandeis's conduct at the investigation of the Interior Department awed the editor of *Collier's*. Hapgood adopted much of Brandeis's economic outlook, and after 1910 or so, and certainly after the 1912 election, his economic views followed those of Brandeis very closely.

Brandeis sharpened Hapgood's awareness of the trust issue. Brandeis was a vigorous supporter of Wilson, thought the trust question the main issue, and argued that Wilson stood for "regulated competition," while Roosevelt was for "regulated monopoly." Hapgood himself gave this issue considerable prominence and predicted that the trusts and the tariff would be the decisive questions. He later contended that, largely influenced by the trust and tariff problems, he had resolved in late 1911 or early 1912 to support Wilson, if the contest were between him and Roosevelt. Such a conclusion was not substantiated by contemporary evidence. Although Hapgood appeared to lean toward Wilson in early 1912, during the summer of 1912 he apparently had some difficulty making up his mind. In a letter written in early July 1912 Brandeis seemed to be trying to persuade him to back Wilson. More convincingly, George Rublee, a close friend of Hapgood's since their Harvard days, reported in mid-July that Hapgood, just before he had left for a vacation in Europe, was still "undecided." Within a few days, Hapgood endorsed Wilson.[45]

The challenge, Hapgood informed his father, was "to support Wilson energetically while still giving T. R. his due." Hapgood conceded that this was a tough problem, and he never really solved it. He did reject an article by Ray Stannard Baker sharply critical of Roosevelt and deleted a reference to George W. Perkins from a Brandeis editorial in order not to further antagonize Sullivan, a devoted Bull Moose, and to preserve some balance. But the difficulty was more intricate than excluding a Ray Stannard Baker article. Hapgood never appreciated the depth of his dilemma: how could one who subscribed to Brandeis's outlook —and by late summer there was nearly complete adherence— give the Progressives anything like the credit they thought they deserved? To Brandeis and eventually to Hapgood the trust issue was the crux of the campaign. All other reforms were secondary. Since Roosevelt was wrong on trusts, all that could be imputed to the Progressive party was that they were well intentioned if not terribly clear headed. This attitude resulted in an occasionally condescending tone—words of praise without the substance of praise, referring to the Progressives's social platforms as "Lloyd-George declarations," or concluding that "it is extremely likely that the Bull Moose party will find itself in better condition if it almost wins in November than if it actually wins." [46] In the meantime, Sullivan was boiling.

XI

The 1912 campaign was Hapgood's last at *Collier's*. Hapgood's letter of resignation, dated October 16, was accepted on October 18; the October 19 issue of the *Weekly* was the last he edited. Hapgood charged that Collier, through extravagant living and debauchery, had severely weakened the financial structure of the magazine. As a result, in September 1912 E. C. Patterson, for many years the advertising manager of *Collier's*, was named vice-president and general manager of P. F. Collier and Son. He was given, according to Hapgood, "complete power over every department." Hapgood contended that Patterson soon boasted that he was going to get better treatment for certain advertisers and modify some editorial policies. Hapgood fought him. After Roosevelt was shot in Milwaukee, Robert Collier submitted a mushy editorial praising Roosevelt and reproaching the analytical Hapgood and ordered it inserted. Hapgood resigned and contended that Collier was not really interested in the campaign but had interfered on that pretext to force him out. After Hapgood left, Collier switched the *Weekly*'s support from Wilson to Roosevelt.[47]

That *Collier's Weekly* was in financial distress and that Robert Collier appeared to be at least the partial cause of these difficulties seem well authenticated. Will Irwin, who wrote fairly regularly for *Collier's*, sensed trouble and began to step up his contributions to the *Saturday Evening Post*. Sullivan has recalled that after his father's death in 1909, Robert Collier was unable to manage the bookselling business successfully. Collier borrowed heavily to keep the enterprises going, but the debts resulted in the infiltration of outsiders to positions of importance. *Collier's*, like many other muckraking magazines, was not noted for turning sizable profits. The book business, always the economic marrow of the organization, was facing stiff challenges from *Leslie's*. Even libel suits, in which *Collier's* had been notably successful, were beginning to hurt. During the Ballinger hearings Collier had proposed to Brandeis that he trim his work to shave expenses in part because "I have so many law suits on my hand at present." Collier himself admitted that the organization had been in trouble but contended that he had cut liabilities in half within the past year. Several sources substantiate the role of Collier's life-style in impairing the business. Part of Collier's high living, according to one account, was a fondness for whiskey and chorus girls.[48]

The extent to which the business department tried to dictate to the editorial is harder to ascertain. Collier, denying that Patterson was to control the entire business, contended that Patterson was supposed to run only financial affairs and Hapgood was to continue to control editorial policy. The extent of Patterson's power probably will never be known. The core of Hapgood's argument was, first, Patterson's dominance, and, second, Collier's insertion of the Roosevelt editorial as a guise for asserting the suzerainty of financial considerations. Hapgood, despite pride in his standards of evidence, presented little that was conclusive on these critical points. The heart of his criticism of Patterson was remarks Patterson had made at a dinner. Hapgood should have waited to get something that showed that Patterson had Collier behind him.

Collier, alleging that Hapgood had not given Roosevelt enough credit, pointed to the influence of Brandeis, a Wilson partisan. Brandeis had not only written several signed articles for the *Weekly* during the campaign, but, unknown to Collier, Hapgood had had Brandeis do several key editorials. Although Hapgood replied that "I have printed editorials by outsiders nearly every week for years," he should not have surreptitiously let Brandeis onto the editorial pages to such a degree at such a time.[49] Collier's charge that Hapgood had not been fair was an appeal to the *Weekly*'s practice in 1904, 1908, and, avowedly, in 1912.

Nothing had irked Sullivan during the campaign more than Brandeis's growing influence over Hapgood. A man of distinguished appearance and the son of Irish immigrants, Sullivan looked too moral to be a politician and too interesting to be a preacher. He had the mix of idealism and practicality that one sometimes found among the college presidents of the day. Fuller faced than his editor, Sullivan had a personality very different from Hapgood's and sometimes misjudged him. He at once underrated several of his qualities and revered others. Sullivan concluded about Hapgood, "It occurred to me that if I could order the universe and have each man where he ought to be, I would keep Hapgood in that country garden, writing just as much and no more than he was moved to write, on topics inspired by the blue delphiniums around him." [50] Of course this ignored the extent to which Hapgood had given up his earlier dreams and the degree to which he functioned best in the fires of competitive journalism. Many of the temperamental differences between Collier and Hapgood, which Sullivan discussed elaborately in his autobiography, were equally applicable to Sullivan and Hapgood.

Hapgood contended that Sullivan, by using the Bull Moose issue, had played into the hands of Collier, who aimed to crush editorial independence. In his autobiography Sullivan, absolving himself of complicity in Hapgood's leaving, contended that "it was not between me and Hapgood that the trouble came. It was between Hapgood and Collier." The elaborate analysis suggested that Sullivan might have been trying to convince himself. More to the point was a letter written by Sullivan to Roosevelt shortly after Hapgood had departed from the *Weekly*. It revealed that Sullivan was not so uninvolved.

I am glad to be back at Armageddon. It caused me a good deal of pain to have provoked the break with Hapgood; but there was no other way possible after he had declined to let me have freedom of expression and after our editorial pages had said things about you and the [Progressive] Party which I knew to be untrue. I was a good deal humiliated early in the campaign, and am glad to be back at Armageddon.[51]

Thus Hapgood thought that Sullivan had been duped by Collier, while Sullivan felt that he had manipulated Hapgood. Exactly what Collier believed is unclear.

Although there are too many gaps in the evidence to yield definitive answers about the break at *Collier's*, some tentative conclusions can be put forward. The bad relations with Sullivan—largely political—and continuing economic difficulties combined to create a strained atmosphere and to make Hapgood suspicious. What motives prompted Collier to insert the editorial about Roosevelt may never be known, but that move resulted in Hapgood's resignation. He might have quit because he thought that business considerations were becoming dominant, but political difficulties could have had some influence. Besides contributing to taut emotions they might well have led Hapgood to realize that the situation at the *Weekly* would not improve during the Wilson administration. Curiously, he did not raise the economic problem in his letter of resignation, which blamed Sullivan for using Collier.[52] Why Hapgood did not make business control a major issue, then, is one of the unanswered questions of this episode. It seems likely that at the time he had wished to avoid a personal attack on Collier and so chastised Sullivan, for whom he understandably had lost affection and who was not guiltless. His letter also indicated that Hapgood could hardly have thought Collier as cunning as he claimed shortly afterwards, for accusing Sullivan had left Collier a great opening.

Whatever Hapgood's motives, his conduct did not raise issues clearly. Although much of the dispute between Collier and Hapgood was hazy and although Hapgood had not definitively exposed Collier's misconduct, it was Collier, not Hapgood, who suffered most from the affair. Collier found himself and the *Weekly* attacked from both the left and the right. Speculation was widespread that some business interests were stifling muckraking, and much of the left was willing to accept this as another such incident. Rumors even eventually circulated that Standard Oil had done Hapgood in. The right was happy to see *Collier's*, which for so long had taken a holier-than-thou attitude toward much of the press, discomforted by serious charges against its integrity. The *Springfield* (Mass.) *Republican* spoke for much of the press, liberal and conservative: "This is a curious situation for an office from which was conducted a campaign of exposure of the advertising crookedness of other publications without parallel in American journalism." [53]

A combination of Collier's predicament and the conciliatory intervention of Louis Brandeis resulted in a truce. Brandeis, out of friendship for Hapgood and possibly out of a realization that continuation of the dispute would not benefit Hapgood, Collier, or reform, persuaded both to stop discussion of Hapgood's departure. Despite his close friendship with Hapgood, Brandeis was able to bring about an accord with Collier, because Collier, already chafing under allegations of subservience to the counting room, could not afford to alienate such a critic of big business as Brandeis, whatever Collier may actually have thought of him. Significantly, Collier tried to secure articles from Brandeis. It was years before Hapgood and Collier could be called even cool friends, and they were never again intimates.[54]

XII

Hapgood's leaving the *Weekly* ended an epoch. Combined with other factors, it pretty much meant the end of the *Weekly*'s days of thickest glory. *Collier's* had lost its innocence in the Hapgood-Collier affair. Neither Hapgood nor Collier would prove as effective alone as they had together. They had shared their greatest moments, and each had contributed to the success of the other. They had complemented each other beautifully, a journalistic Mr. Inside and Mr. Outside. Hapgood, despite some significant further adventures in journalism, would never again have the influence that he had enjoyed at *Collier's*. He would recognize his years at the *Weekly* for what they were, superbly productive. Collier edited the *Weekly* for a couple of years and died in 1918, a shadow of his former glory and in shaky financial condition. Hapgood led a happier life than Collier after 1912.

CHAPTER 7

Wilson Partisan

I

WHEN HE LEFT *Collier's Weekly* in 1912, Norman Hapgood was still in his prime and not likely to slip into unnoticed retirement. Protruding ears gave this lean, angular forty-four-year-old a somewhat boyish appearance. Thin-lipped, his mouth was dour looking and reminiscent of Woodrow Wilson's. Perhaps his most prominent feature was his nose. Hutchins recounted how Norman had used it to distract his infant daughter, Ruth, from her uncle. "It was taking an unfair advantage," Hutchins wrote in mock protest, "thus to make use of the largest and queerest object in sight, in order to assert his superior position in the Baby's world." [1]

After he resigned from *Collier's,* Norman Hapgood did not expect to return to journalism for quite some time. Rumors circulated that he would take a position with the Wilson administration, perhaps in the cabinet. Before returning to magazine work, he became involved in the Fusion movement, a coalition of anti-Tammany reformers that ran John Purroy Mitchel for mayor in 1913. Mitchel, who won, became Hapgood's favorite urban politician. Hapgood thought Mitchel's defeat for reelection in 1917 a sad commentary on the American electorate. The Fusion episode was significant in two respects. It vividly illustrated Hapgood's growing partisanship—during the campaign he had been forced to play a less conspicuous role by Fusion leaders who thought he had been too much of a hatchet man—and it illuminated Hapgood's somewhat narrow attitude toward urban politics, for Mitchel, preoccupied with efficiency, spent little effort in meeting the city's complex needs, and, in the words of his biographer, his administration took an "upper class" nature.[2]

After leaving *Collier's,* Hapgood had little desire for immediate journalistic employment. Two factors changed this. First, Robert Collier, during the controversy with Hapgood, had derogated Hapgood's contribution to the success of the *Weekly* and claimed that he and Sullivan, not Hapgood, had directed the paper politically. This inaccuracy stung Hapgood to reply that the accusation "is so ludicrous that all members of the organization and thousands of the public must wonder just what state he was in when he wrote it." Retribution would be sweet, and there was no better retaliation than a triumphant return to journalism. Secondly, the bundle of offers Hapgood received soothed his ego and impressed on him the estimation others put on his work. Within ten days after his resignation had been made public, he had received about a dozen offers, several quite lucrative.[3] His well-publicized stand against the encroachment of the business office had increased his value. What better way was there for a magazine to prove that it was untouched by foul economic interests than to hire one so consistently identified with fighting that kind of influence? His presence would be de facto proof that the publication was pure, a certificate of chastity.

Aggravated by Collier's charges and flattered by being wanted, Hapgood began to shop for a nice position. He felt "it would be a very great mistake for me to go back as an anticlimax." What he was looking for was implicit in his rejections. He was wary of accepting an inconspicuous government job, for "men are forgotten with amazing speed these days," and he refused one journalistic proposition, although it promised great power, because "it did not give me an organ to build up." Another's readership was too select to give him the kind of influence he sought. A third offer, from a prestigious periodical, Hapgood turned down because he did not wish a career in what C. M. Francis has called "non-combatant thirty-five cent magazine journalism." What might have been irresistible a decade before seemed flat after *Collier's*. Hapgood finally concluded, "I have decided to consider no monthly, no daily, and no syndicate proposition." He insisted on control of the enterprise or at least enough say to avoid a repetition of what had occurred at *Collier's*.[4]

Nothing was more appealing than *Leslie's Weekly*, which had a large circulation, a bookselling business that was giving P. F. Collier and Son trouble, but little political influence. Hapgood, believing that he could upgrade *Leslie's* as he had once strengthened *Collier's*, boasted that if he were at the helm of *Leslie's*, he would "take the Collier prestige in a few months." The cost of *Leslie's Weekly*—about $500,000 to purchase and another $500,000 to finance a good start—was more than Hapgood's chief backers, Charles R. Crane and Maurice Wertheim, were willing to put up. *McClure's*, a monthly Hapgood had once revered, was available for conversion to a weekly, but the *McClure's* scheme stumbled over the high initial investment, eventually about $750,000 for a minority interest, and questions about Hapgood's jurisdiction. Hapgood also considered the *Outlook*, but the Abbotts, not inclined to sell, demanded more than could be raised. He also looked into the *Washington Daily Herald*.[5]

As early as November 1912 Thomas W. Lamont of J. P. Morgan and Company, but formerly of the *Harvard Monthly* of Hapgood's day, had informed him that *Harper's Weekly* might be for sale. Hapgood was interested but fascinated by other possibilities. As some doors closed, *Harper's* looked better. By late April 1913 serious negotiations were under way, and in the late spring *Harper's Weekly* was purchased from Harper Brothers for $100,000.[6]

II

Hapgood's career at *Harper's Weekly* was not the triumph of the *Collier's* years. In fact, the *Harper's* episode was a failure from several angles, but an interesting and well-documented failure. In the days of Thomas Nast and George William Curtis, *Harper's Weekly* had been distinguished, but the twentieth century had been unkind to the *Weekly*, which was in the red every year from 1901 to 1912. Under Col. George Harvey's editorship it had opposed most progressive reforms and no longer cut an important figure in American journalism.

When Hapgood took over *Harper's Weekly*, he promised radical change. The issue of August 16, 1913, the first under his editorship, proclaimed the transformation. The pages were smaller. This was a nice way of emphasizing that this was a new *Weekly*, not merely something dressed a little differently from Harvey's. Fiction policy sounded a keynote. "We do not intend to use fiction to build up circulation in a way that would collect for us a mass of readers who care for little else. We are not to be a high-brow publication, in the limited sense, but we do not intend to collect a lot of low-brows." [7]

This disdain for popular fiction was not only a proclamation of high standards but probably a reflection of Hapgood's frustrations with fiction at *Collier's* and a recognition of the tough competition in the short story and serial market. *Harper's* was slightly more risqué than *Collier's;* Oliver Herford's verses were a little bolder than they had been at *Collier's. Harper's,* contending that it was geared to "intelligent adults," not "to all members of the family at any age," gave more attention to books and the theater than had *Collier's.* Art also helped to establish the *Weekly's* personality. Influenced in part by German periodicals and the *Masses,* the *Weekly* featured work by such artists as John Sloan, William Glackens, and George Bellows.[8] Many of the early contributors, such as Dr. Eliot and Mrs. Fiske, were Hapgood's kind of people. Hapgood's interest in Jews and Zionism was reflected in *Harper's Weekly.* The *Weekly* became a broth of Wilsonian politics with a dash of the avant-garde. No one confused it with the *Masses,* or with the *Saturday Evening Post* for that matter.

III

The leading authority on Wilson's presidency has described *Harper's Weekly* as "a spokesman of the Wilson administration." [9] To anyone familiar with Hapgood's experience at *Collier's* and his almost obstreperous independence, this conclusion seems surprising, almost shocking, but Arthur S. Link's assertion is not exaggerated. As was pointed out in the preceding chapter, Hapgood had gradually become more of an activist. Muckraking, the

Norman Hapgood in Petersham, Massachusetts, c. 1927. (Courtesy of Elizabeth Backman.)

battles against conservative politicians, and the 1912 election prepared Hapgood for the kind of support he was to give Wilson at *Harper's Weekly*. After all this is conceded, however, a gap remained between the *Collier's* and the *Harper's* experiences. This difference was attributable in large measure to Woodrow Wilson.

Although one might expect that Wilson would have particularly appealed to Hapgood's emphasis on style and expression, this was not really the case. Hapgood, who had not read much of Wilson's scholarly work, did appreciate his use of language, although, interestingly, he later thought it inferior to Al Smith's. More than any liking for the scholar in politics, more than Wilson's legislative accomplishments, Wilson's standing as a great progressive leader, as a builder of a moral atmosphere, captivated Hapgood. When foreign affairs became more prominent and Hapgood praised Wilson's skill in that field, it again was mood or tone that most intrigued him.

There was seldom censure of Wilson in the pages of *Harper's Weekly*, almost never in the editorials. Hapgood explained, "We have no intention of criticizing the President in order to gain a reputation for impartiality. We are glad to have somebody to rave about, and shall not stop raving as long as he continues to perform in a manner that gives us such unwonted satisfaction." *Harper's Weekly* was not Democratic, but Wilsonian. Hapgood, who must have been nettled by Secretary of State Bryan's appointments' policy, only murmured, "I have refrained from criticizing him, but cannot make up my mind to justify him." It would be hard to imagine such indecision a few years before. A. J. McKelway, who, under the name of McGregor, wrote a column for *Harper's Weekly*, was never averse to reminding Wilson of the steadfast support he received from the *Weekly*. Not everyone was as adulatory of Wilson as Hapgood's *Weekly*. Philip Littell dryly observed that Wilson was treated as if he were "half saint and half trustee and all great man." Alvin Johnson remembered his keen disappointment with *Harper's Weekly* and claimed that Herbert Croly's expression of dissatisfaction to Dorothy Straight was responsible for the founding of the *New Republic*. In early 1915 Hapgood confessed to his managing editor, "We are under such suspicion of defending everything the administration does in most absolute terms that we are likely to lose our influence." Interestingly, Hapgood's sharpest editorial outburst against Wilson took place at this time.[10] He was peeved at Wilson's Indianapolis speech, a highly partisan address, but the displeasure was only a bark, not a shift to greater independence, and certainly not the beginning of sustained criticism.

In his autobiography Hapgood claimed, "While I was free as editor of *Harper's Weekly* to follow my own ideas, the new owners had put their money in the magazine partly to have an intelligent exposition of Wilson's policies and I stressed that duty as much as I legitimately could." This was hardly conclusive. Although the backers, all Wilsonians, had some influence on editorial content, it was probably less than they had on the organization of the *Weekly*. The fundamental reason why *Harper's* was so pro-Wilson was simply that Hapgood was so pro-Wilson. Hapgood was to no significant extent at odds with Wilson's policies until the last years of his presidency. Hapgood's most important friend intellectually, Brandeis, was also quite pleased by Wilson's performance during his first administration.[11] Exactly what Hapgood would have criticized to any degree is unclear, but it would have been detail rather than purpose.

Hapgood, in effect, interpreted his role as editor of *Harper's Weekly* to be that of a political supporter of Wilson, an ally of the president. Hapgood later recalled that "I seem to have acquired an ardor verging on partizanship in 1912 and never lost it. By partizanship I do not mean belief in the superiority of party, but intensity about my side of a given situation." Although one can trace the roots of this commitment to at least 1908, he undoubtedly practiced advocacy journalism on occasion at *Harper's*. The correspondence between Wilson and Hapgood was suggestive. Wilson, of narrower interests than Roosevelt, was not particularly attentive to the press in general, although he did show some concern for *Harper's* and wrote to Hapgood essentially to ask political advice or to use him as a bridge to independent progressives. By the approach of the 1916 election the extent to which Hapgood considered himself an auxiliary of Wilson was evident. Although *Harper's Weekly* did not survive to the 1916 election, Hapgood's plans were revealing. Hoping to wage the campaign as "a moral question," he promised the president in the spring of 1915, "When I get back from Europe in July I want to give practically all my time and thought for fifteen months to dramatizing this idea." [12] His move from New York to Washington to do a column, "The Nation's Capitol," which first appeared in the January 1, 1916, issue of *Harper's Weekly,* was symbolic. Written in a whisper, this page seemed to be so surely "in the know" that it rejected bragging as the baggage of the less knowledgeable. Hapgood, once an advocate of detached journalism, was now a peddler of inside stories and political gossip.

Among the dangers of this sort of partisanship were that Hapgood would lose his influence with independents and that the *Weekly*'s political reactions would become predictable. One reason why *Harper's Weekly* did not become the national force that Hapgood wished it to be was its lack of objectivity. Support for Wilson could contradict other goals of the *Weekly.* In no instance did this prove more embarrassing than in its coverage of the woman's movement. Although feminism was not a chief concern of Hapgood's when he purchased *Harper's* in the spring of 1913, in his first issue he proclaimed, "We intend, if possible, to make ourselves the official organ for the Feminist Movement." [13] It was a shrewd attempt to develop a characteristic, exploit the growing importance of the movement, and attract women readers.

Harper's Weekly carried a good deal of material on feminism. This brassy interest seemed to signify a major intellectual development between Hapgood's work for *Collier's* and *Harper's.* At *Collier's* the relativistic Hapgood, feeling that women did not have a natural right to the ballot, advocated gradualism and thought that women would get the vote when they really wanted it. In the meantime he was quite content to praise their value to cultural and family life. The hoopla at *Harper's* left the impression that it was a great champion of the suffrage, but the increased prominence of that question forced Hapgood to show his hand. Although favoring a constitutional amendment eliminating obstacles to woman suffrage in state constitutions, he was

Elizabeth R. and Norman Hapgood in Petersham c. 1927. (Courtesy of Elizabeth Backman.)

Norman Hapgood c. 1935. (Courtesy of Elizabeth Backman.)

against grant of the suffrage by amendment. In other words, he had not really changed. It was even more discomforting when the suffragists harassed the president. Hapgood censured them, yet he never questioned the sincerity of the president's position. Wilson actually had little or no concern for woman's suffrage, although under pressure he termed it a state rather than a national issue. Hapgood himself later opposed the Nineteenth Amendment on the ground that it "imposed the civilization of Massachusetts on Louisiana." [14] His inability to make *Harper's* profitable was only in part a result of his failure to develop an independent stance; organizational and economic difficulties were immensely important.

IV

The business side of the *Harper's* experiment was more interesting than Hapgood's lackluster intellectual performance. Hapgood, wary of subservience to commercial demands, cautiously secured the money to purchase and finance *Harper's Weekly*. All the investors were businessmen of progressive sympathies. The chief among these was Charles R. Crane, a heavyset, wealthy manufacturer and veteran of good government fights in Chicago, who had been Wilson's top financial backer during the 1912 campaign. Wilson, rumored to have considered him for secretary of war, wanted him to be ambassador to Russia. Others who contributed to *Harper's Weekly* were Cleveland Dodge, Julius Rosenwald, David Benton Jones, Thomas David Jones, and George F. Porter. Walter S. Rogers and Franklin MacVeagh eventually helped support the *Weekly*. The aim of the investors was not profit but influence and the bolstering of reform. Hapgood summarized: "The men who own *Harper's Weekly* do not care to make much money out of it. If in a few years it pays interest on preferred stock and makes a small amount on the common stock, the owners will be entirely satisfied." [15] Sheltered from conservative interests and demands for quick returns, Hapgood hoped that *Harper's Weekly* would not suffer from the usual weaknesses of periodicals.

During the first few months of his editorship, *Harper's* became bogged down in economic difficulties. Hapgood had intended to write few editorials and had hoped to spend much of his time roaming the country for ideas. This proved illusory. He became so involved in the details of running the *Weekly* that he felt he was losing intimacy with the political scene. Hapgood also admitted that he had purchased too much material. By December debts to the McClure Publications were causing him much anxiety, and several of the backers were slow to meet their pledges. Brandeis warned Walter S. Rogers that the "present financial uncertainty seriously impairs Normans [sic] health and work." [16]

Continuing losses, in the neighborhood of $15,000 a month, growing discontent among some of the owners, and dissatisfaction with the arrangement with McClure brought matters to a head in January 1914. James Phelan reneged on a commitment of $5,000, and Cleveland Dodge, one of the more important owners, was disconcerted by the character of *Harper's Weekly*. Dodge, with the concurrence of the Joneses, felt that *Harper's* should be more solemn, more committed to politics. Crane, milder in his objections, wanted *Harper's Weekly* to be less influenced by European fashion, especially of the avant-garde variety. Hapgood countered to Dodge that "the weak point of a perfectly solid and serious publication is that it appeals only to the citizen in us, not to the other aspects of us as men and women." In a few days, however, Hapgood conceded. After consulting his associates, he decided to change the *Weekly* gradually, and concluded, "It is unsound, whatever our beliefs may be, to be making a paper that does not give decided satisfaction to the men who are furnishing the money." Even after the modifications William Kent considered the *Weekly* too "highbrow" and thought it ought to appeal more to "the 'yap' trade." [17] This switch certainly disappointed Hapgood, who had counted heavily on the gayer aspects to lend character and color to *Harper's* and to make it a more sophisticated organ than, for example, *Collier's Weekly*.

The organization was revamped at about the same time. *Harper's Weekly* had had an agreement under which McClure Publications provided a variety of personnel and services, particularly in the business department, and some editorial work; *Harper's Weekly* shared expenses for some salaries. When *Harper's* continued to lose money, many at the *Weekly,* including Hapgood, suspected that the arrangement was not worthwhile. Sentiment grew that McClure Publications, which owned several magazines, had mixed feelings about *Harper's* and was not safeguarding the *Weekly*'s interests. Services from the McClure Publications, salaries in the advertising department, and the number of copies of the magazine printed were cut. Losses were reduced to between $10,000 and $12,000 a month. Norman Hapgood, who had once placed much hope in Frederic L. Collins of McClure to help him with the business end of the enterprise, began to look for a managing editor and a business manager to relieve himself of some responsibility. He eventually hired Howard D. Wheeler, recommended by E. W. Scripps, for the former position and E. F. Chase for the latter. Under the reorganization, which was completed by the early summer of 1914, "Mr. Wheeler and Mr. Chase are responsible to the owners for the practical side and I only for the public affairs." [18]

Many of the ills of *Harper's Weekly* fell into a pattern. Specifically, there was substantial overconfidence about what Hapgood, who had the aura of success, the success of the stirring years at *Collier's,* could do. The owners and Hapgood assumed that he would compensate for whatever deficiencies *Harper's* had. Many of the backers probably overestimated his sizable contributions to *Collier's,* and Hapgood, indulging in fantasies of administering the coup de grace to *Collier's Weekly,* was not in the best position to make realistic appraisals. Hapgood conceded that he, along with Brandeis and others, had expected too much of the McClure connection, but this was only one in a series of errors. One of the most glaring lacks was the unavailability, until at least the reorganization of 1914, of anyone to administer the details of the *Weekly,* to take some pressure off the editor. In the beginning Hapgood thought that he could handle most things and even planned to travel across the country. He failed to bring topflight journalistic talent with him and did not hire any full-time reporters of established excellence. Consequently, *Harper's Weekly* suffered from inferior performances that involved it in libel suits it should have avoided. No one played the important auxiliary role that Sullivan had at *Collier's*. There was no stable of first-rate journalists. What should have been a prime concern was pushed into the background. Charles R. Crane unsuccessfully tried to hire Ray Stannard Baker as Washington correspondent for *Harper's*. It might have been a good move, especially since Baker, an able journalist, was not yet the adulator of Wilson that he later became.[19] Hapgood mistakenly expected unanimity among the backers. That they were all good, progressive, rich Wilsonians did not preclude marked differences over the content of the magazine. In his first issue of *Harper's Weekly* Hapgood wrote editorials and three signed articles. Intended as an alert effort to display the *Weekly*'s chief asset, it was, in retrospect, a grim preview of one of its most harmful inadequacies.

Harper's Weekly was troubled by a persistent inability to get circulation or advertising. At the beginning of the enterprise Hapgood felt that a circulation of one hundred thousand would be about right, large enough to have political impact but small enough to nourish the cultural pretensions of the *Weekly*. *Harper's*, under his editorship, never came close to reaching this figure. Indeed, at its peak, paid circulation barely, and only briefly, surpassed forty thousand.[20]

As dangerous as the small circulation, and in part resulting from it, was the shortage of advertising, which at times was so conspicuous that one might wonder whether Hapgood was considering dispensing with advertising entirely. In fact, he did not disdain advertisements, he told E. W. Scripps, one of whose papers was run without them. It was just that he could not get many. Not that Hapgood's vocation was pursuing advertisements—a too eager chase would endanger a journal's integrity. Several factors hurt the *Weekly*'s solicitation. The *Weekly* of Harvey's time had a very poor reputation as an advertising medium, and much of the stigma stuck to the new *Weekly*. It was also a time of general cutbacks in periodical advertising, and potential clients understandably preferred to await developments. Since the *Weekly*'s gain in circulation was less than spectacular, advertising was always slight and amounted to only $11,318.37 from June through December 1914.[21]

Although the reorganization of 1914 helped a little, troubles continued. Losses for the year ending June 30, 1914, were over $200,000. In June 1914 Hapgood informed A. J. McKelway that *Harper's* could pay him only $100 a month for his work in Washington. McKelway, who had earned almost twice that from his regular column the previous month, continued to write for *Harper's*, but a few months later, after he had offered some hints to improve newsstand circulation, added that there was no charge. When Hapgood went to Europe in the spring of 1915 to cover the war, the cost of sending him left the *Weekly* so short of funds that it had to postpone paying McKelway. In late May 1915 the managing editor confessed, "I am not in a position to buy a line of material this month." When *Harper's* lost $72,671.85 for the year ending June 30, 1915, Hapgood remarked. "Our losses now are a little more than ⅓ of what they were a year ago." He concluded, "It has been a disappointing year but that gain is something." [22]

Hapgood relied greatly on muckraking series to break the grips of low circulation and scant advertising. Charles Johnson Post detailed the antidemocratic aspects of the army in February and March 1914 and shortly thereafter exposed the Powder Trust. Hapgood supervised several attacks on the patent medicine industry, thought a series of brief comments on the First World War by leading political figures might give circulation a shot in the arm, and, in general, devoted much attention to the war and hoped that coverage might stimulate sales and ultimately advertisements. Many of Hapgood's efforts mimicked his experience at *Collier's*. The patent medicine crusade was a child of his service at *Collier's*. Hapgood thought of getting into a controversy with Thomas W. Lawson, just as he had during earlier days, and he considered provoking suits for publicity.[23] A few of the ventures, notably Post's efforts, caused some stir, but they never achieved the impact of the best work at *Collier's*. Times had changed, and *Harper's* never developed the *Collier's* expertise at producing and directing a cause célèbre.

Several of the undertakings at *Harper's Weekly* proved very embarrassing. The campaign against patent medicines brought three suits. *Harper's* never swaggered about these; it had little cause to. One of the suits seems never to have been tried, but the second, *Hehmeyer* v. *Harper's Weekly*, was important. Hehmeyer, owner of the Bower Chemical Company and the sole American distributor for Sanatogen, a proprietary remedy, sued *Harper's Weekly*, McClure Publications, and Hapgood for $250,000 plus costs for a George Creel article, "Doc Munyon and His Pals," which had derogated Sanatogen. The attorney for *Harper's*, Emory R. Buckner, believed that *Harper's* regretted that it had mentioned Sanatogen. Buckner did manage to win the case, however. Of the third and most dangerous, *Patten* v. *Harper's Weekly*, Buckner warned that the *Weekly* could very easily lose a trial. Buckner delayed long enough to allow a similar suit against the American Medical Association to be heard first to save money for the *Weekly*, which had trouble finding $1,000 to pay him. Buckner, seconded by Brandeis, argued that aggravating Patten might prove costly in court. The A.M.A. case tried in Chicago was spectacular. The letters from Buckner, who was in the audience, remind one of a poor boy pressing his nose against the bakery window. What a contrast to the days at *Collier's*, when Robert Collier would have used precisely this type of event to magnificent advantage. Patten died during the trial, but his brother continued the case and won a verdict of one cent. Luckily for *Harper's*, which would have been hard pressed to finance a court fight, only the deceased Patten and not his brother had been the plaintiff in New York and the case was dropped.[24]

Hapgood was harassed by another suit, by Henry Lane Wilson, which was not tried until after *Harper's Weekly* was defunct but stemmed from an article by Robert H. Murray critical of Wilson's service as ambassador to Mexico. Despite assurances from President Wilson and Secretary of State Lansing, who had access to the diplomatic records, that he had nothing to worry about, Hapgood lost and had to pay a verdict of six cents.[25]

By early 1916 it was evident that *Harper's Weekly* was collapsing. In the fall of 1915 Hapgood had considered selling the *Weekly*, but Hapgood and Crane refused to sell to anyone hostile to either progressivism or Wilson. The January 1, 1916, issue adopted a standardized cover—in succeeding weeks only the color of the ink changed—a sign of desperation. Still losing money by the thousands, the *Weekly* grabbed only $627.88 in advertisements for the month of January, a paltry haul by any standards. Two days before an April meeting with Crane and Rogers in Washington, Hapgood declared, "Sale of the weekly imminent." Later that spring *Harper's Weekly* died as an independent entity. Its circulation was taken over by the *Independent*, a weekly edited by the competent Hamilton Holt, who had supported Taft in 1912.[26]

V

Hapgood's experience with periodicals during the Progressive Era was of more than biographical interest. His career provides a nice vantage point to examine certain issues. Upton Sinclair charged that substantial business pressure helped to end muckraking. That *Collier's* came under the sway of financial interests is fairly certain, although the precise nature of this control is difficult to ascertain. There is no important evidence to back Sinclair's contention that the National Association of Manufacturers "not only applied the advertising boycott to 'Collier's,' they set the banks to work . . . and they took away control of the magazine from Robert Collier, and put it into the hands of a banking committee, where it stayed." It seems more likely that Collier's ineptitude and various economic factors rather than a conspiracy put *Collier's* under the direction of others. It is true that Thomas W. Lamont tried to get control of the *Weekly* in 1912, but this was probably a shrewd move to snatch the book publishing enterprise, and, perhaps on the side, to curb the *Weekly*'s muckraking.[27]

The opportunities available to Hapgood, a certified muckraker, in 1912 and 1913, indicate that many chances to muckrake were available to one who had the money. Furthermore, Lamont, often cast as a villain, encouraged and aided Hapgood in his efforts to buy *Harper's Weekly*, which obviously would do a good amount of exposing under Hapgood's direction, and Hapgood thought well of Lamont's help. Both Sinclair and Louis Filler have argued that *Harper's Weekly* fell to "the advertising boycott." Whether they meant an organized effort is not clear, although both used boycott in a context implying coercion. Hapgood, never claiming the *Weekly*'s lack of advertising was a result of an attempt to alter his policies, contended that the difficulty was due to the *Weekly*'s inability to build circulation, its previous poor reputation, and a general constriction of advertising in the periodical field. One must avoid seeing muckraking and advertising as necessary enemies. One reason why Hapgood, a muckraker with good credentials, was so wanted after he left *Collier's* in 1912 was the feeling among many in journalism that he could draw advertising. He referred to "the pull of my name with advertisers, because of public confidence. Colliers has been soliciting advertising almost exclusively along that line." C. W. Post, according to Sinclair, was the leader of efforts to make magazines more responsive to the will of advertisers, but advertisements for his products often appeared in *Harper's*.[28]

Robert S. Maxwell has pointed out that a lost libel suit had helped curb muckraking at *McClure's*.[29] Hapgood's work at *Collier's Weekly* and at *Harper's Weekly* revealed a more subtle if no less interesting impact. In Hapgood's case it was not that lost libel suits were expensive but that fighting a large number of suits, even if successfully, led to attrition. For a magazine like *Collier's*, which prided itself on accuracy and whose prestige was on the line, every suit seemed to necessitate heavy expenditures for defense. Only a few of the cases, notably *Town Topics*, were ultimately profitable. The cost of libel suits hurt most when the magazine was having trouble from other causes. The expense of legal battles shook already delicate economic structures at both *Collier's Weekly* and *Harper's Weekly*.

VI

Most of 1916 had not been enjoyable for Hapgood. The *Weekly* started the year critically wounded and died in a few months. The collapse of *Harper's Weekly* would certainly not boost his reputation, and his ex-wife Emilie, concerned for his future, asked Brandeis to look after his interests. Norman, Emilie observed, "does not seem to give himself a thought." Hapgood hardly had a rest before he labored for the Woodrow Wilson Independent League, organized by Colonel House, Joseph M. Price, Franklin K. Lane, Frank Polk, Crane, and others. Hapgood, the vice-chairman, actually did most of the chairman's work.[30] With progressive credentials, a wide range of contacts with reformers, a reputation for some independence, a disdain for parties, yet a loyal Wilsonian, he was well cast in this role. During his remaining years he would head or serve on the executive committee of countless organizations. His prominence, respectability, and association with liberal causes made him serviceable.

Despite Wilson's reelection the campaign proved disappointing to Hapgood, who thought that Wilson's superiority to Hughes was self-evident and had predicted a stunning triumph for the president. Believing that the real argument for Wilson was his splendid record and that there was no need to indulge in sensationalism, he was taken aback by Wilson's slim victory and particularly upset that the emotional "he kept us out of war" appeal was so powerful.[31] Hapgood became more pessimistic about the nation's political atmosphere than he had been at *Collier's Weekly*.

Fortunately, 1916 closed on a nice note for Norman Hapgood. In December he married Elizabeth Kempley Reynolds, an attractive twenty-two-year-old, who had studied at the University of Paris and was already establishing herself as a leading American translator of Russian. They honeymooned in Europe. His remarriage was not without its lighter moments—in retrospect. A young niece, on seeing Norman with his second wife, asked ingenuously, "Where's Aunt Emilie?"[32]

VII

Norman Hapgood did some syndicated work in 1917. During 1918 and part of 1919 he contributed a biweekly column to

Leslie's Weekly, a conservative magazine. Hapgood and the editor disavowed responsibility for the opinions of the other. Hapgood had once alleged Standard Oil influence over that periodical, but he seemed to enjoy being its showcase liberal.[33] The *Leslie's* experience was an omen of his joining Hearst's organization within two years. Hapgood lived in Hanover, New Hampshire, most of this time—Elizabeth was founding the Russian department at Dartmouth College.

Foreign affairs were a major concern of Hapgood's throughout Wilson's presidency, but particularly during the second Wilson administration. The First World War of course predominated. Hapgood early accused Germany of starting it. In an editorial called "The Blame" in the August 15, 1914, issue of *Harper's Weekly,* he found the Kaiser guilty, and *Harper's* sported such covers as "Who Made Germany Crazy?" Although he vigorously condemned Germany, he pleaded for a just peace, one that respected self-determination and one that would not cripple Germany.[34]

Much of Hapgood's outlook toward foreign affairs was characteristic of other progressives. Hapgood certainly shared the optimism of Robert Wiebe's "new middle class." "Foreign relations . . . assumed a particularly benign cast because these men saw their ideals gradually materializing about them," Wiebe has argued. "They sought smoothness in the conduct of world affairs, an absence of violence and disorder and all wasteful conduct." By September 1914 Hapgood concluded, "This is the whole question of the war: Is the future to be decided at the Hague or by the Bismarckian method of 'blood and iron'?" In the summer of the next year it was evident to Hapgood, who often lumped together democracy, respect for neutral rights, and peace, that Germany must become democratic if peace were to last. Given his optimistic outlook and the belief that democracy was winning throughout the world, he could argue "that the world is likely to pay now, once for all, the bill that grows out of despotic government." Christopher Lasch has written of his "anti-imperialists," "If they invented 'peace without victory,' they were among the first to abandon it in favor of the dream of total victory: the annihilation of autocracy everywhere." [35]

VIII

Hapgood was tested by the Russian problem. He had been interested in that country for some time and, having an especially deep faith in its destiny, followed Russian affairs closely, particularly after the overthrow of the Czar. Wilson, under the guidance of Colonel House, offered Hapgood the ministry to Copenhagen, partly because it provided a good vantage point on Russia, but, probably, partly to reward a loyal supporter. Hapgood had apparently been considered for some kind of post for a couple of years and for Denmark since 1918. Formally nominated on February 27, 1919, he encountered trouble quickly. The Senate Foreign Relations Committee, controlled by Republicans, did not consider the nomination. Assistant Secretary of State Frank Polk thought it wise to drop the whole matter and avoid antagonizing the Republicans, but Wilson differed and made a recess appointment; Hapgood would be the American minister until the Senate reconvened in the fall, and his name would be resubmitted at that time.[36]

Hapgood arrived in Copenhagen in June 1919 and assumed his post. By the summer of 1919 he had already reached many conclusions about the Russian Revolution and the proper American reaction. Cheering the collapse of Czarism but wary of the Bolsheviks, Hapgood hoped to encourage contacts and trade with the Russian cooperatives, which at this time were still fairly autonomous. Alerted to the significance of the cooperatives by his wife, Elizabeth, he was fascinated by them, wrote of them often, and has been called their "most persistent advocate . . . in America."[37]

Hapgood thought the cooperatives a means of associating with Russia, yet of avoiding endorsement of the Bolshevik government. It was a chance to identify with a great popular upheaval but still be aloof from the Bolshevik dictatorship. It was also an alternative to intervention. Arguing for the withdrawal of Allied troops, Hapgood believed that Bolshevism, without the strong nationalist appeal made possible by foreign intervention, could not survive. The Bolsheviks would either be destroyed by more practical men or become more practical themselves and thus drop much of their creed. This view was common to American liberals.[38]

Hapgood had been in Denmark two months when there was trouble at the State Department. Breckinridge Long, an assistant secretary of state, heard allegations that Hapgood had tried to raise money for the Soviet government and that he was sympathetic to the Bolsheviks. Long confided in his diary, "It is a grave charge." Almost as distressing as the accusations, which were based on remarks Hapgood had supposedly made at a dinner with officials of the Guaranty Trust Company and, more important, on a letter he had written the day after the dinner, was that Henry Cabot Lodge, the powerful and truculent chairman of the Senate Foreign Relations Committee had gotten wind of the story. When Secretary of State Robert Lansing questioned Hapgood about the episode, Hapgood replied, "Facts are simple, I never tried for or recommended loan for Soviet Government. I did recommend credit to cooperative associations." Long was not persuaded and an entry in his diary summarized: "Today I recommended the recall of Norman Hapgood as Minister to Copenhagen. I did it because I believe he is a Bolshevist in sympathy and because he wrote a letter in April proposing financial loan to the Soviet Gov't itself—which he now denies. . . . The Sect'y [of State] took the recommendation to the President and left it with him." Long warned Lansing, "There will be a scandal if he is not removed." [39]

The president refused to buckle to Long and stood by Hapgood, but the State Department had little sympathy for Hapgood. One assistant secretary of state called him "Hapgoody-goody," and another informed Lansing that there was general agreement in their attitude toward Hapgood. Hapgood in turn wrote the president, "I am going to inflict more letters on you hereafter and confine my dispatches to ordinary business." In September, when Lodge renewed his interest in the case, Lansing defended Hapgood, probably unenthusiastically; Lodge was not persuaded.[40]

In October it became evident that Hapgood would not be confirmed when the Senate reconvened. He was willing to fight, but he begged the president to consider only the national inter-

Elizabeth R., Elizabeth, Norman, Jr., Ten Eyck (David), and Norman Hapgood picnicking in Germany, 1931. (Courtesy of Elizabeth Backman.)

est. Above all, Hapgood did not want to jeopardize ratification of the treaty. In mid-October he decided to resign and formally notified the president on November 16, 1919.

Hapgood's withdrawal did not end the affair. Reports appeared in the press that he had been recalled. More important, *Harvey's Weekly* rehashed the old charges in spectacular fashion and referred to Hapgood's "activities as a plenipotentiary of Messrs. Lenine and Trotzky." Hapgood, returning to the United States on December 23, was anxious to disprove Colonel Harvey, but he said nothing until his resignation was accepted by the president—though technically his recess appointment automatically expired when the Senate reconvened. Hapgood considered the attacks revengeful—he had criticized several of the senators in *Leslie's Weekly* and when he was head of the League of Free Nations Association, a pro-League group.[41] Harvey's articles, based on information supplied to him by Lodge and by the Senate Foreign Relations Committee, surely irritated Hapgood. Although there was not an explicit understanding that if he resigned he would be spared a public controversy, it was not unlikely that Hapgood thought he would be allowed to fade away. To the outmaneuvered Hapgood, Harvey's attacks must have been salt on the wound.

Many of the charges against Hapgood were without foundation. The most damaging accusation was that he had sought loans for the Soviet government at the dinner with Guaranty Trust officials. He claimed that he was merely searching for knowledge that would be useful if changes were made in American foreign policy. There was considerable confusion among the witnesses, but he did seek a loan to the cooperatives probably through the Soviet government. Hapgood certainly did not seek a direct loan for the Soviet government, for the next day he wrote Brandeis, "I did not bring up the point of contracts made directly with the Russian government." In his April 9 letter to Willis Booth, one of the Guaranty Trust officials, Hapgood asked: "I should like very much to know whether contracts with the Soviet Government itself based on credits established in neutral banks, with the deposit referred to, would not avoid the danger referred to last night growing out of the absence of private property in Russia." This letter, used so often against Hapgood, might have been more of an inquiry about a possibility than a check on a means already decided on. Besides these specific pieces of evidence much was made of his leftish associates.[42]

After he left office, Hapgood persisted in the campaign to alter American policy toward Russia. "This issue is more important than domestic issues, because domestic errors can be undone in four years," he argued in 1920. "It is more important than the League of Nations issue, because unless we can solve this question the League is a menace and a fraud. This issue is paramount, and it will not wait." For some time he felt that only foreign harassment prolonged Soviet rule. He was a staunch critic of America's Russian policy during the 1920s and especially that of Secretary of State Charles Evans Hughes.[43]

Hapgood's outlook toward Russia was a combination of realism and moralism. His weakness was not that he was pro-Bolshevik, as some of his critics alleged, but that everything tied together too nicely. If anything attracted him to Russia it was his progressive belief that democracy was gradually unfolding throughout the world. Russia, a large and significant country, was naturally exciting. It was inconceivable to him that a great popular movement—especially one overthrowing Czarism and the Russian upper classes, both of which he detested—with some democratic elements in support, could desire other than at least crude democracy. Being democratic, it must be good; being democratic, it ought to share interests with the more enlightened segments of the West. Bolshevism itself could not last. His optimism about the chances for representative government in Russia, a nation inexperienced in that field, was not only misplaced but surprising in one who had once been a mugwump and who always stressed the importance of educated leadership. Within a few years he appeared to revert to gradualism. Hapgood, hardly appreciating the extent to which a harsh Bolshevism was a genuine outgrowth of the upheaval in Russia, offered cheap solutions. He exaggerated the extent to which cooperatives, which Lenin began to assume control over shortly before Hapgood left for Denmark, could maim Bolshevism, and he overrated the victories that friendly gestures might win.[44] Although Hapgood effectively debunked the atrocity stories and ridiculed the State Department, he was less successful in subjecting his own opinions to careful testing.

IX

The last years of Wilson's presidency shaped Norman Hapgood's outlook for much of the 1920s. Hapgood had been disturbed by the president's call for the election of Democrats in 1918 and disliked his neglecting to bring prominent Republicans with him to Paris, but he remained friendly toward Wilson and did not become disillusioned with his Russian policy. Hapgood opposed the suppression of civil liberties during the Red Scare, was greatly interested in the wartime experiment with a regulated economy, and was disappointed by Wilson's failure to develop a comprehensive reconstruction policy. Although Hapgood became less enthusiastic about the League within a few years, his support lasted through most of the rest of his life.[45] Loyal to internationalism, he voted for Cox in 1920.

CHAPTER 8

From Labor to Emotional Crisis

I

HUTCHINS HAPGOOD'S WRITINGS in the second half of the first decade of the twentieth century nicely indicated the shift of his interests. His two most important books of this time were *The Spirit of Labor* (1907) and *An Anarchist Woman* (1909)—*Types from City Streets* (1910) was basically a collection of earlier pieces. Above all, Hapgood was veering toward issues of social importance. If the ghetto and the Bowery were the preoccupations of his earlier years, labor, radicals, and Greenwich Village were the chief topics of his prewar work. His outcasts now usually had some kind of political implication. He now claimed that conservative newspapers were not only stuffy—the charge he had made at the *Commercial*—but also antilabor.[1] As Norman Hapgood's years on *Collier's* marked his politicization, so at about the same time did Hutchins become more socially concerned, but to a different degree, in a different way, and to a different result.

Hutchins Hapgood's interest in the labor movement marked a new enthusiasm and was an important development, but in many respects it flowed from old conceptions. Workers, like Jews and toughs, were outsiders. As such, labor touched a temperamental quality of his. Workers promised a fresh literary field, but labor also differed from either the ghetto or the Bowery. The ghetto, Hapgood had discovered, however beautiful and moving, and whatever it might potentially add to American life, was declining. The Bowery, less evidently retrogressing, was essentially static. After all, the colorful characters were pretty much sui generis, and a good part of their appeal at best was novelty. Hapgood soured on criminals; he simply could not see their ultimate importance.

Hutchins Hapgood discovered labor in Chicago. Like his

older brother, he enjoyed the midwestern flavor in politics, although Norman's orientation was much more middle class. Hutchins wrote his wife from Chicago, "My relations in past years with thieves, vaudevillists, etc. etc. seem now to me quite unimportant, socially. But these working people and the radical atmosphere in which the thought of the working class results— this seems significant to me in a tremendous almost terrible way, and the personalities—many of them—fascinate, please and sadden and excite me." Just a short while before, he had thought that the labor movement lacked literary potential, but his midwestern experience altered his view.[2] His reversal suggests the extent to which literary value was still necessary to energize him.

Hutchins's absorption in the labor movement followed his own pattern. Part of the intellectual baggage he brought into the relationship was the human document approach. If this genre had as one of its purposes shedding light not only on the character of the individual but on his environment, what could be more valuable than exposing a movement of widespread ramification? Hapgood, realizing that he must pick a subject carefully, scoured Chicago. Finally he found Anton (Anton Johannsen) and persuaded him to submit to a series of interviews. After Hapgood left the *Chicago Evening Post,* he made a special return trip to Chicago to question Johannsen over an extended period. *The Spirit of Labor* had many of the trademarks of earlier efforts in this genre: an emphasis on the real, firsthand experience, and the deep and simple, all heavily seasoned with personality. Its technique deviated from previous human documents because Hapgood found that the complexity of the labor problem made it necessary to go beyond an autobiography of Anton into a biography. Hapgood played a more active role.

Anton, no mass-produced revolutionary, had a robust sense of individuality and a clearly etched personality. Like Marie and Terry (Terry Carlin), the heroes of *An Anarchist Woman,* Anton was basically a maverick. A former tramp and drifter, he berated conservative trade union leaders, but he also flustered anarchists, socialists, and miscellaneous colorless radicals. In addition to all this, Johannsen was quite a lover. Anton had at times the forthrightness of a grizzly bear; like the tough, he was direct and sure of his ground. His superiority seemed beyond training, the child of a vigorous, whole personality. Throughout *The Spirit of Labor* Hapgood was more interested in Anton's inversion of traditional morality—Anton in some respects was to Hapgood what political bosses were to Steffens—than in probing, for example, the causes of the strikes Anton was involved in or the backgrounds and personalities of Anton's opponents in the unions.

Marie's experience as a maid allowed her to comment effectively on the hypocrisy of an employer closely associated with Hull House. She also provided scathing criticism of a radical family with whom she had lived for a while. Terry was a scorching, impulsive individualist who had saved Marie from a worthless life. They became lovers, but Marie eventually left Terry. Marie "finally rebelled against an idealism so exquisite that it became cruelty and almost madness. And this is the way with the world." [3]

Hapgood's *The Spirit of Labor* and *An Anarchist Woman* were about radicals. Some of his earlier work had contained social criticism, but these two books were more explicit. May, the heroine of "A Marionette," who indulged in an unconventional sex life, had declared, "I am not a rebel against Society, and gladly believe as good people do. My only excuse is that all through my life I have been unprotected." [4] One could not say the same about Anton, Marie, or Terry.

Hapgood's exposure in Chicago to radicals such as Emma Goldman, Alexander Berkman, and George Herron prepared him for his subsequent work for the *New York Globe*. His zeal for labor served not only as a bridge to prewar Greenwich Village radicalism but also to the Columbia Conserve Company and to the liberalism of the 1930s. He confessed in 1939, "As I look back upon my long life, I find there is only one faith that burns in me as brightly or more brightly than ever. That is what may be called roughly the faith in the labor movement." [5] Labor gave Hapgood a hard base, something to supplement and toughen his cultural radicalism.

II

An Anarchist Woman was one of Hapgood's last efforts in the human document. Indeed, only one subsequent work, "Cristine," was composed in precisely this form, and it was never completed. Hapgood's assets as a writer were a willingness to appreciate a variety of characters, an ability to deal with subjects and situations not commonly discussed in American novels at that time, a good, quite readable style, and an ability to write epigrams. None of his ventures were financial successes, although he did have a following, including Eugene O'Neill, Theodore Dreiser, and Fremont Older. Hapgood's human document deserves recognition as a rough precursor of what William Stott has called the "informant narrative" so popular in the 1930s.[6]

All Hapgood's human documents suffered from organizational weakness. Many harbored orphan chapters. *The Autobiography of a Thief* included a chapter that did not fit the rest of the narrative. Much of *An Anarchist Woman* was epistolary in form—Hapgood did not have the opportunity to finish the interviews. *Types from City Streets,* perhaps his most frustrating book because it might have been his best, too often contained incongruous material, too much resembled a scissors-and-paste job in organization, if not in perceptions.

Hapgood's troubles lay deeper than this. The document approach was loaded with pitfalls. He might pick the wrong horse as he clearly did a few times. Certainly he never got a winner of the stature of William Riordon's George Washington Plunkitt. His tendency to sentimentalize was part of his liking, and his weakest characters were usually pathetic. This was certainly true of his women; May, Marie, and Cristine were basically warm, sensuous victims. More than great sympathy hurt Hapgood. "David," a human document about David Edstrom, the sculptor, was Hapgood's one work in this genre in which he detested the subject. While both were in Italy, Edstrom had convinced a reluctant Hapgood to do a study of him. After Hapgood had completed the interviews, Edstrom changed his mind, fled with the manuscripts, and claimed that he had been emotionally unstable. Edstrom had revealed, among other things, that he had had a diseased testicle removed and that beating his wife had given him a thrill. One might expect some hard-hitting comments in this study, and there were, but the book lost focus when Hapgood used it to defend himself from the charge that he had exploited Edstrom's mental condition. James R. Mellow has recently noted that Gertrude Stein's "Men," which described a homosexual episode, referred to Maurice Sterne, Edstrom, and Hutchins Hapgood. Stein's story was detailed though often obscure about Sterne and Edstrom, and only briefly mentioned Hapgood's involvement. It is difficult to say how much weight this evidence ought to be given. This writer has encountered no other direct reference to homosexual behavior of Hutchins's part. At most Stein's article might mean that Hapgood had at least one homosexual experience.[7]

Hapgood was more interested in personality than in complex background. His study of Anton was one of his better pieces, but it explained the complications of the labor movement with only moderate success. Indeed, Hapgood was so absorbed in personality that his human documents rarely, if ever, gave much attention to physical setting. The drama was always in characters. He lacked Stephen Crane's knack for creating atmosphere and mood through the description of colors, smells, and things. While Hapgood was working on *The Spirit of Labor,* Neith wrote to Hutchins, "You were not interested primarily in the labor question, but in the human element . . . you were really a novelist though you didn't like the conventional form."[8] This was only partly true. Hapgood was more concerned with character than ideology, but he was also more interested in personality than in literary craftsmanship. His romantic preoccupations with authenticity and the ennobling quality of suffering and his belief in the ultimate importance of the outcast and the rebel made him careless in method. His concern for the deeper meaning often placed his books in a rut. One will probably enjoy Hapgood's human documents more if one has read only a couple than if one has read four or five of them. Never enthusiastic about painstaking research, he too often took a ride on the interview. Several of his books might have been better had he followed an approach more akin to *The Spirit of the Ghetto* and used a series of sketches to describe a milieu. But Hapgood was too interested in personality, too tied to seeing one individual as a type, to escape confinement in his literary method.

It is difficult to apply one of the traditional labels to Hapgood's human documents. He certainly was not a naturalist. Although he recognized the importance of environment, he was enthusiastic about personality and rejected naturalism's amoralism. His work seems to have been chiefly influenced by a combination of realism and romanticism. His concern for the underside of life, particularly in an urban environment, was fairly typical of realism, but his emphasis on spiritual values, on seeing man as Man, and his sentimentalism were indebted to romanticism. One finds in Hapgood's writings characteristic journalistic concerns of the time handled with romantic assumptions. This mix might appear peculiar, but it is important to recognize that in much American writing at the turn of the century, realistic and romantic ideas were often combined.[9]

III

After he finished research on *The Spirit of Labor*, Hapgood, his wife, and their children Boyce and Charles went to Europe and remained there for two years. Hutchins found this visit productive. "Our two years abroad have been most interesting," he informed an aunt, "but I shall be glad to get back to America where the big bulk of my friends and my real work must be, and where it is best that the children should be educated." [10]

Returning to America without a position, he went to work for the Columbia Conserve Company, a canning business that Charles Hapgood had bought for William Hapgood. Hutchins's year with the struggling Indianapolis concern was scarred by emotional and marital strain. Searching for other employment, he asked Robert Morss Lovett to try to secure a position for him teaching sociology. Another possibility was taking over a daily newspaper in Charlottesville, Virginia. Hapgood observed, "I think the people would be satisfied with little and I could give them hot[?] Jeffersonian democracy!" Neither of these schemes amounted to anything, but he did manage to get a position with the *New York Evening Post* doing some literary work and writing editorials. He soon grew discontented with the *Evening Post*. After he had dined with the editor, Hapgood told his wife, "I like [Rollo] Ogden, but his respectable intelligence in which there is some wit and much form, has not an iota of temperament and made me feel like getting drunk." Hapgood, who did not stay at the *Post* long, turned to free lance journalism; he also composed a few editorials for the *New York Press*.[11]

Hapgood finally made a breakthrough. He got a job on the *New York Globe*, the new name of the *Commercial Advertiser*. His years on the *Globe* rank with the *Commercial* days as his most significant journalistic employment. Probably more prominent during his *Globe* years than at any other time, he prowled for topics and claimed, "I could write about anything that was in my head or my senses. The warm spring day, a French girl, a picture at Stieglitz's, an inspired bum in a saloon, a suffrage meeting, an interview with Bill Haywood, or a strike at Hastings." Although reminiscent of his service for the *Commercial* in flexibility and delicacy of approach, the *Globe* experience was quite different. There were no packs of eager, young reporters and the *Globe* was not an experiment. Hapgood had a signed column in the *Globe;* his work on the *Commercial* had been almost always anonymous. Although he pursued his interests at both times, he traveled to different places. The old haunts had been the Bowery and the East Side and his subjects usually Bowery toughs and ghetto intellectuals. He would occasionally write about these for the *Globe,* but they were no longer his fascinations. He was still interested in personalities, but of a different sort—Wobblies, anarchists, socialists, reformers, and artists. His readers, he asserted, were basically liberals, reformers, and radicals. He was likely to be found at Mabel Dodge's salon or at Stieglitz's "291," or in Greenwich Village, but also at the Brevoort Hotel or Luke O'Connor's Working Girls' Home.[12]

IV

Political activity was a significant though not major concern of Hapgood's *Globe* years. Dismissing socialism as too rigid and confining, he sometimes referred to himself as a philosophical anarchist, by which he meant, not anarchism, but restlessness, individualism, and an inability to subsume himself to a group's or a party's outlook. He also kept his distance from most progressives. As was pointed out earlier, the *Commercial* and the Griffou Push had questioned many reformers, and Hapgood in *The Spirit of the Ghetto* had warned against taking a narrowly uplifting viewpoint. A suspiciousness of reform inhered in his love of outcasts. If they were admirable and their excellence was in part caused by their situation, one might have mixed feelings about reforming or changing them. This dilemma faced others beside Hapgood. Jane Addams observed that "self-sacrifice and generosity," were part of the immigrant's "reward for living in the midst of poverty." John Sloan wondered, "I can't help feeling that the movement [socialism] is right in the main. I am rather more interested in the human beings themselves than in the schemes for betterment. In fact, I rather wonder if they will be so interesting when they are all comfortable and happy." [13] The labor movement, springing from below, helped Hapgood out of his difficulty, just as Addams's faith in a social ethic and cultural pluralism reassured her.

The goals of the turn-of-the-century reformers were more limited than those Hapgood had to deal with when, during the high tide of progressivism, he was with the *Globe*. His relations with labor and radicals had given him newer, more ideological criteria. Although Hapgood praised progressivism in the sense that he maintained it had on the whole done good, he decried elements in it and was never comfortable with it. His critique was based on three charges: class bias, antilabor feeling, and intellectual shallowness reflected in personality. He was upset by the elitist character of the movement and had little use for eugenics or for efficiency experts. Hapgood, who had a genuinely antielitist slant, felt that government should be broadly based and declared about his town, Dobbs Ferry, "We want a

From Labor to Emotional Crisis

Hutchins Hapgood c. 1938. (Courtesy of Elizabeth Backman.)

Neith Boyce Hapgood, 1934. (Photograph by Carl Van Vechten, courtesy of Miriam DeWitt and Joseph Solomon.)

good government, to be sure, but we also want a representative government. We do not want a class government. Even inefficiency and easy-going political immorality is better than that." Although he opposed motion picture censorship, he preferred censorship by the democratically elected mayor to that by a select board.[14]

The muckrake impulse was wholesome, but Hapgood feared that it might wound the cause of the workingman. He argued that "in the labor movement, there is the possibility of a state of mind where a man will on account of his ingrained ideas of property morality, or other current morality, neglect a larger, less defined, less worked out morality." The emphasis on "a larger, less defined, less worked out morality" was at the root of another fundamental critique. Hapgood prided himself on his knack for getting to the essential, for brushing aside details. Indeed, he was more at ease dealing with tendencies than with platforms or programs. He wrote Steffens, "It is not necessary to be right, I think, in any exact & definite way—Taft and Hughes & Norman [Hapgood] could not be right except in that exact & definite way. When religion or emotions or imagination come in to play they are filled with distrust." One must grasp imaginatively. The Bureau of Municipal Research, Samuel Gompers, Woodrow Wilson, Charles Evans Hughes, George W. Perkins, and Morris Hillquit were all of the same type, something like what Walter Lippmann would later call "routineers."[15]

Many of Hapgood's judgments of individual progressives paralleled his feelings for his older brother: Norman was too arthritic, too unimaginative, to tackle the really significant, which often moved rapidly and zigzagged. Hutchins used Brandeis, Crane, and Wilson, three whom Norman greatly admired at this time, as targets in a shooting gallery. Although praising all three, he struck each hard. Of Brandeis, Norman's idol, Hutchins said, "If we were all as moral and as efficient as Mr. Brandeis desires there would be no art or poetry in the world, and we doubt whether there would remain a permanent possibility of a still deeper justice. For efficiency, carried to its logical point, might well result in greater exploitation than we now have." Brandeis was too preoccupied with the business values that Hutchins wanted people to get away from. Hapgood called Crane "a good man, but . . . a conventional man, without imagination." Wilson had "a clear mind, a good record and a high purpose," but little else. Hapgood contended that "it is only the radical mind . . . that sees the dangers and weaknesses of the progressive movement." He would probably have been critical of Crane and Wilson anyway, but a radical position further sanctioned his beliefs. Christopher Lasch has noted that Oswald Garrison Villard "apologized" for his political position to the allegedly more radical Hapgood, and Hutchins no doubt relished evaluating his brother in an olympian manner.[16] Recognizing the middle-class texture of progressivism and uneasy with the bourgeois, Hapgood did not distinguish sufficiently between the reformers of 1900 and the progressives and was prone to miss change and resort to stereotypes.

Hutchins's reaction to the 1912 election was interesting. Unlike Norman, he did not back Wilson. At first unenthusiastic about all the candidates, Hutchins eventually supported Roosevelt. He interpreted the election as a contest between intuitive, spiritual understanding and precise intelligence. The country needed more than "a logical and coolly balanced progressivism." Hapgood had felt that politicians should embrace the profound emotional forces of society, and although Roosevelt was not completely trustworthy, he at least showed some awareness. "Whatever Mr. Roosevelt may personally be," Hapgood concluded, "he is at present representing this deeper mood of the people." [17]

V

Hutchins Hapgood dissented from most progressive analyses of urban politics. Asking why an obviously corrupt Tammany Hall survived, he reached a different conclusion from Norman Hapgood, who had blamed the people and indulged in jeremiad. Hutchins, who had more faith in the people, declared, "The reformers need to reform themselves." Hutchins, like Jane Addams, Herbert Croly, Frederic C. Howe, Lincoln Steffens, and others, saw some redeeming traits in the boss. Suggestively, Hapgood emphasized the social qualities of the boss, gave less attention to his welfare functions than did Addams, and was less occupied with the boss as leader than Steffens.[18]

Hapgood championed the saloon, hoped that it would be cleaned up, and at one time had wished that the upper classes would infiltrate it. He defended the saloon for three reasons. First, he had spent good socio-intellectual times there. Second, in Chicago it had been a center of the labor movement. Third, he stood by the saloon all the more because its detractors were the kind of people he had been battling all along. Favoring regulation, he urged the repeal of laws against gambling, prostitution, and drink.[19]

Mayor William J. Gaynor, who had been elected with Tammany's support, was Hapgood's favorite urban politician in the Progressive Era. He asserted that "he has been the best and ablest Mayor that New York has ever had." He particularly delighted in Gaynor's awareness of complexity, his apartness from good-government reformers, his antielitist tendencies, and his respect for civil liberties, although Hapgood was somewhat critical of the mayor's police policy, which he felt had not been pushed far enough.[20]

VI

Was Hutchins Hapgood a progressive? That is a tough question partly because progressivism is difficult to define. His chastisement of reformers and his appreciation of the boss and the saloon were not typically progressive, but there was an impressive body of similar progressive literature. Jane Addams often spoke critically of reformers, and such classics as Herbert Croly's *Promise of American Life* and Walter Lippmann's *Preface to Politics,* hoping to establish a more viable movement, often threw bricks at other reformers. Howe and Addams, among others, saw some worth in the saloon, although neither's appreciation was of the same sort as Hapgood's. After all, Hapgood wrote a partial autobiography about his experiences with alcohol. Addams, Steffens, Croly, Lippmann, and Howe demonstrated some awareness of the boss's functions. After this is pointed out, however, there still were barriers between Hapgood and the progressives. One was his prolabor position, certainly to the left of progressivism. His vigorous anti-middle-class sentiment was another stiff difference. His aversion to self-righteous reformers, especially those who wished to impose their standards on people he liked, kept Hapgood apart, and his estimation of many reformers as wooden and unimaginative was significant. Progressivism simply did not satisfy him; in a basic sense it was not life-enhancing. He should not be considered a progressive, although he reflected some of their influences and although some progressives agreed with some of his criticisms.

VII

Although political outlook was a convenient measure of Hapgood's thought during these years, he did not care much for politics. His portrait could not be painted in political colors. In 1912 he complained that politics has been "uninteresting ever since the civil war," and, unlike Norman Hapgood, he did not believe that it had greatly improved in the early twentieth century. With the exception of a flash of interest in the campaign of 1912 and his enthusiasm for Mayor Gaynor in early 1913, Hutchins Hapgood did not become involved with any campaign until a generation later. In some respects he assigned politics a back seat.

Our politics will never be of any great consequence until our general civilization is better. Good politics follows, rather than leads, an advance in culture and civilization. When we have better art, better literature, better schools, better industrial conditions, better habits, less snobbishness, greater love, more poetry and philosophy, we can then have better politics, but then there won't be any need of politics.[21]

Hapgood believed he promoted the deeper things. Preoccupied with philosophical values, not ballots, platforms, or party labels, he raked not for muck but for gleanings of the spiritual. He hoped that the movements he associated with in the prewar years would develop a richer "spiritual" life. Comparing his *Globe* days with the *Commercial* ones, he realized that then he had sought to invest the common with meaning; now he courted the "exceptional." He explained, "Bergson, Post-Impressionism, the I. W. W., anarchism, the radical woman movement, the thrill of the socially and politically new, and the sophisticated pleasure of pouncing on any event or incident or fact which interprets these exceptional things, these make up the sum and substance of my existence." [22]

Hapgood was not flitting about; his method had a purpose. The movements of the time were not random, but connected, and converging to rattle existing standards. Robert Henri and Big Bill Haywood had this in common. Hapgood observed:

There seems a vague but real relationship between all the real workers of our day. Whether in literature, plastic art, the labor movement, science, journalism, philosophy, wherever we turn and find something vital in form, we find a common quality—we find an instinct to loosen up the old forms and traditions, to dynamite the baked and hardened earth so that fresh flowers can grow.[23]

This belief in confluence unified Hapgood's columns and energized his interests in a variety of areas. On the other hand, like his earlier work on the Bowery, his *Globe* writings became too predictable, glibly lumped things together, and often lost a sense of distinction.

Hapgood played the role of integrator of the radical movements in New York. In his columns radicals and avant-garde artists could usually expect favorable exposure, but journalism accounted for only a part of his effectiveness. Hapgood was a man of unusual warmth and sympathy who liked drink and women and craved social intercourse as a calmative. He often served as an unofficial social chairman of the intellectuals. Brand Whitlock thought Hutchins "delightful, much better in all ways than his brother Norman." There were many testaments to the great value put on his companionship, including, presumably, his extramarital affairs. "Everybody loved Hutch," Mabel Dodge Luhan remembered. "Your father was so full of love for mankind (and womankind)," Neith Hapgood wrote one of their sons. Their daughter Beatrix recalled that her father had told her that he found something to like in everyone he had met—except in Thomas W. Lamont. Robert Morss Lovett emphasized, "No one has ever been more ready to share his friends with one another.... For myself I owe to him Lincoln Steffens, Jo Davidson, John and Katie Dos Passos, Maurice Aisen, Mary Heaton Vorse, Susan Glaspell, Bayard Boyesen, Luke O'Connor, and above all Neith." Hapgood used his talents as a recruiter for Mable Dodge's evenings. Dodge—wealthy, as intense a seeker as Hapgood and every bit as passionate—was eager to experience new social and cultural currents. In the intellectual circles of prewar New York, this often meant an interest in Wobblies and anarchists, Freud and avant-garde poets and artists. At one of her celebrated open houses one might find such diverse personalities as Walter Lippmann, Carl Van Vechten, and Bill Haywood. Dodge acknowledged that Hapgood "brought all his friends to see me and took me to see them." [24]

Ray Stannard Baker recorded his impressions of one of Hapgood's performances at Mabel Dodge's: "With half a glass of whisky and soda in one hand, a cigarette in the other, and leaning far forward, he seemed to be groping for language to express something only half thought. An intensely personal man, he evidently felt the minds of those in the room whom he knew working upon him." [25]

In Greenwich Village or Provincetown, Hutchins Hapgood was always bringing people together. He performed a somewhat similar function to that of Norman Hapgood at *Collier's Weekly*, introducing individuals of like interests to one another. Norman did it mainly through official capacity, Hutchins more by personal qualities. Each did it largely for different groups. There probably were not many important intellectuals in prewar New York who did not know, at least in passing, Norman or Hutchins Hapgood.

VIII

Hapgood's thought always involved something more than his opinions on politics or on the latest in the arts. A craving for philosophical unity was never far below the surface. He conceded in his autobiography, "I have been conscious since my childhood of the unseen cause of all seen things, which gives to all seen things their superlative beauty; and have been engaged in the hopeless quest of the Cause. Ever since I studied Hegel at Strassburg, and before, I had been on the trail of the Infinite; and still the Infinite torments me." At Harvard Hapgood had been intrigued by metaphysics and seems to have written a study of free will, but he came to realize that the great problems of metaphysics were unanswerable. As if relieved, he turned to life more completely.[26]

Hapgood never rid himself of the desire for unity. In the breathless style of *The Story of a Lover* he moaned, "Oh, why do I need the Impossible? Why, oh why?" He told Mabel Dodge, "O, that terrible strenuousness that makes us strive for what we have not, even when our Natures recognize it as alien! I want the Beyond but I want it to have the qualities of the Here! Impossible, maddening." He argued that religion "begins where all our definite knowledge ends. But our knowledge is limited about everything, so that religion is inherent in everything. As long as we feel the deeper meaning of our experience we are religious." His sharpest criticism of the prewar radicals, as it was of the Communists in the 1930s, was that they were too materialistic.[27] Despite his spiritual searching, Hapgood was not religious in a clearly defined sense.

Hapgood often threw a lot of normative words around what he sensed. Neith Hapgood observed, "He made a philosophy out of his temperament and this to him was truth." Ray Stannard Baker acidly called Hapgood's quest for the "Absolute" "a small boy playing in a muddy puddle!" Although Hapgood constantly spoke of the complexity of life, the futility of dogmatism, his thought was always based on fat assumptions. Leo Stein growled, "I'm going to ask Hutch some day to compile a list of the things that are obvious or which everybody knows, that is, everybody except me—it will make a volume about the size of Webster's Unabridged." [28]

IX

Hutchins Hapgood vigorously mixed his ideas with his personal life; he never compartmentalized his thought or separated it from his emotions. An understanding of his relationship with his wife is indispensable to a recognition of his character and intellect.

Hutchins Hapgood fell in love with prim-looking Neith Boyce at first sight. She did not reciprocate his affection, not for quite a while anyway. A good portion of their relationship is told in that fact. The reddish-blond-haired, green-eyed Neith had an oval face, with thin arching eyebrows standing as sentries against easy familiarity. Her nose was nice if a little arrogant, and her lips frowning. In all, she looked attentive but slightly bored, with a suggestion of lurking displeasure. Although a photograph of Neith, obtained under false pretenses, became a cigarette card, she had a cool beauty, not the high-stepping sort like Emilie Hapgood's. Max Eastman remembered Neith as "a slim, pale, silent woman whom we used to describe as an 'early Italian stenographer.' " "She moved like a slow river" and "she always seemed partly absent," Mabel Dodge Luhan remarked.[29]

The distant Neith was a vivid contrast to Hutchins. She made him look impetuous, excitable; he made her seem cold, unalive. Steffens, when he heard they were going to be married, presumed that it would be unsuccessful. She confessed that "for . . . many years human relations did not touch or move me very much, they were not real to me." [30] Neith's self-possession and reserve probably appealed to the troubled and fervid Hutchins.

Neith, the daughter of Henry Harrison and Mary E. Boyce, was born in Indiana in 1872. Her father, a Civil War hero, had been active in a variety of ventures including the *Los Angeles Times,* the *Arena,* banking, mining, and real estate. While living in Milwaukee, the Boyces had lost all their children except Neith to diphtheria. Later another baby died although two sisters survived. Neith's parents, like Mabel Dodge Luhan's, were cold, although they were untouched by the perverse, decadent qualities of Luhan's. Neith "had never been able to talk to them." After a suicide in the house, "Iras [Neith] was even apart from herself as she observed other people," Neith remembered. She wrote her autobiography in the third person. She was in her mid-twenties before she got over a fear of sleeping in the dark. Her mental collapse after almost leaving her husband and her grief at the death of her son Boyce, a grief so profound that for a few years Neith seemed to stare past people and was often unapproachable, even to her children, revealed a capacity for powerful emotion, but also a tendency to turn inward and difficulty in seeking release. Unlike Hutchins, Neith did not make her feelings a perennial topic of conversation.[31]

Self-reliant, independent, Neith Boyce was one of hundreds of young women in New York journalism in the late 1890s. She was quick on her feet, as a later incident she recorded showed. Bernard Berenson, asking her impression of an acquaintance, implored, " 'Tell the truth now. Don't say something unpleasant to please me.' I said 'Why should I want to please you?' He said, 'You're an impudent creature.' "[32] The capable Neith Boyce worked next to Steffens, the city editor, on the copy desk of the *Commercial*. Like others of the staff, she was an aspiring writer and eventually wrote many short stories and several books: *The Forerunner* (1903), *The Eternal Spring: A Novel* (1906), *The Bond* (1908), *Harry* (1923), and *Proud Lady* (1923). She was one of the few *Commercial* products who stuck to a literary career.

X

Hutchins Hapgood and Neith Boyce were married in June 1899. No one called their relationship calm. An entry in Neith's diary in 1903 stated, "Ended by quarrelling about the usual things—beginning with the fact that I am not sociable with the Americans at the pensione and ending up with the fact that I am a bad wife—as it was in the beginning, is now and ever shall be, amen." [33] Hutchins experienced the bittersweet sensation of discovering that one's spouse was one's most perceptive critic.

Although each had moments of disillusion, both eventually thought their years together extremely worthwhile. Considering the experiences of many of their friends, they believed themselves quite fortunate. Hutchins strove with fierce intensity to make his union with Neith complete, to satisfy all his spiritual longings, but she usually maintained some reserve. Partly influenced by the sexual theories he had encountered in Chicago, Hutchins had several affairs after marriage. In *The Spirit of Labor* he argued that in a successful marriage "interest in others helps them to be more interested in one another, and their relation together. It makes it more exciting, more rich." A monogamist who experimented, he really loved only Neith. He encouraged her to become interested in other men but was envious when she did, largely because she had not fully realized him yet. Recognizing that his feelings did not mesh with his ideas, Hapgood thought he was like other experimenters, who "were not only crudely and madly jealous but they also hated themselves for being so!" [34]

The Hapgoods' stay in Indianapolis severely tested their marriage. Neith had to choose between Hutchins and a lover, Arthur F. Bentley. She picked Hutchins, but collapsed mentally. The relations between Hutchins and Neith improved after Indianapolis, but Neith's "discovery of . . . long-continued secret relations" brought on more strain. Hutchins's affair with Lucy Collier, the first wife of John Collier, became general knowledge, or at least Mabel Dodge found out. Hutchins and Neith claimed to be mature and unruffled and recognized that this dalliance involved no fundamental tie, which could only be to each other. Later Neith conceded that she had been maintaining a front. "How noble I was! how patronizing! And of course all the time I was nothing of the sort," she confessed. During one of Hutchins's affairs, Neith and the children moved to Vermont. When he visited, the usually ebullient Hutchins was subdued and their youngest child remembered that although she could not grasp the gist of her parents' conversations, "there was a lot of talking." [35] The Hapgoods' marital practices sometimes took more of a toll than either admitted.

XI

The starkest fact of Hutchins Hapgood's intellectual life between 1914 and 1939, when his autobiography, *A Victorian in the Modern World,* was published, was the scarcity of his writings. He wrote *The Story of a Lover* in 1914, although it was not published until 1919, and *Enemies,* a play coauthored with his wife, was finished in 1915. "Cristine," never completed, was done about 1918 or 1919. "My Forty Years of Drink," his fourth and final work before the autobiography, was composed between 1932 and 1934. Why he produced so little is of as much consequence as what he actually wrote.

The reasons for Hapgood's lack of output were an emotional crisis, or rather a series of them, and a shift in interest. The discussion of his childhood has pointed out the conflict of his youth, and though his condition had improved greatly at Harvard, even after his world tour he "was subject to frequent attacks of extreme lassitude, when physical effort of any kind would play me out completely." His stresses seem to have disappeared or become submerged when he worked for the *Commercial.* Hapgood, aware of violent, possibly destructive, powers lurking within himself, feared serious involvement with music because it stirred his soul too much. He had valued the distractive worth of friendship and recognized the disciplining, relaxing effect of work. He observed in 1909, "Work takes one away from life, is a buffer between sensitive nerves and intensest experience. Strong natures who for some reason are dislocated and therefore do not work or work only fragmentarily, come too much in contact with life and often cannot bear it; it burns and palls at once." [36]

The rougher stretches of his marriage affected his emotional state. Neith was not the only one who agonized in Indianapolis. Hutchins pleaded with Steffens to help him find a job, not creative but mindless employment that might knock out his anxiety. He complained that "my life has been so terribly personal that it has only been at rare intervals that I have even partly succeeded in getting out in the 'larger atmosphere.' " Recognition of the therapeutic value of work sometimes made Hapgood opportunistic. He castigated the *New York Evening Post*, for which he worked shortly afterwards, as stodgy and stifling, but the character of that sheet was well known, and it is inconceivable that he would not have been aware of it. Laboring for the *Evening Post* less for intellectual reasons than for psychological relief, he took out his anxiety, aggravated by dependence, on that paper. In 1912 Hapgood lamented that when he became worried he became severely introspective, when he became severely introspective he could not work and in fact became immobilized.[37]

Hapgood shook these earlier crises. This was not the case in 1913. The years from 1914 to 1922 were ones of great anguish. He recalled:

The hope and buoyant faith, which had been mine during my work on the *Globe* and at the time of Mabel's salon, had changed in a few brief years or even months into something almost incomprehensibly different. It was almost as if I had returned to the ignorant misery of my boyhood, as if the happy and quiet years at college and my cool and interested trips abroad and my mature work on the newspapers, had ceased to be. The old questionings between me and my soul returned with greater, because more passionate, feeling. I was rudderless, like the rest of the world.[38]

Exactly what triggered Hapgood's difficulty is uncertain. Actually he appears to have been under great stress in 1913, when he became antagonistic both toward himself and his friends. His leaving the *Globe* was related to this stress. Hapgood had resented the editor's increasing his columns from four a week to six, but even before this, Hapgood had believed that his days on the *Globe* were numbered. He asserted in his autobiography that "the dark clouds gathering on the world's horizon and the disturbances in my own life" had destroyed his desire to write. Precisely what part world affairs played in either his crisis or his quitting the *Globe* is hard to determine but probably slight. His combative summer and the end of his service on the *Globe,* both loudly suggesting psychological turmoil, occurred in 1913, well before the war. Hapgood, feeling that he was partly to blame for the First World War, proclaimed, "We were the Cause of the War: the violence and inconsistency of our emotions, the impotence of our ideas. What were our ideas worth? Had they contributed to make the War impossible?" [39] One detects in this excessive guilt not so much the decisive impact of the war on him, as the feeding of an eagerness to blame himself, a search for atonement. Hapgood later did some newspaper work—he wrote editorials for the *New York American* in 1922—but his departure from the *Globe* was the meaningful end of his journalistic career.

"I am disturbed about everything," he noted; "about my work, about what is *value,* about Neith, about life in general." In 1918 his eldest son, Boyce, died of influenza in Colorado, and Hutchins, already badly shaken by emotional problems, was crippled by the loss. He rebuked himself severely for letting his son go west. It took him a long time to recover some sort of stability. Neith Hapgood began to have mystical feelings, and Hutchins read the Bible. Hutchins declared, "I shall never write again—unless I am 'called' with unhappy force." [40]

XII

Hapgood's self-preoccupation was evident in his literary products of this period. *The Story of a Lover* was an account of his relations with Neith. Written while their marriage was particularly turbulent, *The Story of a Lover* was in some respects an outgrowth of his human document approach. Only this time he, not Jim Caulfield or Anton Johannsen, was the subject. Hapgood's paradoxical attitude toward the book disclosed many of his ideas about literature. Written in 1914 but withheld from publication from fear of upsetting his father, it was published anonymously after Theodore Dreiser had recommended it to Horace Liveright. Its first sales were good—better than any of Hapgood's other books—but it suffered a setback when members of the New York City Police Department's Vice Squad seized it. Although it was found not to be obscene, he felt that the publicity ruined further sales. Those were days when scandal of this sort was not good business.

In 1919 he thought the book biased and not representative of his 1919 feelings. He later explained, "I was intensely true to my own emotion and that made a good bit of autobiography. But writing as I did about things outside of myself, the picture was distorted." Despite this qualification, in his autobiography Hapgood designated it "the very best thing I have written." He evaluated the book this way because it had accurately pictured his sentiments at the time he wrote it. Not only that, but through the torrid intensity of love he had caught the universal. "It came from something not so much me," he marveled, "as something beyond me, in my unconscious. I wrote it at one stroke; and therefore, from the point of literary style, it is, I really think, as perfect in form as anything we Americans have written." Nothing displayed Hapgood's identification of the real, the accurate, and the intense with great literature better than *The Story of a Lover*. He had spoken "literature" to Neith during their courtship. His story not only transcribed his mind but was "a universal book, . . . all human beings who feel at all must feel as I feel." [41] If one were only truthful enough, if a powerful emotion could push one far enough, one might turn out great literature.

The Story of a Lover was aggressively sincere and its breathlessness reflected the outpourings of a troubled soul. The fiber of the book was introspection; incident was used as illustration to prove or suggest a conclusion. The prose was choppy, overemphatic, speckled with capitals, overwritten. Hapgood had a tendency to run to alliteration when he got excited, and he often got excited in this book. More serious than peculiarity of style was the book's weakness as anything but an autobiographical document. His misunderstanding of Neith was a serious flaw that he later recognized. His contentions about approximating the universal would simply not be credible to many. Hapgood, who had spoken so often of the best reaching all, at times isolated himself by his philosophical and temperamental idiosyncrasies.

Enemies also concerned the Hapgoods' marriage. This one-act play was marked by conflict between its two characters, He and She, but as in *The Story of a Lover* there is a reconciliation, although on unconventional grounds. She asked, "I've never bored you, have I, Deacon?" He replied, "You have harassed, plagued, maddened, tortured me! Bored me? No, never, you bewitching devil!" They embraced.[42] The play's tendency to see marriage as educative conflict extended that of *The Story of a Lover* and previewed that of *A Victorian in the Modern World*.

"Cristine" suggested Hapgood's quandry. A human document about Greenwich Village and Provincetown, it was Hapgood's first use of this genre to discuss his intellectual crowd. The effort failed. Cristine, surely Christine Ell, was simply not a sturdy enough vehicle.[43] Cristine lustily embodied the changing sexual mores, the rootlessness of the Village, but she was not perceptive enough to be a commentator; thus the best chapters were the early ones, before she confronted a complex milieu. Unable to keep himself in the background, he often left her to dash to some other concern, and his opinions of people dominated hers. Perhaps he never finished "Cristine" because his device had broken down.

Hapgood might have handled his predicament in one of three ways: he might have created a fictional character of greater breadth than Cristine; he might have used a series of vignettes of different people to scan Village life as he had done with the ghetto; he might have dumped Cristine and leaped into the ring himself. He lacked the originality for the first, and his fascination for the individual personality and his commitment to the human document made the second unlikely. It would be almost another twenty years before he would successfully exploit the third. "Cristine," however weak, was Hapgood's last chance to get outside himself. The Greenwich Villagers and the Provincetowners were the last significant groups of people Hapgood knew, that is, the last he could have done a book on. By 1920 or 1921 it mattered little to him whether he could have written a better human document. His mind was fixed on different problems—problems, doubts, and agonies that would engross him for the rest of his life. While Hutchins Hapgood was becoming more locked into his difficulties, William P. Hapgood was beginning to cut a figure as the leader of an industrial experiment. As Hutchins's star was setting, indeed, as Norman's was setting, the youngest brother's was rising.

CHAPTER 9

The Columbia Conserve Company

I

IN SOME RESPECTS William P. Hapgood was unlike his brothers. Only a couple of years younger than Hutchins, William had been a sickly child who grew up somewhat apart from his older brothers. Although he also went to Harvard and was interested in cultural matters, he did not immerse himself in literature and philosophy as did Norman and Hutchins. Unlike his brothers, he felt little urge to write epigrams. Norman was an editor in chief of the *Harvard Monthly* and Hutchins did some writing for it, but William served as business manager. Associated with the same organization, William played a different role.

William P. Hapgood loved sports, "the most interesting activity of my early life." Many of his youthful letters abounded with references to hunting, fishing, mountain climbing, and sailing. The once fragile William grew to be the largest and strongest of the brothers. He loved to pit his muscles against unyielding New England mountains and his seamanship against the choppy Atlantic. Always an avid outdoorsman, he would maintain a rural cabin for many years and often took his nieces and nephews camping and sailing. He was the only one of the Hapgoods to participate in intercollegiate athletics. Amply nosed, like Norman and Hutchins, blue-eyed and parting his brown hair just to the left of center, he had perhaps the most distinguished appearance of the three. He was the only one who looked dapper. Like his brothers, he possessed a distinct personality. William had little of Norman's self-examination, much less the gruelling introspection of Hutchins. Hutchins recognized William's "health, saneness, [and] unnervous intelligence," and Norman noted his youngest brother's "serenity, ardor, and youthful heart." [1] William's conflicts were usually close to the surface.

After receiving his undergraduate degree, William Hapgood did not undergo a crisis of social adjustment. He did not attend the Law School, nor did he need a world tour. He hoped to work in Boston, but failing to find anything suitable there, in November 1894 he moved to Chicago to join Franklin MacVeagh and Company, a wholesale grocery headed by an old friend of Charles Hapgood. William's experience contrasted with Norman's anguish at a Chicago law firm and his longing for the intellectual atmosphere of Cambridge. William's displeasure was not that his surroundings lacked concern for the latest in literature. "I do not like Chicago," he mentioned to an aunt, "principally because it is not on the ocean and also because I do not know many people whom I am interested in. Besides this the city is very dirty, noisy and hot." His choice of a business career distinguished him from his brothers. While Norman was reviewing plays and Hutchins was discovering the East Side and the Bowery, William was learning the grocery trade. William Hapgood became a department head, the chief of manufacturing at MacVeagh.[2] Assertive and self-confident, he sought greater responsibility.

II

Indianapolis could hardly compete in glamor with the New York of the other Hapgoods, but this midwestern town was the scene of William Hapgood's triumphs and failures for most of the next half-century. Eager to run his own business, William had persuaded his father to purchase the Mullen-Blackledge Canning Company, a small plant in Indianapolis, in 1903. Why they chose this particular enterprise is unknown, although the decision bore some relation to William's prior work for MacVeagh. William was the president, but his father was the largest stockholder in the Columbia Conserve Company, the new name of the concern. Experienced in business and with one success under his belt, Charles Hapgood was surely consulted by his son before important decisions were made. Columbia did so poorly that in 1910 it fled to the country and reincorporated with $125,-

000 of capital stock. "I was largely responsible for the loss of the first company," William Hapgood later confessed. The company's first board of directors was Charles Hapgood, his three sons, and Eleanor Page Hapgood, the large-eyed, firm-mouthed, small, sincere woman William had married in 1898. The outlook was not bright. Charles Hapgood, complaining of the strenuous efforts he had to make, lamented his youngest son's business ineptitude and warned another son that "I fear this is a constitutional weakness which will ever torment our well beloved son from acquiring these requisites to success and the question now troubling me is what to do about it." Although Columbia declared a 10 percent cash dividend in 1912, instability and distress continued to haunt it.[3]

III

The Columbia Conserve Company did well in 1916 and showed, according to William Hapgood, "our first real profit in the thirteen years of our business life." The next year he transformed the company by declaring that the workers were to share in the earnings and eventually become the owners. He also established a seven-member council and the committee that could set wages, subject to a board of directors' veto. This was fairly daring, for although profit sharing was not new, it was uncommon in 1917. The council of workers was even more unusual.[4] Unlike most cooperative experiments, Columbia was not a response to immediate economic grievances. It was not a reaction against either high or low prices, nor did it aim to abolish the middleman.

Certainly, there was much interest in cooperatives in the early twentieth century. Farmers, social gospelers, and progressives often were among the enthusiasts, but it is difficult to discover the sources of Hapgood's ideas. He was not one to sort carefully the origins of his thoughts. In explaining the beginnings of the Columbia experiment, he recounted his dislike for the favoritism shown to the upper classes, discussed his interest in uncovering ability and in proving himself, and also mentioned that "for a number of years I had debated with my friends and discussed with my brothers the social wisdom of resting the control of industry on ownership." The historian of Columbia has contended that Hapgood "was raised in the home of a businessman who held very liberal ideas toward labor and who would have accepted socialism. It is, therefore, probable that William P. Hapgood developed his plans of a worker's council from his own ideas based upon those of his father rather than from any other source." [5]

The legacy of Charles Hapgood to his sons was more in the nature of valuing hard work, a contempt for riches, and a democratic philosophy than a radical social outlook. Certainly William Hapgood's seriousness, his desire to overcome obstacles to prove his worth, should not be taken lightly. Growing up in an atmosphere in which the father feared softness as much as anything, William noted, "In my own case I knew that it was not mainly, or even chiefly, through ability that I held my place.... Perhaps, too, I was stimulated by the thought that later on my own ability might be tested by an environment less favorable to me." [6] Whatever his father imparted to him, it is unlikely that William would have initiated his changes in 1917 if Charles Hapgood were alive. Regardless of what the senior Hapgood would have thought of his son's move toward worker control, he would hardly have approved of the step at that time, after only one profitable year. It is very likely that Charles Hapgood would have checked or at least curbed his son.

William Hapgood's brothers played some part in the origin of his industrial experiment. Hutchins, noting William's interest in *The Autobiography of a Thief, The Spirit of Labor,* and *An Anarchist Woman* and that he had introduced him to his radical friends, speculated that "perhaps it was at this time that the seed was laid in my brother's mind, which promised and still promises to be of initiatory value." Norman, intellectually closer to William than Hutchins was, probably had more direct impact. Keenly interested in business ethics and in cooperatives, Norman was also an obliging middleman for the ideas of Brandeis, ideas that appealed to William. Norman, just before the purchase of *Harper's Weekly,* had hoped eventually to include the major executives "and perhaps even the general run of employees, in profit sharing." The performance of *Harper's Weekly* precluded such efforts. William's boldness went beyond that of his brothers. Although Mabel Dodge Luhan's recollection that Norman and Hutchins were aghast at William's conversion of the Columbia Conserve Company sounds more like a good story than an accurate one, she certainly touched a truth.[7] It would be hard to conceive either Norman or Hutchins acting with such fearlessness. Self-assurance was one of William's prominent characteristics.

The happenings of 1917 marked only a stage in the growth of industrial democracy at the Columbia Conserve Company. "With the formation of the council in January, 1918," it has been observed, "the history of Columbia Conserve is no longer a normal business history, but rather an account of a group of people striving for the success of their factory in terms of human relations as well as finances." In 1920 the council was setting salaries, advising on the appointment of foremen, and awarding vacations. In 1924 the committee was merged into it.[8]

The council, more than any other institution, embodied the company's commitment to workers' management. In 1922 Hapgood wrote with pride that "the outstanding result of our work during the last five and a half years has been the progress members of council have made in their grasp of the intricacies of business, of manufacturing, of sales problems and economic principles." The council was the crucial test not only of how well workers could manage a factory but also of the educational value of Columbia. The right to vote was at first restricted to elected members, later expanded to all interested salaried workers, and, finally, wage workers were permitted to attend meetings. "Between 1923 and 1925," it has been noted, ". . . the employees began to manage the company through the Council."[9]

Before the reorganization in 1917, about 95 percent of the workers had been on wages, but by the end of the year almost all were transferred to salary. Salaried workers, placed in various classifications, the lowest of which was supposed to be a living wage, did not receive overtime, but their pay was not deducted for days missed because of lack of work or because of sickness.

In 1925 Paul Douglas found an average pay increase of 40 percent among Columbia's salaried workers since 1917 and concluded that Columbia's rates were "very much above the competitive level." Because of Columbia's concern for a minimum standard of living, executives probably earned less than they might have elsewhere.[10]

Columbia hoped that virtually all its workers would be salaried, but the seasonal nature of the business prevented this. Throughout the 1920s Columbia was still heavily dependent on tomato products. Since the tomato season was relatively brief, Columbia was forced to take on many wage workers during the pack. It hired them by the week, guaranteed a certain number of hours of employment, and established minimum wages. Wage earners during the rest of the year were viewed as sort of apprentices, and the promising ones were placed on salary as soon as practicable.

In the late 1920s Columbia switched from compensation for efficiency, which the earlier scales basically represented, to payment "by needs." William Hapgood championed this new method and argued that "there is in my judgment no other really satisfactory conclusion which a group of free and democratic people can reach." As early as 1926 the council had established special pay for fathers. By 1930 the salary rates were twenty-two dollars a week for single workers, thirty-three dollars a week for married men, and nineteen dollars a week for married women. Columbia gave allowances of two dollars a week for each child under sixteen years old, up to a total salary of thirty-nine dollars a week.[11] Special requirements were determined individually.

Although Hapgood claimed that this system was easier to apply than bickering over efficiency ratings, it also involved a good deal of discussion and individual attention. It would be hard to imagine a large plant enmeshed in all the personal scrutiny that it required. Although the workers voted for it enthusiastically at first, their reactions became mixed, and eventually widespread discontent developed. Over Hapgood's objections, by 1935 Columbia gave extra money for responsibility, but still paid basically by needs. There was always some question whether this mode of compensation could retain the necessary experts, and some evidence indicated that Columbia was hurt by the loss of young men.[12]

IV

Regularity of employment for the salaried was a cornerstone of the Columbia plan. Hapgood, arguing that "full-time employment should be our most important objective, and the main justification for our existence," warned that "on the solution of that problem depends practically all the steps beyond. Without regularity of work it is idle to attempt to bring workers into intimate and effective relation with the problem of management." He quite likely got the idea of steadiness of employment from Norman Hapgood, who had early favored it, and Norman was undoubtedly exposed to this concept, as to so many others, by Brandeis, probably its chief American advocate.[13]

Russell E. Vance, Jr., has observed of the initiation of the program, "If there were other companies at this time that had guaranteed annual employment they were so small that they did not receive recognition in national reports." Columbia's achievement was all the more remarkable because year-round employment was practically unheard of in the canning industry, where concerns tended to be very small, often rural, and wages were low. Since investment in equipment was, compared with heavier industries, slight, savings from using machinery throughout the year were not great. With labor a relatively high percentage of cost, canners released most of their employees until the next season. The Women's Bureau found that only "2 percent . . . worked all 52 weeks in canning plants in 1937." Compared with the seasonal canneries, Columbia's record was extraordinary. Evaluated in terms of its own class, "Seasonal and Non-Seasonal Product Canneries," Columbia's performance was excellent. For this type "the average number of weeks over which canning was spread was 32, more than double the time of most plants that operated on seasonal products only."[14]

The Columbia Conserve Company had fairly progressive

working hours, but reducing them was never one of William Hapgood's principal aims. Hard work was good if it was stimulating. Paid vacations, old age, and sickness benefits were conspicuous. Most impressive, perhaps, was Columbia's health plan. At one time it provided complete health care for workers and their dependents, including daily visits to the plant by a physician; later, dependents were not covered. Hapgood contended that Columbia's medical policy had saved at least six lives including that of his son, Powers. By 1931 William Hapgood concluded, "The most important protective measures for workers in industry are those against unemployment, sickness and old age. Ultimately, these protections must be afforded by some form of state and federal insurance, although more private companies will eventually experiment with their own plans as we have done." Attempting to complement the welfare programs, Columbia offered courses in various subjects, but the classes were not popular and were disbanded.[15]

V

One of the outstanding characteristics of the Columbia experiment was that the salaried workers came to own the business. The generous 1917 plan had entitled the employees to a form of profit sharing, and by the mid-1920s strides had been taken toward worker management of the company, but controlling ownership eluded the employees until a new stock-purchase agreement was instituted. Under the 1917 accord profits were paid in stock, but employees were able to sell their holdings to the company for cash, and in any case the stock was owned individually. Douglas concluded in 1925 that "by the end of 1924, it was . . . apparent to all that it would probably be impossible for the workers to acquire economic control of the company within at least a generation by the voluntary reinvestment of the workers' share of the profits." William Hapgood, on behalf of the major stockholders, submitted a new proposal to the council in December 1925. After the payment of 10 percent dividends on stock and salaries, one-tenth of the remaining profit was to be placed in a pension fund, with most of the rest of the earnings used to buy stock at $150 per share with the goal of worker ownership. When the first profits under the new system were declared in the next year, the workers decided that their holdings should be owned collectively and voted by trustees elected by the council. This important provision sped the drive toward worker ownership, prevented control of the workers' stock from resting with a few upper-level and veteran employees, and solidified the workers' voting strength. Columbia prospered during the late 1920s, and by 1930 the workers had title to 51 percent of the common stock. This event received wide national publicity and in some respects marked the apogee of the Columbia venture. In 1931 Hapgood predicted that the workers would own all the common stock by July 1933, but by then they had only 63 percent. The depression had ripped apart the timetable.[16]

VI

The unfolding of the Columbia experiment was based on a degree of economic vitality. If the business failed, the social plans would perish; the size of the profits to some extent determined how quickly the social program would go. Columbia began to do well in 1916, and the rest of that decade was generally profitable. Although sales dropped substantially from 1918, 1919 was a very good year because of the lower cost of material and a particularly wide margin of profit on Columbia's two most important products, tomato soup and catsup. Columbia did particularly well in these years with goods packed under private labels; that is, Columbia would manufacture for various jobbers under their labels. Hapgood had been especially effective in developing this trade. Nineteen twenty was a bad year, "the most serious . . . the canning industry has yet encountered," according to the secretary of the National Canners Association. In the early 1920s the Columbia Conserve Company experienced not only the trials of other canners but also a decline in the sale of soups in the private label market.[17]

Columbia fared better in 1925 but because of weakness in vending chili and catsup was beset by another sales decline in 1926. Although Columbia enjoyed initial success with jobbers in 1928 and 1929, retailers simply were not able to move its merchandise quickly enough. Campbell's continued to have a stranglehold on much of the condensed soup market. Despite these annoyances Columbia managed to turn a profit, its attempts to develop greater worker participation were evidently successful, and the outlook was very optimistic in 1929. Based upon the showing with private labels, strength among wholesalers, and the quality of Columbia's products, Hapgood had predicted spectacular sales for 1930. In 1930 sales did not leap forward as he had prophesied, but at least they did not take a dramatic plunge. In fact, 1930 was gratifying. The next year the depression hit Columbia hard and the hopefulness of 1929 and 1930 withered. Faulty decisions at Columbia aggravated a rough general economic situation. Although Columbia contracted for less acreage in the 1930 season, it was still oversupplied with tomatoes. It did not lower prices sufficiently, and its inventory glut was swelled still further by the next year's pack. In 1932, because of an unmanageable stock on hand, so little tomato acreage was purchased that a profit was unthinkable.

Since Columbia was thoroughly committed to regularity of employment, it could not cut expenses by releasing its salaried workers. On the other hand, the council noted that it was unable to place qualified wage workers in the salaried force because of the business slump. In the spring of 1931 the company decided to "release all wage workers on May 28th with the exception in sales, demonstration, and publicity work." Finally, by the end of May, Hapgood asked the council for a temporary 50 percent cut in salary. Initial reaction was less than enthusiastic, but after several months the workers agreed to some decreases. They would spend a large part of the next years on reduced salaries, initially to minimize losses, but in 1932 to finance the pack. From July 1930 to July 1938 the average salary at Columbia was 68.4 percent of the 1930 rate, and although reductions at Columbia were severe, Hapgood contended that its workers continued to be better off than those in other canneries.[18]

The Columbia Conserve Company

Most of these actions were defensive. Columbia required something positive, something to expand sales. Like most small businesses, it had little control over the prices of the raw materials it purchased or of the products it sold and found itself faced with stiff price competition in 1931 and 1932. Cheap tomato soup flooded the market, and Columbia was hard pressed to meet the challenge. The private label business, which had often accounted for a sizable chunk of Columbia's gains, did poorly. Although Hapgood would have preferred to continue to stress private labels, the company's weakness and the need for some sort of breakthrough virtually ordered Columbia into the factory label field. Hapgood's efforts to quicken business became a source of contention.

VII

Economic adversity formed the background to the fighting that nearly destroyed the Columbia Conserve Company and did change William Hapgood's outlook. He had been miffed at the council's reluctance to reduce wages, but by late summer of 1931 he whistled, "We as a group have now achieved the psychology which worker-owners must achieve, namely a combination of employer and employee point of view, which will cause them to deal effectively and realistically with any economic situation which may develop and at the same time stress social values when the economic situation permits." [19]

Within a few months he again chastised the employees for not tightening their belts enough. Hapgood, growing more defensive, lamented his critics' inexperience, a theme he would sound frequently during the next few years. Dissension began in earnest in 1932. Leo Tearney, a salesman, accused Hapgood of "autocracy" in the management of Columbia. Arlie Myers, an influential figure on the council and a long-time employee, denied several of Tearney's assertions but had to admit that Hapgood could be "autocratic" at times.[20]

A. A. Heist, a minister who had joined Columbia because of interest in its social program, quarreled with both Norman and

William Hapgood. Norman had not only an intellectual interest in Columbia but had been one of its largest stockholders for some time and had increased his holdings by buying up most of Hutchins's stock when his younger brother badly needed the cash. In January 1932 Norman became a salaried worker at $2,000 a year to do publicity and advertising. He requested a 20 percent cut, a reduction that other employees had been operating under. Norman, who had been using Columbia as a depository for funds, for which he was paid interest, now needed the money and began to withdraw it at the rate of $1,000 a month. This created some resentment among workers, whose paychecks had been diminished by the depression. In the summer of 1932 Heist charged that "wages should have prior claim to either dividends or capital. If Norman made a mistake by leaving his earnings here why should the wives and families of the workers suffer." [21]

Norman Hapgood resented these allegations. In his defense it was pointed out that his willingness to sell some of his stock had saved Columbia about $20,000. Hapgood did not relish the council's peeking at his financial affairs and reminded them that he had been put on the payroll only to help his brother. He also noted that Heist had confused funds on deposit with stock, and he denied that the private stockholders were responsible for the low wages. Then, indulging in an escalatory rhetoric characteristic of many of his comments over the next year, he "wished the responsibility for the whole financial structure could be shifted from the only shoulders that can carry it and see what would happen." Norman had slight faith that Columbia could survive without William Hapgood. Indeed, a year before, Norman had tried to remove his investment. He informed Brandeis, "I wished . . . to get my money out and invest in conservatively for the family, but now I am willing to freeze part of it in order to save something if there is a collapse." A year or so before he tried to get out of Columbia, Norman had entitled a chapter on the Columbia Conserve Company in his autobiography, "Happiness for All." Although Hapgood had felt his actions justified, he asked not to be paid until business improved, and

The Columbia Conserve Company

he left withdrawals from his account to the treasurer's discretion.[22]

Columbia's reputation as an experiment in industrial democracy had attracted a good many labor figures and persons of leftish political beliefs. One of the most significant was William Hapgood's son, Powers. Very idealistic, he had ardently supported American entry into the First World War. At seventeen he complained, "My age is a terrible one to be in at the present time. Too darn young to be in France acquiring manhood and a *real* education, not one of a bookworm." Like his father and his uncles Norman and Hutchins, Powers attended Harvard. At Harvard he was influenced by some radical friends and the writings of Carleton and Cornelia Parker. After college he became a coal miner, did some union organizing, and became a lieutenant to John Brophy. A slender, gentle-faced man with resolute eyes, Brophy was devoted to trade unionism and Catholicism. In 1926 Brophy and Hapgood had led the left-wing challenge to John L. Lewis's control of the United Mine Workers. Defeated, both Brophy and Hapgood were at Columbia by 1929. Although they would later become prominent in the CIO, in the late 1920s the opposition of Lewis and the operators had made it difficult for them to find work. In 1928 Hapgood had married Mary Donovan, a socialist whom he had met while both were trying to prevent the execution of Sacco and Vanzetti.[23]

The major battle was fought over the publicity campaign, which attempted to promote the sale of Columbia label goods by exploiting the social experiment, and the conduct of the sales department. William Hapgood hoped that news of the Columbia venture would arouse the idealism of college students and various religious groups. Publicity in a less formal sense had long been a part of Columbia's activities, but it had never been tied so closely to sales. Nowhere was the combination of social concern and business pitch so forthright as on the Columbia tomato soup label:

> No wonder we make such fine soups, catsup, tomato juice, and other products. We, the workers, own the business. We are proud that we

have succeeded, and succeeded because we have done better work because we cared. Not one of us has been discharged on account of hard times. For there is no unemployment. There are 52 pay envelopes a year, old age pensions, expert care in sickness and in health, three weeks vacation with full pay. Why should we not make good products?

If you think this plan should spread, and if you find this product better because it is made by cooks who care, please tell your friends about it.[24]

The label then mentioned that a free pamphlet was available.

Precisely when conditions were worst and when some of the more radical employees were disgruntled, the publicity drive was flaunting Columbia's virtues. The confrontation took place in the council meetings of December 29, 1932, and January 4, 1933. Ethyln Christensen, speaking for the sales department, disparaged the effectiveness of publicity and criticized its expense. "More important," she concluded, "the foundation on which the publicity was based has been gradually destroyed. Many of the elements which made the story valuable do not now exist." Tearney ridiculed Hapgood's business acumen: "Mr. Hapgood could have gotten valuable information about our prices had his mind not have been on tomato vegetable, name on the can, panels on the label[,] church organizations, and such items. We remember when women's clubs in California were to put us on the map. Now it is the schools and colleges in New England who are to put us over." [25]

During the meeting of January 4 Dan Donovan, a former supporter of publicity, challenged Hapgood's program. Brophy, resorting to unabashed demagoguery, moaned that the publicity campaign had been the chief explanation for the pay cuts. In some respects the comments of Arlie Myers, no radical, were more suggestive. Myers caught the feelings of many in a phrase in a manner that Hutchins Hapgood might have appreciated. Myers asked, "Is our effort to sell democracy or to sell soup?" Frank Eustis drew the battle line by introducing a resolution that would stop spending on publicity for six months. William Hapgood questioned the competence of his critics and vigorously objected that he had already made commitments for the next several months and threatened that if the council did not let him

fulfill them, he would resign from the sales department. Eustis's motion passed thirty-six to twenty-seven, with sixteen not voting.[26]

In the next session of council, on January 6, Norman Hapgood alleged that a clique had been plotting against his brother. The accused defended themselves by saying that they stood for democracy, but Norman, unconvinced, argued that "there are two groups here, the 'old guard' or the builders, and the hot-air artists, whose platform is to fight, organize and speak." The council unanimously refused to accept William's resignation. Norman, trying to break the deadlock, moved that the council vote to support either his brother or the Brophy-Tearney faction, and the one who lost would leave the company. Norman was attempting to isolate the opposition, but the council would not bite. Several schemes for compromise proved unsuccessful.[27]

On January 30 William, Norman, and Powers Hapgood offered a three-point program. Powers, recovering from an accidental gunshot wound, served, at least for a while, as a mediator, one who had ties to both the radicals and William Hapgood. Powers's emergence as a conciliator testified to the breakdown of his father's authority. The Hapgoods' proposal asked that Eustis's plans for reorganization be dropped, that a sixty-day cooling-off period begin, and that William Hapgood be warned of any significant attack on him. William threatened that if Brophy, Donovan, and Tearney failed to accept this arrangement, he would request the board of directors to fire them. The radicals refused and the board, four votes to one, released them that afternoon.

Until a few days before, it had been supposed that only the council could discharge. This surprise did not enhance William Hapgood's chances of disproving that he was a despot, and, in any event, was no compliment to his leadership. Brophy and Donovan were furious. More important, a council resolution disapproving of the releases passed, forty-four to twenty, with seventeen not voting. The board, prodded by Hapgood, had, in effect, gone against the wishes of the majority of the stockholders. In the meeting of February 3, William Hapgood, apparently buckling to the council, consented to an investigation by an outside committee. Brophy and Donovan were reinstated. A few weeks later the council agreed that it would accept the findings of a committee made up of Paul Douglas, Sherwood Eddy, Jerome Davis, and James Myers, all prominent and respected in the liberal community.

On March 17 the council accepted Powers Hapgood's resignation. William Hapgood felt relieved. About this time William signed an agreement with the Continental Can Company, a principal creditor, guaranteeing the release of employees who threatened Columbia's equilibrium. In return, Continental Can financed the 1933 pack. With tightened discipline in effect, Norman Hapgood predicted of Brophy, Donovan, and Christensen that "it seems unlikely that they will remain long." In a few days Christensen and two others quit. On May 8 William declared that either he or Brophy and Donovan must depart; he would resign if they were not let go. The council, reluctant to forfeit Hapgood, voted heavily in favor of releasing Donovan and Brophy. The Committee of Four protested that the firings violated Columbia's agreement with it and that Brophy and Donovan were entitled to a review. The council then proceeded to cancel the agreement with the Committee. By June, Norman reported, "With Powers, Donovan, & Brophy out, quiet is restored, and Billy serene. Also there is a little improvement in business." [28]

VIII

Although the formal fighting had ended, it had badly bruised Columbia and scarred the company's reputation. The bright optimism of earlier days was tarnished, and, like *Collier's Weekly* after the dispute of 1912, Columbia would never again be the same. William's not always commendable behavior during the controversy appeared even worse in the council minutes, which excluded much of the story. He sometimes reacted quite emotionally, as when he stomped out of the council session. Norman's attempt to force an exclusionary ruling from the council on Hapgood versus Brophy and Donovan could hardly reassure

Powers, Eleanor, and William P. Hapgood c. 1910.
(Courtesy of Barta Monro.)

those who feared a Hapgood power play. Deciding whether to keep a man many considered indispensable or others who happened to oppose his views was not the kind of choice that would encourage the workers to question policies in the future and would certainly not stimulate democratic participation. The first dismissal of Brophy and Donovan was a genuine blunder. William Hapgood should have explained his reasons to the council thoroughly, but he did not and was forced to backtrack. He later considered the establishment of the Committee of Four "the greatest mistake of our entire experiment," but if he had not alienated the council, he would hardly have sought outside intervention. It would have been better had the council inquired into specific allegations against Brophy and Donovan. The minutes recorded that Donovan "asked if there were any charges made against them by Wm. P. Hapgood. The chairman [of the council] answered that there were not." [29] The mishandling of the Brophy-Donovan affair contributed to the estrangement of the Committee of Four, which hurt Columbia in the religious and liberal press.

William Hapgood reevaluated his reliance on popular rule within the factory. In short, he thought that in the controversy of 1932 and 1933 he should have taken a harder line against the dissidents sooner. In 1934 a revised and expanded version of his original pamphlet was no longer called *An Experiment in Industrial Democracy* but *The Columbia Conserve Company: An Experiment in Workers' Management and Ownership*. He argued that the original title had raised too many expectations and thus caused too many disappointments. Influenced by the New Deal, he surmised that power had been too diffuse at Columbia, that more executive discretion would have been beneficial, and that Columbia should have had a strong board of directors all along.[30]

Hapgood developed a greater appreciation of leadership. More conservative about the role of the worker in business decisions, more like his brother Norman and more like Brandeis, he thought that the workers should have gained control more gradually. William Hapgood continued to maintain that technicians must help the laborer, but he now accented the spheres in which expertise should dominate. In an unpublished addition to *The Columbia Conserve Company: An Experiment in Workers' Management and Ownership* he explained his position in 1941:

> In the beginning of our experiment I took the average liberal point of view toward democracy, that increasing industrial freedom and greater economic security would of themselves make a more efficient, happier, and more generous group and one more insistent upon equality. It has been the liberal assumption that democracy grows by what it feeds upon, that the potential of collectivism is democratic. I have increasing doubts that this is so. I am coming to believe that a fascist tendency is more inherent in collectivism than a democratic one, and that collectivism may degenerate into a counter-revolutionary movement.[31]

IX

The year ending on June 30, 1933, had been one of Columbia's most disastrous ones. The company's small profits during the next four years were not large enough to erase the heavy obligations of the earlier years. Furthermore, Columbia suffered financial setbacks during the late 1930s. Russell E. Vance, Jr., has written, "With the severe impairment in capital from unpaid stock dividends and debts, together with continued losses in sales, few people could foresee any future for the Columbia Conserve Company." [32] The Columbia experiment would last only a few more years.

In the 1930s Columbia dabbled in trade unionism. Hapgood long had recognized its educational value, but many at Columbia felt that since the business was worker-owned, it was in an exceptional position and might find union membership constricting. Indeed, William Green of the American Federation of Labor had agreed with the workers' conclusion. Hapgood, whose chief hope was cooperation, also feared that a union affiliation might involve the company in unionization activities. After the 1932–33 battle with his critics, who often came from union backgrounds, he became even warier of membership. By the late 1930s, however, Hapgood again encouraged Columbia's workers to join a union, but the workers, fearing a recurrence of earlier troubles and wondering whether a union would mesh with Columbia's goals, were only reluctantly persuaded. In early 1939 all Columbia workers affiliated with the CIO, but interest was so slight that a little over a year later the union disbanded.

X

What can be said of the Columbia experiment? During its halcyon days it received much praise. In 1925 Paul Douglas concluded that Columbia "has been most heartening to all who wish for a better social order." W. Jett Lauck, in a curious book, declared that "the plan and performance of this company affords probably the most complete and perfect illustration of direct industrial democracy which exists today." The widow of Edward Bellamy, author of *Looking Backward,* commended Columbia. Even as late as 1935, a book on industrial relations called William P. Hapgood "perhaps the leading proponent in this country of sharing management with workers." [33] Obviously, Columbia was significant and accomplished something.

William P. Hapgood occasionally moved where few had tread. In some respects he was more audacious than his brothers, who often gave the impression of being tucked into reference groups. His commitments to worker ownership, regularity of employment, and social welfare put him in the vanguard of liberal businessmen. Indeed, Hapgood's boldness had a mixed impact on Columbia. Without his will and drive, the experiment would not have been attempted, yet his impatience sometimes subjected Columbia to risks a more cautious individual might have avoided.

Columbia's ability to serve as an example for other enterprises depended upon its survival. Although Columbia was not a stunning financial success, it did not fare badly. William P. Hapgood noted that from 1917 to 1939 Columbia made a total net profit of $568,564.53. The lion's share of this was, however, earned in a few years. Perhaps Columbia's fundamental economic failure was its inability to achieve stability. Profits were unpredictable and bore only slight relation to volume of sales. As was emphasized many times at Columbia, much of this was because Columbia, like most small businesses, had little control over the prices of either its raw materials or its finished products. Columbia had begun early to search for nontomato items to enable it to produce year-round and to get away from overdependence on the tomato.[34] The company diversified somewhat, especially by the late 1930s, but the large variety of its products signaled incomplete solution. It was unable to develop sufficiently a few really significant items.

Sales, perennially weak, was Columbia's most maligned department. Columbia had great difficulty developing the necessary personnel, and sometimes paid extra for efficiency to get vital help. The persistence of the sales problem was more likely a reflection of Columbia's situation than of individual culpability. Certainly, if over a period of years the salesmen were as inadequate as Hapgood contended, it was a mark against his executive ability.

Hapgood admittedly often suffered from overconfidence. His optimism was conspicuous in the first edition of *An Experiment in Industrial Democracy*. He wrote, "I might say, in all modesty, that at the close of our fiscal year, June 30, 1929, we had become more competent than 95 per cent of American industrial enterprises." He explained, "We have had no unusual advantages over our competitors except the opportunity to govern ourselves. To that fact alone I think our increasing success may be attributed." [35] The speed with which earnings were used to purchase stock for the employees under the 1925 agreement might have hurt Columbia. If more of the money had been diverted to the reserve fund and to sounder financing of the social programs, some of the edge might have been taken off the depression and less harsh measures might have been needed. Hapgood was inclined to see hard proof of the value of Columbia in hard cash. His eagerness to reinstitute higher wage rates during the depression was related to his anxiousness to keep Columbia a conspicuous example of success. One suspects that one reason why he hired so many radicals was that he believed he could make them witnesses to Columbia's excellence.

There are also reasons for skepticism about Hapgood's hopes that cooperation would catch on. It would be hard to imagine the officers of a large corporation doing what Hapgood did, or their stockholders supporting them if they did. Also, a large corporation would be likely to get involved in intricate questions of capital investment and technical decisions. Hapgood's plan was perhaps feasible only with a small concern controlled by an individual or a small group. William Hapgood failed to appreciate the difficulties of creating an effective coalition for cooperation. In this there was a parallel to Norman Hapgood's inability to understand the obstacles against developing politically viable antitrust policies.[36]

Breadth was one test of the success of Columbia's social programs. Douglas remarked in 1925 that "probably the majority [of the Columbia workers] are hostile to negroes and foreigners." In 1929, when the council debated hiring Negroes, the minutes recorded that "it was note-worthy that a greater number of people took part in the discussion than is usually the case with most of our problems." The vote was 74 against, 15 for, and 1 undecided. Few if any immigrants were associated with Columbia, and the wage rates discriminated against women. Health care and pay-by-needs had checkered careers, and Hapgood was often more deeply committed to these programs than were the employees. Regularity of employment was one of Columbia's chief accomplishments, but even this needed qualification. Norman Hapgood conceded to Brandeis in 1932, "The severity of measures taken to meet the financial situation has had the advantage also of squeezing out some of the force. Sixteen men and ten women have resigned in 12 months. Of course there would have been some resignations anyway, but mainly these 26 fall into two classes,—those who do not like hardship and those who disapprove of the majority policy led by W. P. H. but certainly influenced by you." [37]

Turned into a cooperative, not founded as one, Columbia had the advantage of being a going concern but the disadvantage of the workers' questionable loyalty to its new goals. When unions and government offered more in the 1930s and 1940s, the commitment of many workers to Columbia decreased.

Columbia claimed that self-government would develop the workers. The proceedings of the council supported the conclusion that employee involvement performed valuable educational functions. On the other hand, as might be expected, a core of workers largely dominated the council. Efforts were made to be less dependent on William Hapgood's guidance; it was necessary to take some of the strain off him. More important was the issue of whether Columbia could be a triumph in workers' management if it relied so much on an individual and if it could not produce its own leaders. Columbia was never able to replace William P. Hapgood.

Columbia intended to be an example or at least an inspiration. Through much of its career it received many applications for work from those, including foreigners, who were concerned with industrial democracy. By 1927 the Columbia Conserve Company had "attracted a great deal of attention, both in this country and abroad." Columbia did not win this fame passively. Interpreting its role as not merely helping itself but helping others, Columbia aided Pennsylvania miners, was greatly interested in other cooperative enterprises, and joined the CIO in the late 1930s in order to give moral support to the labor movement. Hapgood wanted to promote a foundation for the advancement of cooperatives.[38]

XI

The Columbia venture adversely affected the financial standing of the three Hapgood brothers. By parental gift and by inheritance all were involved in the company. The Hapgoods certainly could have made more profitable investments or could have exploited Columbia more to their own advantage, but all three supported the Columbia plan, though at times grudgingly. Each Hapgood brother at one time or another held a position with the company. Hutchins, who did not work for Columbia after it began its social program, though he was a director for a while, had the fewest ties. Economic necessity had forced him to sell most of his stock to Norman, who worked for the company during part of the 1930s and was a major stockholder and creditor. William's commitment was obvious.

Columbia appealed to the idealism of the Hapgood brothers and gave a certain unity to their economic thought. The concept of an experiment attracted all three, who rejected socialism but also disliked existing American capitalism. Norman was more conservative and elitist in his support of Columbia than were his brothers. Hutchins, despite his associations with radical labor and skepticism about his younger brother's abilities, was an enthusiast. Norman and Hutchins supported William's stand against the radicals in 1933.[39]

The Hapgoods had been upset by the more traditional type of trade union activity. Norman, who wanted labor to be more creative, more responsive, more imaginative, craved a Brandeis in overalls. Hutchins, a little more radical than Norman in his attitude toward the labor movement, was probably most attracted by Columbia's self-help aspects, the firm initiative it gave labor. All three brothers were preoccupied with individual development and education, and for a time the Columbia method seemed effective in these respects. The Columbia Conserve Company, as much as anything else, struck the Hapgoods as the right sort of thing to do, a good adventure to participate in.

CHAPTER 10

Final Years

I

NORMAN HAPGOOD CONTINUED in journalism long after Hutchins had turned to other interests. During the 1920 campaign Norman stumped for Cox and was a contributing editor to the *Independent*. Hapgood had been considered for an important position with the *New York Evening Post,* but the *Post* delayed offering him employment because of his "wide reputation for radicalism." In 1921 he began writing regularly in the Hearst press. This must have surprised many, for Hearst hardly had had a more persistent critic than Hapgood's *Collier's Weekly*. Hapgood had called Hearst, to pick only a few highlights, "entirely without conscience," "an utter demagogue," a "liar," "a cheap and vulgar hypocrite—who would inflict any injury upon his country if it blew him any nearer to the centre of attention." Frederick Palmer and Arthur H. Gleason had done pieces for *Collier's* that certainly did not please Hearst. In 1911 *Collier's* was publishing a series, "The American Newspaper," by Will Irwin. Before Irwin reached Hearst, Hearst's attorney threatened Collier and Irwin with a libel suit if they printed anything scandalous; Hearst knew what to expect. At *Harper's Weekly* Hapgood had paid less attention to him, but contended, "If you wanted a person absolutely lacking in morality of any kind, you would go a long way before you would find one equal to Hearst." [1]

Despite this hostility Hearst, who was known to hire former critics if he thought it advantageous, had made offers to Hapgood in 1912 and 1916. By 1923 Oswald Garrison Villard was lamenting "the long list of men of distinction who have accepted the shilling of this king of sensational journalism." If Hearst's advance was understandable, why did Hapgood accept? Hapgood had a reputation as an advocate of journalistic ethics, and in his autobiography he was defensive about his work for Hearst. He explained that he had rejected earlier proposals "mainly on the ground that they were editorial in nature, that the Hearst newspapers were run as a unit, and that therefore I should find myself at times seeming to support policies in which I did not believe, more especially in regard to foreign affairs." [2]

True, Hapgood's column in the *New York American* was roped off from the rest of the paper, and his experience at *Leslie's Weekly* had been a precedent. On the other hand, his presence on Hearst's pages indirectly sanctioned them, and at times, for example, when Hapgood quite favorably covered the Washington Naval Conference while Hearst was cannonading it, the incongruities were glaring. Hearst's emphasis on the leering, the criminal, and the superficial sometimes made Hapgood seem out of place.

In his autobiography Hapgood failed to mention that in 1918 he had turned down an offer virtually identical to the one he accepted in 1921. One element present in 1918 but absent in 1921 was his feeling that working for Hearst might embarrass the Wilson administration. Hearst's offer was handsome—$20,000 in 1918 and presumably as much or more in 1921.[3] Furthermore, opportunities in liberal journalism were restricted; there was not a bull market for muckrakers in the 1920s. Hapgood's reputation had probably declined somewhat. He had left *Collier's* about eight years before, and his most significant later work had been the fiasco at *Harper's Weekly*.

In 1922 Hapgood became the editor of *Hearst's International*, a monthly. Largely responsible for its political content, he remained until 1925, when *Hearst's International*, because it was competing too directly with Hearst's *Cosmopolitan*, was absorbed by the latter. At the beginning of his editorship he explained to William Allen White, "We want to take up the effort that lapsed when McClures [sic], Collier's and Everybody's dropped it—the stirring of the public mind on fundamentals." *Hearst's International*, popular, a little gaudy, prosperous, was reminiscent of *Collier's*. Hapgood could tell a potential contributor, as he could not at *Harper's*, "We would rather have you name the price yourself." [4] Hapgood's short editorials, in the *Collier's* and

Harper's manner, were, if anything, simpler and briefer than his earlier efforts.

Such valuable soldiers in the *Collier's* days as Arthur H. Gleason, C. P. Connolly, Will Irwin, William Hard, and Louis R. Glavis saw action for *Hearst's International,* and Hapgood launched several muckraking crusades, against the Ku Klux Klan's penetration of American politics and Henry Ford's anti-Semitism. It is difficult to ascertain how much Hearst interfered in the management of the monthly. Conceding that Hearst suppressed some material Glavis had uncovered about Secretary of the Interior Albert Fall, Hapgood still claimed control over the magazine's editorial policy. Since Hapgood considered the new conservation scandal "so much worse than the Ballinger trouble," his equanimity was surprising. Paul de Kruif, a frequent contributor to *Hearst's International* during Hapgood's editorship, has also recalled that a story of his critical of Douglas Fairbanks was denied publication because that actor was a friend of Hearst.[5] On the whole, it seems likely that Hapgood called most of the shots on the political side of the *International.* Although in some respects Hapgood's work was more satisfying than at *Harper's Weekly*—he was fighting again and he was not bound to a hero—his efforts did not have the significance or impact of those of the *Collier's* years. They simply failed to stir the America of the 1920s.

II

Through most of the rest of his life Hapgood maintained an active interest in public affairs. In foreign policy he continued to be heavily influenced by the concerns of the Wilson years. Hapgood supported the League, but in a low key, ridiculed American policy toward Russia and France's belligerent conduct toward Germany, and early warned of the aggressive intentions of Nazi Germany.

On the domestic front he continued to fight for liberalism. In the early 1920s he toyed with the idea of a third party patterned after the British Labour party. Although he had doubts about

Robert La Follette, particularly in foreign policy, in 1924 he had *Hearst's International* endorse the Wisconsin politician for the presidency. In 1930 Hapgood perceptively evaluated the failure of the Progressives in 1924: "It was not that we should have had perhaps a couple of million more votes if the voting had come three months earlier,—that was due to rising prices for grain; what mattered was that we came out of the fight with nothing left in the public mind, except that there had been some sort of a protest against the conservatism of the two big parties." [6]

In 1928 Hapgood was an Al Smith enthusiast and had coauthored a campaign biography with Henry Moskowitz the year before. Two things in particular attracted Hapgood to Smith. First was Smith's Lincolnesque quality. Smith came from the people, had a gift for language, and knew how to educate the public. Secondly, Smith was a master of the governmental process and appealed to Hapgood's passion for knowledgeability and expertise. Although Hapgood preferred Smith or Newton Baker in 1932, he supported Franklin D. Roosevelt after he got the Democratic nomination. Hapgood generally favored the New Deal and campaigned for Roosevelt in 1936, but his enthusiasm was tempered by his Brandeisian outlook. Indeed, Hapgood often served as a go-between for Brandeis and President Roosevelt. Hapgood disliked the National Industrial Recovery Act but applauded the Tennessee Valley Authority and the Public Utility Holding Company Act.[7]

Hapgood kept busy after *Hearst's International* shut down. Although he rejected an opportunity to edit Hearst's *Washington Herald*, he worked for the Hearst papers in 1925 and 1926, then for United Features, and later composed a weekly newsletter. His powerful, almost overwhelming, sense of service did not atrophy during his later years. A dozen times in his writing he must have referred to Jefferson's self-composed epitaph, mentioning his association with the Virginia Statute for Religious Freedom, the Declaration of Independence, and the University of Virginia. Jefferson's attitude struck Hapgood as ideal, a superb outlook toward life. In late 1927 he noted that "I have managed to get too much on myself for this winter, with two books to write, an unconsciounable [*sic*] number of speeches, and a good many magazine articles." Hapgood, a liberal publicist, did a good deal of speaking, traveled abroad, and did studies of Shakespeare and Shelley, the latter of which was never published. He also worked on a book about the Sacco and Vanzetti case, but never finished it. His autobiography, *The Changing Years,* appeared in 1930. During much of the 1920s Hapgood lived on O Street in Washington, D.C., but he also spent a good deal of time in the Hapgoods' ancestral home, Petersham, Massachusetts. He immersed himself in local affairs, and "his long, lean figure, sloping across the Common on his daily walk to the Post Office, his little boy at his heels, had become a landmark of Petersham." Hapgood loved to play chess and enjoyed a good mystery story. He took a great deal of interest in the intellectual development of his children. A daughter remembered that the conversation at the dinner table was varied and stimulating. He gave pennies to his children for memorizing lines of poetry. Hapgood also dealt with the lighter aspects of parenthood, such as deciding to allow his children, against the objections of his mother-in-law, to wear blue jeans.[8]

Hapgood became active in the Unitarian Church. His membership resulted from a desire to identify with a useful organization, rather than conversion. An outgrowth of his concern for Petersham and the church was his becoming in August 1936 editor of the *Christian Register,* a Unitarian weekly published in Boston. Hapgood wrote editorials and solicited unpaid contributions from such people as William Hapgood, Henry Moskowitz, Charles R. Crane, and Lillian Gish. He was interested in establishing the grounds on which religion could adapt to science and hoped to expand the *Register*'s appeal to the laity. His work for the *Christian Register* differed from his earlier editorships in that it was not in the national spotlight and attempted to stake out areas of agreement rather than to be abrasive. Within a year after joining the *Christian Register,* Hapgood died unexpectedly on April 29, 1937, the same day as his friend William Gillette, after a prostate operation. He left a widow, a daughter, Ruth, by his first wife, Emilie, and three children, Elizabeth, Norman, and Ten Eyck (later David), by his second wife, Elizabeth.[9]

III

The last twenty-five years of Hutchins Hapgood's life were curious. Between the publication of *The Story of a Lover* in 1919 and his autobiography in 1939, he did almost nothing that attracted attention except, perhaps, his exposure of Dreiser's anti-Semitism in 1935. In 1932 a friend during the *Globe* days wondered what had become of him.[10] Shaken by emotional disorder, Hapgood wrote little but produced perhaps his ablest book, *A Victorian in the Modern World.*

During the 1920s he was especially troubled. Hoping to expand into some new forms of writing, he explained to Alfred Stieglitz, "I have felt for Some time past the need of another creative step (I don't mean by creative any definite work, though it might be that), another shaping life impulse—but it doesn't come. Some impediment, perhaps." Hapgood summarized his problem years later: "I . . . felt I would never write again unless it was on some religious or mystically philosophic subject. Writing to write seemed meaningless. Even the best books seemed to me irrelevant. I could see they were well done, beautiful, but what of it? What care I how fair she be, if she be not fair to me?"[11]

Hapgood, faced with tragedy and seeking to heal his emotional wounds, desired the ultimate. His viewing of final understanding as calmative resembled his seeing friendship and intellectual concerns as emotional stabilizers. When Mabel Dodge appeared to be enduring the loss of her lover with a splash of stoicism, he cheered, "I believe your readiness for the Cosmic Sense accounts for a fine way in which you are able to take what would ordinarily be a very severe blow." There was a sense of melancholy, of fatalism, in Hapgood's work. Mabel Dodge Luhan argued that "Hutch had always extolled the *inevitable* in any relationship; he admired the fated and helpless victims of the heart and the nervous system, for he was not, himself, one to challenge destiny and overcome the stars, and one perforce grows to find significant values in one's own limitations."[12]

Hapgood often spoke of his inability to get outside himself

Final Years

and believed that he was "a thing divided against itself." He warned Alfred Stieglitz of "the *essential* maladjustment between what is most ourselves and what is most fundamental in life." The only exit from this predicament, Hapgood continued, was to "renounce *ourselves*—not merely the material, worldly self—before that horrible problem of fundamental maladjustment can be solved!" Several years before, at Mabel Dodge's famous peyote party, he stammered, "I saw the death of the flesh occur in my body and I saw the Soul emerge from that death." [13]

Hutchins Hapgood could not extricate himself. Finding his old work tasteless and insisting that only the grandiose had flavor, he sought to unravel the ultimate, but he was least competent at this sort of task. Since his Harvard days he had been aware of his inability to explain the greatest truths—when he got near the profound he stutttered. To use one of his favorite phrases, he could not "express the inexpressible." [14] He fumbled for years trying to do a book on metaphysics but did not write much. He was cornered. Not only a gap between importance and understanding but his inclination toward self-punishment pushed him into an impasse and kept him there.

Hapgood found some compensation in dancing, driving, and sex. He had first danced in postwar Paris, and dancing became, he noted in 1940, "my greatest experience since 1919." He also confessed that driving about in his Ford was thrilling.[15] Both pastimes alleviated his malaise. Above all, the unthinking rhythm, the escapism of these two amusements delighted him.

In 1927 he was in Europe ostensibly trying to find journalistic subjects. Actually, if diaries accurately reflected his state, he was more interested in sex. "I do feel that I would benefit from a new sex experience," he maintained. He concluded, "I know it would be good for my continued activity & would do my relations with Neith no harm. But I simply cannot. My 'unconscious' refuses to allow me an 'erection!' " He could perform sexually only with his wife. He tried two French prostitutes "(at different times)," but to no avail. In Mirano he met a young harlot, Maggie, "not a bit commercial," who entranced him, but without the desired result. Finally, he triumphed after another encounter. He had "met a refined whore and she succeeded! at last! . . .

I ought to do it every now & then, for my health, but I fear disease and also the thought of prostitution is disagreeable." [16]

This episode was revealing. Although he had patronized four prostitutes and disliked prostitution, he was not remorseful until he had had his pleasure. His "involuntary fidelity" indicated that his immersion in the new sexual theories outdistanced his emotional commitment. A couple of weeks after these sexual meanderings, Neith asked Hutchins if he had been carrying on. He replied: "You gaily hope that I have had a 'few little adventures' to cheer me up! It is swell of you to love your old child so much, but although I have sometimes wanted a lady to cook for me and keep me warm, yet the desire was all there was to it. The desire was not vital enough to get into action!" [17] His experiences with dancing, driving, and whoring did not lead anywhere. They were releases rather than cures.

Digestive problems advertised his anxiety. Hapgood, claiming that the exercises described in Frederick A. Hornibrook's *The Culture of the Abdomen* "in the course of time . . . *cured* me of constipation and largely removed the toxins that had so thoroughly poisoned my physical being that I had been unwell for years," recommended the book to relatives and friends. A recent discussion of digestive disorders has concluded: "The role of exercise in the treatment of constipation has been exaggerated, but for some it may have an important psychic effect. It tends to divert the thoughts from working and business cares and household worries and thus confers the sense of relaxation which facilitates a bowel movement. Massage of the abdominal muscles is a waste of time." [18]

Hapgood's emotional stress became more intense in the 1920s and early 1930s. Informing his son that "for the first time in my life I am bored," he complained to his wife that it was because of "the feeling which I have never had before that I am 'doing' nothing." He wished that he had developed a work "habit." [19] Like his quest for menial work after the crisis in Indianapolis in 1909, this confessed his inability to cope with himself, to develop sufficient self-discipline. Hapgood was moody. He could jump from a joie de vivre to depression without losing his breath partly because in spite of his heavy anxie-

Final Years

William P. Hapgood c. 1930. (Courtesy of Elizabeth Backman.)

Powers and William P. Hapgood c. 1935. (Courtesy of Barta Monro.)

William P. Hapgood tending his garden c. 1940. (Courtesy of Barta Monro.)

ties and the ultimate failure of his efforts to relieve them, he had a will to live. He explained to Steffens, "With my mind (so-called) I condemn life and regard it as a bad joke, from which we have no escape, unless death is one—But there's an unreasonable instinct in me—the deepest thing—which approves of all instinctive life." In a short story Dreiser characterized this aspect of Hapgood's makeup with bite.

He was a man of broad understanding, sensitivity, and some learning, yet intellectually convinced of the futility of everything—life, death, energy, faith, disillusion, men—whatever you will. . . . At times he appeared to wonder why he or any one else chose to exist. On the other hand, he appeared to be sufficiently sound and vigorous and voracious materially or physically, as to enjoy himself hugely, to eat, drink and make merry with the best.[20]

IV

The Great Depression encouraged Hutchins Hapgood to write again. Although usually in comfortable circumstances, he had never been wealthy. He had earned little from journalism and almost nothing from his books. Neith did fairly well, but her earnings were unpredictable, dependent on how many short stories she could write. Hutchins's father helped him for many years. For example, while Hutchins was on the *Globe* he earned $70 a week, but Charles Hapgood gave him an additional $250 a month. His father also presented him with a large house in Dobbs Ferry, New York, but the residence proved too large for his son's needs and a financial drain. Hutchins spent most of the last two decades of his life in Provincetown and on a farm in Richmond, New Hampshire, which he had purchased a couple of years after selling the Dobbs Ferry property. He was often surrounded by his surviving children, Charles Hutchins, idealistic and serious, Miriam, warm-hearted and attractive, and Beatrix, slim and intense. Hutchins took an energetic interest in the household—sometimes to the annoyance of his wife. A lover of food, he did most of the shopping, and often enthusiastically

Final Years

bought more vegetables than the family was able to use. His relations with Neith did not lack occasional vividness. John Cowles recalled of 1940:

> That was the winter that through some heinous misdemeanor which Hutch must have committed, Neith packed a bag and said she was leaving him forever and for good and he need not bother to try to stop her; just get the car out and take her to a railroad or any other means of far transportation. Though Hutch seemingly persuaded her that his need for her was greater than her desire to get shet of him, she did keep the suit case packed for the ensuing two weeks and Hutch under reasonable control during the in terim [sic].[21]

Hutchins Hapgood invested much of his parental inheritance in the stock market and lost very heavily, particularly because of his holdings of Kreuger stock. In the early 1930s he was forced to sacrifice all his cashable stock to save a Kansas cattle ranch his parents had left to their grandchildren. These troubles had not wiped him out, but he needed more money. From 1931 to 1941 he earned so little that he paid no federal income tax.[22]

Hapgood thought of becoming an editor of a new Provincetown paper and of serving as "a kind of social reporter for the [Roosevelt] Administration, or for some department." He even considered writing about labor again and contacted Anton Johannsen. None of these plans bore fruit. In the early part of the 1930s he also did "My Forty Years of Drink," an antiprohibition piece, which told how alcohol had played a prominent and creative role in his life.[23]

In the spring of 1936 Hapgood thought he would start an autobiography. His old friend Frederic C. Howe, whom he had run into at a dinner in Washington, D.C., had insisted that Hapgood do an autobiography and whetted the interest of Alfred Harcourt, of Harcourt, Brace in the project. Neith kept after her husband and was instrumental in the writing of the book. "Without her I wouldn't and couldn't have done it," he admitted. His two most significant books, *The Spirit of the Ghetto* and the autobiography, were thus indebted to his wife's interest and intervention. His boredom with winter life in Key West and his economic straits made him receptive to work on his memoirs.[24]

Hapgood, like Mabel Dodge, sought emotional relief in an autobiography.

His stumbling into an autobiography seems strange, for the genre was in some respects a logical step for the introspective Hapgood. He had already done explicitly autobiographical writing, and many of his other works had autobiographical overtones. Mabel Dodge Luhan shrewdly commented about his *Globe* work, "Of course, he always wrote about himself, though he was too intelligent to betray this in any crass way." Hapgood had a great interest in personality. It was his "specialty," his older brother had said.[25] Hutchins Hapgood exploited this talent marvelously in this book, which was so expressive about so many people. He had been unconsciously in training much of his life.

Autobiographies were common among his friends. Frederic C. Howe observed that a good number of the old Greenwich Village crowd had written of their experiences. Leo Stein told Maurice Sterne, "Everybody's doing it. You might as well have your turn at telling what *you* think of everybody." Indeed, it had become fashionable to use autobiographies to tell tales and to settle scores. Sterne nervously asked Hapgood whether he planned to expose anything significant about him, and Mabel Dodge Luhan remarked, "I bet you slew me in your book." Neith and Hutchins parodied the liking for infighting. In "The Primrose Path," a play, "She" shot a pistol at "He" during a marital dispute. The bullet missed.

> HE: [*Trembling*] You don't shoot as well as you write!
> SHE: [*While cocking pistol, half smiles in spite of herself—sees pen on table—hesitates. Puts down pistol, seizes pen*] I'll have a greater revenge! I'll write a book about you!
> HE: [*Sinking in a chair clutching his head in terror*] My God! [26]

Hapgood, who had been bothered by arthritis for several years and found writing painful, noted, "I dictated all of my book, except the part about childhood." Ridgely Torrence's remark that its tone was conversational was insightful.[27] Segments of previous autobiographical efforts, selections from books, articles, and unpublished works were incorporated into *Victorian*. Hapgood himself rescued it from being a miscellany.

His aspirations, his struggles, and above all his strenuous personality welded the autobiography together, at least most of it —he did not successfully integrate the last part. He had found a character of sufficient complexity, resiliency, and interest. This was part of the difference from *An Anarchist Woman* or "Cristine." Passages that limped in "Cristine" and "My Forty Years of Drink," ran in *Victorian*.

A Victorian in the Modern World, like Hapgood, was many things. Bulging with sketches of his friends, it has often been mined by historians looking for apt characterizations, but *Victorian* was more than a gallery. Hapgood was preoccupied with temperament, and it was not surprising that descriptions of various individuals were a significant part of his book. His portraits were done with wit, understanding, and fine literary style. The quality was high and many sketches were excellent. They were critical. Hapgood, despite his lovableness, dealt few full houses: Hutchins, unlike Norman Hapgood, had no real heroes. Preoccupied with self-definition, Hutchins sometimes misjudged Neith and his brother Norman. Often subconsciously playing an internal game, evaluating others against himself, Hutchins usually managed to score points. He particularly disliked people who were cocksure and threatened his ego. Gertrude Stein, Max Eastman, and Emilie Hapgood were treated harshly, and in certain passages his brothers did not fare well either. He often labeled radicals dogmatists, challenged the emotions and personalities of stiff rationalists like Leo Stein, Max Eastman, or even Norman Hapgood, and used reason against passionate individuals like Hippolyte Havel or Mabel Dodge Luhan. Leo Stein astutely observed that in *Victorian* "the characters are not created so as to stand by themselves." [28] Hapgood, as usual, was most fascinated by reactions within himself.

If Hapgood asked one question in *Victorian,* it was why he was the way he was. This was important, for it separated his from some other autobiographies. Howe's *The Confessions of a Reformer,* Lincoln Steffens's *Autobiography,* and Norman Hapgood's *The Changing Years,* preoccupied with how their authors came to *believe* what they did, were more interested in their ideas than in their characters. All three of those volumes were more concerned with political ideology, with registering the jumping on and the jumping off of opinions than *Victorian,* which was much more personal. Hutchins's development was much less consecutive.

Hapgood grappled with determinism, particularly in the section about his childhood. Feeling victimized by society and using his own difficulties to chastise the sexual inhibitions of the day, he speculated that much of his subsequent maladjustment, his being nagged by emotional problems, was rooted in his youth. Like John P. Marquand's George Apley, Hapgood seemed to say that "I am the sort of man I am, because environment prevented my being anything else." At other times he realized that such a conclusion short-circuited an indictment of society from a more mature perspective. A second type of determinism crept into *Victorian.* Perhaps his problems were physiological, he sighed at times.[29] Hapgood, despite his restlessness, feared the inevitable.

Ambiguous about his emotional difficulties, he claimed that much of his insight, much of his value as a human being and as a writer, developed from his stresses. Linking the afflictions of his youth to a sympathetic understanding of outcasts and a knack for discovering the deeper currents of life, he concluded that his tensions were painful but educational. His contention that insight grew out of suffering, his concentration on perception rather than action, and his belief that he should be evaluated in terms of his personal qualities, not in terms of his political or social accomplishments, were indebted to the romantic tradition. The goal of Hapgood's introspection was not the discovery of right action but adjustment.

Despite his anguish Hapgood emerged as a spry character. With a nice style, a delightful wit, and a touch of the naughty, he wrote a lively book, one that retains its vivacity even after several readings. His assertion of a love affair with life, the mildly risqué accounts of his drinking, and his appeal to women seemed to reassure him and the reader that fundamentally he was adjusted, if not in a completely conventional sense. After reading a manuscript of a volume of Mable Dodge Luhan's autobiography, he had urged her to be more positive and "take away the negative sting and reconcile the reader by making him feel that you see the Whole, which is the reconciliation of the parts." [30] Hapgood himself sugarcoated his autobiography once in a while, but it was conspicuously frank and honest.

Hapgood's claim that he was a Victorian led one correspondent to quip that if Hutchins was a Victorian, he was Queen Anne. Part of the Victorian impact on Hapgood was that even when he was in opposition, Victorianism shaped him. He disliked much of the new sexual freedom. The young, Hapgood believed, took sex too casually, needed more spiritual and less physical groping. The concept of being within a period of change, a conspicuous theme of his autobiography, was preeminently Victorian. Hapgood's introspection, his intensity, his fear of a conquering materialism, were built of Victorian lumber. Robert Morss Lovett remarked that "Hutch is . . . Victorian in every sense except reticence, and by dropping that veil he has allowed the essential Victorian qualities to appear." [31] Although Hapgood was less the complete Victorian than Lovett claimed, he was very much influenced by Victorianism, although usually subtly.

Carl Van Vechten told Hapgood that *Victorian* was "assuredly your masterpiece and if your work is to live, I think, dear Hutch, it will live by this book." Bernard Berenson commented that "you have written what will long survive anything poor creatures like myself has [sic] ever done." John Dewey, Howe, and Alfred Stieglitz, among others, complimented Hapgood's volume, but *Victorian* sold only 1,500 copies, and it never produced the money that Hapgood had hoped for. Hapgood thought that the war, the high price, the book's complexity, and Carl Sandburg's biography of Lincoln, put out by the same publisher and receiving a great deal of attention, all hurt *Victorian*. Additional explanations might be offered. Mitchell Kennerley contended that the title had hurt—Victorian was an unpopular word. More important, Albert Parry found publishers in the 1930s unreceptive to books on bohemianism. Christopher Lasch has noted of Mabel Dodge Luhan's autobiography that "at a time when political involvement was the fashion among intellectuals, Mrs. Luhan's painstaking investigations of the intricacies of personal intercourse could hardly have commanded a following." [32] Although Hapgood had more of a political slant than did Luhan, a good deal of Lasch's evaluation applied to *Victorian*. By 1939 not only was interest in this kind of work decreasing, but much of the ground had already been covered by other reminiscences, notably those of Luhan and Steffens. Much of the book's appeal depended upon how one reacted to Hapgood. That complex, somewhat moody, introspective person probably did not have that large an audience.

Hapgood's last years were marred by the familiar unproductive attempts to find work, the same perplexities, and poor health. *Victorian,* despite its high quality and its critical recognition, did not give Hapgood as much emotional calm as he wished. In good part a compilation of previous efforts, it did not resolve his metaphysical longings, and it did not branch into fields that might hold his interest over the coming years. In the early 1940s he became, like so many American intellectuals, interested in the past. With Neith he worked on a history of the Hapgoods through their letters. He died on November 26, 1944; Neith died seven years later. Because of their interest in the Hapgood family, both were buried in Petersham, the Hapgoods' ancestral home.

V

The marrow of William Hapgood's carrer has already been discussed. By 1940 his greatest moments were behind him. The Columbia Conserve Company, once a confident experiment in industrial democracy, was deeply troubled. In the mid-1930s Hapgood had been considered for an important position in the Hightstown (New Jersey) Project, a government resettlement program. He wrote in 1936, "Provided the Government accepts my proposal, especially with respect to financing, and still further provided the Trade Unionists carry out their end of the agreement, the chances of success will be greater than the chances of success for the Columbia Conserve Company." Hapgood became too entangled in problems at Columbia and too

Final Years   205

frustrated by government bureaucracy to play an active role, but his infatuation with Hightstown suggested a degree of disillusionment with Columbia.[33]

In 1940 William Hapgood hoped to cancel the agreement put into effect in 1926 and reorganize Columbia, but he failed to get the necessary two-thirds vote from the stockholders. Continental Can, a major creditor, also was against change. The situation was desperate, William informed Hutchins: "Our common stock is now impaired by losses during the last eight years to the extent of $171,000 and that amount will be increased during the next 2 months by at least $10,000 more. Deducting $181,-000 from 211,000 leaves a balance of $30,000 as the book value of the common stock. The actual or market value is very much less." William concluded that "unless we reorganize I doubt we can carry on for more than a few years." In 1941 he reported that a loss of $9,087.14 "wipes out our common stock." [34]

In late 1940 Columbia allowed salaried workers to be paid in wages if they preferred, but any who did so would lose their salary benefits. Wartime regulations, permitting Columbia to pack only five types of condensed soups, further hurt the company. William Hapgood advocated quarterly stockholders' meetings "since Council meetings have died out, to a great extent, through lack of interest or whatever cause," but the council refused to consent. In August 1942 Hapgood proposed to divide the stock, but the council again rebuffed him. In September of that year the employees struck for about a week. He thought it a squeeze for higher pay—he had refused to concede to this demand at the annual meeting. He assured the largest private stockholder that "we shall do our very best, between now and next June, to see that the preferred stockholders are properly protected. Most certainly they cannot be protected as long as the majority of the common stock is controlled by the union." [35]

In January 1943 the management won a trial for receivership brought by some ex-employees, and on February 15, 1943, the trustees instituted a countersuit to break the old trust. While the case was on, the workers were transferred from salary to wages. William P. Hapgood explained to the stockholders:

We are no longer able to furnish all of our salaried workers with collective security. As a matter of fact, the "Columbia Experiment" has ceased to exist, and we are now forced to proceed along the regular standard lines of an American corporation. Many of us, including, of course, myself, regret this great change in the operation of the Company, but we have been powerless to prevent it.[36]

A federal court broke the old trust in July 1943 and ordered the stock divided among the old employees. "This means that the Columbia experiment in workers' control has ended," Hapgood emphasized. The company was formally reorganized in 1944. Careful government regulation of production during the Second World War forced Columbia to close down for long periods, but profits were impressive in the mid-1940s. "From 1947 to 1953," it has been noted, "the net profits averaged approximately $30,000." [37]

In 1953 Columbia sold all its fixed assets to John Sexton and Company for about $515,000 and its private label business to Venice Maid Company for $15,000. Hapgood had considered selling at least since 1943, but he was in his eighties before he let go of Columbia. In fact, he would not have given up the business even then were it not for his concern for the other stockholders, particularly Elizabeth Hapgood, Norman's widow. William had been permanently blinded by glaucoma during the early 1940s and often suffered from insomnia, but his energy did not decrease much. In his later years he often walked four miles a day on a rope walk constructed on his property. Hutchins wrote to him admiringly in 1942, "I couldn't do what you are doing without croaking immediately." In the 1950s an interviewer found that William Hapgood "still advocates the right of the working man to a fair share of the profits of business if he is willing to assume his proper share of the responsibility toward industry and society as a whole." Hapgood disapproved of McCarthyism and supported Stevenson in 1952. A generous man who often helped those in need and was never preoccupied with his own financial position, he could also be very stubborn once he had made up his mind. He remained happily married to Eleanor, a pleasing woman, until her death in the mid-1950s. Although successfully resisting an attempt by his grandson to

Final Years

be appointed his legal guardian, William Hapgood in his last years was placed under the guardianship of his attorney. William Hapgood died on July 30, 1960. "As he had requested," the *Alton* (Ill.) *Evening Telegraph* reported, "news of his death did not reach the newspapers until six days later, and only a handful of persons attended his funeral." [38]

CHAPTER 11

Conclusion

I

THE HAPGOODS REACTED to one another in more than a coolly intellectual way. They were not boxes of ideas. Of the three Hapgoods, Hutchins probably had the most trouble with his brothers. He provided a good perspective because he was more concerned with this type of interaction and because his views are better documented.

Hutchins had been particularly intimate with his older brother. They were close in age, had been chums in college, and Hutchins had his first real job, on the *Commercial*, with Norman. After that time, however, they grew apart. After spending some time with Norman in 1905, Hutchins exclaimed, "All his old charm for me has *returned*." Yet the distance remained. For one thing, Neith was not one of Emilie's admirers, nor was Hutchins for that matter. The two elder Hapgoods got along socially, but differences in outlook prevented the intimacy of earlier years. After meeting his older brother in 1913, Hutchins announced that Norman "was friendly, but he sees things so little as I do, that he had the usual rather chilling effect on me." Norman's not giving him much to do for *Harper's Weekly* annoyed Hutchins. In 1918 Hutchins concluded that "I have enjoyed Norman and feel nearer to him than I have since he married Emilie"; over a decade later Hutchins again had to speak of a new familiarity. By 1931 Norman added, "I hope for very close relations during our remaining years." After Norman's death in 1937 Hutchins developed a renewed appreciation of his older brother.[1]

Neith, probably speaking for her husband as well, complained of Norman in 1905, "I don't enjoy *him* as much as I once did. He is so conventionalized now—all the fringe[?] gone—nothing left but a thoroughly good citizen with the story of success &

the usual ideals—so he seems to *me!*" In a manuscript, "On Respectability," Hutchins Hapgood concluded, "Respectability is the sacrifice made by the individual to Society." On the right-hand margin, he scribbled, "How it changes the idealistic student (Norman etc.)." Hutchins considered *Why Janet Should Read Shakspere* his brother's best volume "because he has dwelt with Shakspere longer and it has more to do with his real, rather than journalistic, mental life." Hutchins thought his brother was his opposite in many respects: "Norman lived, in a way, in the externals of life, active, unsentimental, unreflective, clever, able, extroverted, and ambitious. I, on the other hand, was subjective, moody, maladjusted, reflective, introverted and, in a worldly sense, unambitious, keen only about sensual and spiritual experience." [2]

Hutchins missed much of his older brother's complexity. He was too eager to stereotype Norman, who he thought had made too many compromises, had traded in too many principles. To a degree Hutchins envied his older brother's purpose, calm, and self-control. One detects in Hutchins's scathing comments about Norman's relations with Emilie a mild delight that the analytical Norman, too, could experience marital discord. Norman did not express his feelings about Hutchins often, although Hutchins recorded in the early 1930s that Norman "continues even up to this day, to think me unbalanced in one way or another." [3] Norman was intellectually a more important figure in Hutchins's life than Hutchins was in his.

The relations of Norman and Hutchins with William Hapgood ran a different course. Norman and William apparently got along well. Their habits were similar, and they cooperated effectively at Columbia. Emilie did, however, add some spice to fraternal relations. Neith wrote, "Emilie has not the light touch! She tried to smooth down Billy & Eleanor in reference to her famous remark about Powers, but not very successfully. Billy's sole comment was a snort." Hutchins's relations with William were often openly tense. Hutchins was annoyed by William's complete self-confidence. William once wrote to his son, Powers, accusing him of having more "Hapgood egoism" "than any one of us, except perhaps Uncle Hutch." William also claimed that Hutchins " 'wanted what he wanted when he wanted it,' and he persisted until he made the other party almost scream." [4]

Hutchins had consistently doubted William's business ability and informed Alfred Stieglitz in 1921 that "my activity in connection with it [Columbia] is confined to long letters to my brother trying to prevent him [from] doing things I think foolish." There was friction throughout the 1920s. At one point Hutchins remarked that one of "Billy's letters, though characteristic, shocked me greatly." Hutchins warned his wife, "I would prefer that Charles [their son] should *not* see this letter from Billy. I don't want to influence his relations with Billy." A new peak in animosity was reached several years later when Powers accused his uncles of maneuvering to put William at a disadvantage. Hutchins also suspected that William and Eleanor Hapgood were upset by the not very flattering sketch of William in *Victorian*. In the mid-1930s Hutchins thought it an excellent idea to gather the entire Hapgood family for a reunion at Christmas. Mary Donovan Hapgood, Powers's wife, responded, "So you would like to have *all* the Hapgood clan together. I am doubtful about having a very happy Christmas (or any other time) if that should happen." [5]

Perhaps nothing did so much for so long to fuel discord as the Hapgood estate. Fanny P. Hapgood, who survived her husband, who had died in 1917, passed away in 1922. Her will, drawn in 1917, left her property, including a Kansas cattle ranch, in trust to her grandchildren on a per capita, rather than on a *per stirpes*, basis. Her three sons, who served as trustees, were to receive the income during their lifetimes. The land became riddled with debts and was a source of irritation. During the early 1940s Hutchins and William Hapgood reached new levels of antagonism. Although there were some friendly encounters, Hutchins, in the year of his death, explained to Powers that "I never know whether your father will consent to hear my letters or not, when sent to him directly." William stated that he would "not acknowledge any letter which contains a personal attack upon me." William sighed after Hutchins's death, "If I had the ordering of the world there would be no such things as estates." "Hurrah!" Neith exclaimed when the ranch was finally sold.[6] By then only one of the brothers was alive and much irreparable damage had been done.

II

The Hapgood brothers had distinct personalities and individual careers. Hutchins, sociable and generally well liked, was the most outgoing, and perhaps the only one who had much of a sense of humor and certainly the only one with a metaphysical penchant. Norman, who could be charming, was somewhat deficient in warm personal qualities. Perhaps his aloofness contributed to the misinterpretation of his character apparent in the autobiographies of Hutchins Hapgood and Mark Sullivan. Committed chiefly to ideas, Norman could be inspiring, but in an abstract way. He suffered some severe setbacks—divorce and the mental collapse of his oldest daughter, Ruth—but he rarely spoke about them. The silence indicated not lack of feeling but an aversion to public display of his problems. He could never have written a book like *Victorian,* nor would he have wanted to. William was far less introspective than his brothers. Prone to make snap judgments, he stuck firmly to his decisions. A domineering man, he was termed harmfully overpossessive toward his son by his daughter-in-law.[7] One finds in the three Hapgood brothers a tendency toward extremism in personality.

Ellery Sedgwick recalled that "Norman stretched your brains, Hutchins strained your sympathies." Mabel Dodge observed that Norman Hapgood "was thin where Hutch was solid and thick—and cold-minded where Hutch was warm." Neith commented to her husband that Norman "would never be much of a sinner, nor much of anything temperamentally—you are just the opposite." Hutchins thought Norman stiff and conventional. Norman's opinion of Mabel Dodge suggested his feelings toward Hutchins's circle. "Your little friend [Mabel Dodge] looks as though she'd be very sweet to go to bed with," he reputedly said to Hutchins, "but as a counselor . . ."[8]

The careers of all three brothers were different. Being writers, Norman and Hutchins jousted with issues that did not concern

William. Their experiences on the *Commercial Advertiser* and their attempts to reconcile their literary standards and concepts of culture with journalism found little outgoing parallel in William's career. If Norman's deepest intellectual passion was for that which transcended the immediate, he nonetheless wrote little that was lasting. Certainly achieving more recognition than Hutchins and probably the most historically important Hapgood, he never wrote a book the equal of Hutchins's best. One cannot point to a group of intellectuals who influenced William P. Hapgood, nor did he write much about politics.

The adult lives of Norman and Hutchins Hapgood were not much alike. Hutchins explained that "we went separate ways." [9] Norman, who traveled from service as a drama critic to prominence as the muckraking editor of *Collier's Weekly* and *Harper's Weekly* and recognition as a leading progressive, was the most famous Hapgood. Hutchins prowled the Bowery and the ghetto, mingled with anarchists and revolutionaries, and was intimately associated with prewar Greenwich Village and with Provincetown during the 1920s. One connects Louis Brandeis, Charles R. Crane, Mark Sullivan, Woodrow Wilson, and Robert J. Collier with Norman Hapgood. One associates the Griffou Push, Mabel Dodge Luhan, Alfred Stieglitz, Bernard Berenson, and Leo Stein most readily with Hutchins. There was, of course, an overlap in friendships—Robert Morss Lovett was a good example—but Norman and Hutchins were usually most intimate with different people. It is hard to conceive of Norman putting much stock in Josiah Flynt Willard, and, by the same token, Hutchins did not adore Brandeis or Wilson.

Hutchins's radical shading put him outside the range of Norman's progressivism; Norman would not have prepared an introduction to Alexander Berkman's memoirs. Hutchins once informed his wife, "I had a dispute about the proletariat, crime etc and Norman maintained that my point of view was degenerate. Long discussion, no result." Hutchins accepted what Christopher Lasch has called "new radicals" and Henry May has termed "Young Intellectuals" more readily than Norman did. Norman and Hutchins both advocated a single standard for men and women, but Norman proposed acceptance of the women's standard, that is, premarital chastity and marital fidelity, while Hutchins urged women to have men's sexual freedom. At the Forum of the Church of the Ascension, Norman Hapgood "made everyone sit up straight when in reading from one of the members of the Assembly in the time of Washington he said 'Damn' right out loud." [10] About the same time, *The Story of a Lover* was being tried for obscenity. Hutchins Hapgood never had Norman's audience of hundreds of thousands, nor was he appointed an American minister.

III

If the distinctions were so sharp, William falling outside the spheres of his brothers because of his business career and Norman and Hutchins roaming different fields differently, is it justifiable to group the brothers? In short, did they have anything more than blood, ability, and the Hapgood nose in common? There were important similarities. All had cultural interests, Norman and Hutchins more so than William. Norman inserted editorials on literature and poetry in *Collier's Weekly* and *Hearst's International;* Hutchins quoted Goethe in Bowery dives; William commented on Shakespeare after selling tomato soup. The Hapgoods were fond of the small unit, whether it was the Harvard of the 1890s, the Griffou Push, the *Collier's* circle, Provincetown, or the Columbia Conserve Company. The mid-1920s found Norman active in Petersham, Hutchins at Richmond and Provincetown, and William at Columbia. Norman and William, followers of Brandeis, gave the small unit more precise, more economic defense than Hutchins, but the Hapgoods were most comfortable when dealing with small groups.

Whatever their dissimilarities, the Hapgoods were interested in improvement. *Collier's*, Hutchins's work for the *New York Globe*, and Columbia hoped to benefit society. Despite the disparities of interest in, and approach to, politics, Norman and Hutchins Hapgood usually voted for the same candidates for president. Hutchins's radical and romantic comments often covered liberal-humanitarian sentiments very similar to many of his brothers'. The Hapgoods supported the New Deal, although Norman, like William, was nettled by National Recovery Administration guidelines that troubled Columbia for a time. Shortly before his death, Norman was upset at Roosevelt "because of the excesses of the Farley machine, the folly of the efforts to flood the Supreme Court, and the timidity about introducing taxation and retrenchment for fear of losing votes in various groups of beneficiaries." Despite these irritations, Norman, had he lived, surely would have backed Roosevelt in 1940 because of the international situation and perhaps because of the New Deal's increased attack on monopoly. Hutchins told President Roosevelt that he had been "a consistent adherent of the policies of your administration." Although he was very upset by the draft, "a semi-criminal performance," he supported FDR in 1940. Hutchins, according to his wife, "says for the first time in his life he is getting into a campaign to defeat Mr. Willkie!!" None of the Hapgoods were socialists or communists. All three rejected fascism.[11] As was pointed out in a previous chapter, the Columbia venture suggested a likeness in the Hapgoods' economic beliefs.

IV

All of this establishes a fair degree of similarity, but the real cohesion was deeper than how they stood on this or that program or on this or that politician. It was not so much ideology as principles that bound them together. Their father's impact was decisive. Charles Hapgood, morally tough and demanding, lectured his sons that they must be resilient and careful and hold to moral precepts. His maxims were not roads to wealth but essentials in their own right, and his teachings transcended any need for proof by dollars, although such justification steeled them to an extent. Charles Hapgood loathed fops whether or not they squandered the family fortune. No longer a believer in the old religion, he tenaciously held to most of its ethics.

Charles Hapgood's strenuousness differed from his sons' in that for a long time he was preoccupied with achieving some

Conclusion

economic standing, some security. As a result of his early business failures, he had a greater fear that scarcity was around the corner than did his offspring. When a young grandson mentioned that he was learning a little carpentry, Charles Hapgood was quite pleased. "Learn some trade *well*. . . so you can always . . . earn your own living," he exhorted. Then if one flopped in one's profession, whether it be law, medicine, or whatever, "you will be able to take up the Trade which you have learned and be sure to be able to make an honest living, to get enough bread & warm Clothes." Charles Hapgood was not merely encouraging a youngster's hobby, he was building character. Hutchins Hapgood has recorded an amusing example of his father's determination. After playing tenpins with his father, who was in his sixties, young Hapgood noted, "I beat him, much to his disgust. He cares more for victory in games than I do, and is very intense about it, like a boy." [12]

Charles Hapgood expressed his strenuousness in his business career, but also in child-rearing, indeed more so in the latter. It would have been a profound tragedy to him if his sons did not live up to his standards. He would have preferred the pauper's home. In his diary he concluded: "The hardest problem of my life was how best to assist in the moral and intellectual development of Fanny P's and my children, and when solved, for better or worse, a heavy load was lifted. I doubt if any parents have had better material on which to work, or material harder to spoil, but we did not fully realize its nature while handling it." Each of his three sons followed in his footsteps in concern for their children. To pick only one highlight, in 1928 Norman Hapgood and his family left the United States for a two-year stay in Europe mainly because he believed that such an experience would be of enormous value to his children. [13]

Charles Hapgood gave all his sons an example of shaping their own destiny, of directing their future. He implanted a feeling of responsibility and an awareness of the necessity for self-control in each of his sons. When he was a boy, Norman Hapgood had shot his sick dog with a pistol, but he botched the job and the incident was very unpleasant. Norman wrote in 1914 that "scarcely has a month passed in all the years since then that

I have not remembered this deed with horror. It was not that I was cruel. It was that my mind was affected by the pistol." He was haunted by the fact that he had lost control of himself. Norman's emphasis on accountability gave an interesting twist to his defense of small enterprise. "It is size that seems to be sending things to the devil. Empires are too big; business passes from small expert and personal units to huge trusts; the resulting complications are such as men have neither the brains nor the morals to handle usefully." [14] This was not merely the cry of one who wanted more efficiency or a tear for the closing of the entrepreneurial frontier, but a lament over a situation in which men could no longer prove their moral worth.

The Hapgood brothers led fairly rigorous and unluxurious private lives. Hutchins noted that his brothers were "extreme examples of sobriety." Hutchins, of course, could not be described in precisely those terms, but he had scant regard for extravagance. His wife remarked, "Neither Hutch nor I have expensive personal tastes—amusements & clothes costing us practically nothing." Norman said in 1937 that "a wish for the year might well be that the lessons of the great depression may not be lost; that children may grow up in homes where there is more talk of principles, of generosity, and less continued stress on worldly prizes." Hutchins speculated that "this 'depression,' may indeed be a blessing in disguise; for misfortunes of this kind tend to open our minds to the fundamental things, to the value of the simple facts of existence." [15] These comments were not panglossian, but products of seriousness and wariness of wealth.

Charles Hapgood's general strenuousness and his beliefs in hard work, thrift, and honesty were absorbed by Norman, Hutchins, and William Hapgood. Charles Hapgood seems to have put his rules within a generally democratic framework. His emphasis on learning and achieving accounted in part for his sons' great concern for education in the broader sense. The gist of much of Charles Hapgood's outlook was that one must seek and adhere to moral principles. Norman's autobiography contained a page of homilies. Hutchins's was loaded with epigrams, and William's few writings showed some interest in moral concepts, his life even more. All were, at least in part, paying tribute to their father's influence. Indeed, Hutchins's preoccupation with personality, his great concern for character assessment, so evident in *Victorian,* was partly a reflection of his father's absorption in moral evaluation.

The Hapgood brothers did not seek Theodore Roosevelt's "strenuous life," which was greatly affected by militarism and imperialism. Although William's building himself through athletics paralleled Roosevelt, the Hapgoods' striving was less sweaty and less likely to result in smashing someone's mouth. Their exertions were more in the nature of earnestness. For the Hapgoods, weakness was much less related to cowardice than to lack of seriousness. Their testing was more internal, more inclined to be introspective. The Hapgood brothers' movement to reformist or leftist positions was not impelled by status anxiety but was significantly encouraged by anxiety about themselves, their regard for their worth. Walter E. Houghton, noting the prevalence of particulary "earnest" types in the Victorian Era, has commented that to the Victorians, "to be in earnest *intellectually* is to have or to seek to have genuine beliefs about the most fundamental questions in life, and on no account merely to repeat customary and conventional notions insincerely, or to play with ideas or with words as if the intellectual life were a May-game." [16]

Seriousness had been highly valued at the *Harvard Monthly,* and it has been pointed out that Norman Hapgood's dramatic criticism was frequently described as "serious" and "earnest." His early days at *Collier's* were marked by an almost inhuman desire to be fair, to be correct, and not to place partisanship or friendship above principle. His increasing identification with causes was a redefinition of the expression of his earnestness. He energetically sought to realize his aspirations; Hutchins remarked that in his last days Norman "was as full of plans, as active as ever." [17]

William Hapgood, who believed in meeting challenges, was more inclined than his brothers to display his earnestness in actions rather than ideas. He argued, "It is difficulties and not ease which educate mankind," and one thing he saw in Columbia was a personal test. His love for work was manifested in his position on lowering working hours:

> I am not in sympathy with the desire to reduce greatly the length of the working day, nor am I in harmony with the general opinion that manual work should be reduced to the lowest possible minimum. On the contrary, from experience I know that hard manual labor is beneficial to my body, to my mind and to my spirit, and I do as much of it as is safe for a man of fifty-eight. But for hard work to educate and stimulate, it must have a creative element.[18]

A comment of eighteen-year-old Powers Hapgood indicated the extent to which William had passed on his outlook: "No matter at what age I go [die], I'll go happily if only I've completed or helped to complete some work which will permanently help the world. The tragedy of death, it seems to me, is not in just the mere leaving of the earth and friends. But in the leaving of it before one has had a chance to do something of value." [19]

Hutchins Hapgood's concern for being earnest took particularly grueling forms. He claimed that "to me a strenuous morality is the highest way in which the human spirit expresses itself. . . . Stern sincerity is the largest element of a morality that does not concern itself with the pious, the hypocritical or the conventional." Despite Hutchins's liking for wine, women, and socializing, Leo Stein remarked to Mabel Dodge Luhan, "You know I used to say that until I met you Hutch had been the least frivolous person I had ever known, that I had never heard Hutch make a pun." Like Norman Hapgood's editorials in *Collier's*, Hutchins's work was sometimes called too serious. "I made up my mind that I would write a light article," he once notified his *Globe* readers, "since I am accused of being too earnest." Hutchins Hapgood was always striving. Bernard Berenson, after learning of Hutchins's death, asked Neith, "Did he attain a mystical vision before the end?" [20]

Hutchins Hapgood did not define his earnestness in his father's spartan life-style as much as his brothers. Indeed, he rejected large parts of it, including its abstemiousness, its discipline, and tendencies toward respectability and conventionality, but he retained a strong sense of accountability and he did go on quests. Neith shrewdly interjected in her deep, rich voice after Hutchins had been bewailing his life and exaggerating his failures, "Well, I never expected to be perfect." Norman and William, like their father, emphasized the importance to judgment of balance and detachment. Hutchins, influenced by romantic concepts, trusted the imaginative, intuitive, and emotional more than did his brothers. Hutchins Hapgood brought to soul-searching and love the energy his father had devoted to business. Late in life he explained, "I constantly realize that if I continue a letter, a talk or a piece of writing, a little distance beyond the beginning it almost always results in a certain mysticism." Hutchins exhorted, "Marriage is a strenuous occupation. To make it a good marriage is a constant work of art. It needs resourcefulness, good will, imagination of a creative kind. Only artists in life can fully realize marriage." Hutchins, however, never found in love the bliss that he had hoped for. He carried his feeling of inferiority, his introspection, sensitivity, and longing for the spiritual into his relationship. He displayed his tensions by concluding of woman:

She is like the rotation of the crops, the attraction of gravitation, the ebb & flow of the sea. She has the power and the primitiveness of the earth. *Woe* to the more artificial male, dependent on the unconsciously remembered civilization—woe to his delicate spiritual organization if he gets in her way! It is like opposing a force of Nature—*with* which the wise man works, not *against*.[21]

His self-destructive analyses were fruits of his inability to place his earnestness within a satisfying framework. To a degree his hunting for the "Absolute" or the "Infinite" corresponded to his brothers' search for reconciliation through journalism or through the Columbia Conserve Company. As was pointed out in the first chapter of this study, young Hutchins's guilt feelings and dreams about a disparaging "Presence" and "Reproach" seem to have been rooted in his inability to meet paternal expectations. His lifelong fatalism, a sense of helplessness, was perhaps related to his not performing up to his father's norms and a consequent feeling of deficiency. This was the source of much of his frustration, although he was only partly conscious of it.

His father had whipped him only once and punishment was internalized as guilt. Hutchins Hapgood's culpability was somewhat formless; he had trouble pinning it down. In an important passage in an early autobiographical work he wrote, "In his dreams Sydney [Hutchins Hapgood] sometimes had strenuous unhappy spiritual interviews with his God, whose vague and terrific form had a family resemblance to his father." Here was a possible bridge between his spiritual striving and his unsatisfactory relationship with his father. Much of his interest in metaphysics was a craving for relief of his anxieties. His tendency to place himself in punishing situations was a probable child of his guilt feelings. He spoke of Neith's "perfection," but she was ultimately impenetrable, and he was, therefore, inadequate. His insistence on writing about the spiritual, although he acknowledged his inability to do so, had a note of self-chastisement. His calls for mindless work to rescue him from his deadlocks were feeble imitations of the outward form that earnestness often took for his brothers. He confessed to Mabel Dodge Luhan that agony "would leave me in moments of creative work, of great and satisfying love, of physical exertion in the face of Nature—but it was always there, in the background, lingering[,] waiting." [22] Whether creating, loving, or suffering, he was intense. Indeed, his agonizing to an extent satisfied his striving's demand for activity.

It is difficult to find the precise psychological roots of Hutchins Hapgood's inability to meet his father's expectations. Three of his four earliest memories either outrightly or suggestively involved acquisition. His feeling of loss, that something was missing in him, his desire to share in Neith's pregnancy or to become pregnant himself, and his suspicion that Neith thought his love for her had a childlike quality might point to some problems in his early relations with his mother.[23] It is hard to explain why Hutchins and not his brothers had such difficulties. Also, as psychologists have frequently noted, mere amount of stress does not predetermine adjustment or maladjustment. As one might expect, detailed information about his early life is scant, but it is possible that some disruption of family life might have had a detrimental impact on him. This early insecurity might have left him too weak emotionally to meet his father's expectations. This interpretation is offered for consideration rather than advanced as a near certainty.

Charles Hapgood lamented, "I have done nothing to benefit the World—only grubed [sic] for money." He was hardly fair to himself, but his comment indicated his disapproval of those who merely accumulated wealth. Without poverty nipping at their heels, his sons searched for new outlets, careers other than conventional entrepreneurial ones. Norman Hapgood found fulfillment in his critical work and eventually as an editor and liberal. Muckrake journalism's self-importance and its increased awareness of the value of the press peculiarly appealed to him. For a while Hutchins Hapgood thought journalism satisfying, but his love for the deeper meaning, for the news behind the headlines, and his penchants for metaphysical speculation and agonizing were ultimately more compatible to his straining. William Hapgood, who had been active in conventional business, became infatuated with the idea of giving the workers more say and eventually ownership of his company. William once said, "I should far prefer the life of a recluse, than that of an active and acquisitive business man." [24] In redefining entrepreneurship in more gratifying terms, William differed from his father. Norman, Hutchins, and William Hapgood did not follow the path of Charles Hapgood. Had they been born fifty years earlier, they might have been content to be businessmen who took an interest in community affairs. Much of the story of the Hapgood brothers is about their efforts to channel their earnestness. Nonmaterialistic, anxious to earn a living consistent with their standards, and relating seriousness to striving, all three brothers proved susceptible to many of the social and political concerns of late nineteenth-and early twentieth-century America. Their intensity about life, usually beneficial, was sometimes detrimental. Norman Hapgood, eager to stand for the best, occasionally became too much the partisan of some causes and criticized unfairly those who differed with him. Indeed, one often senses a tension between his desire for fairness and his need to show his commitment through action. Hutchins Hapgood's introspection often crippled him, and William Hapgood's dedication reinforced his self-confidence and audacity. Norman, Hutchins, and William P. Hapgood differed in many ways, but their earnestness, a combination of strenuousness, seriousness, and idealism, made them intellectual and moral brothers.

Notes

Selected Bibliography

Index

Notes

Abbreviations

BP   Louis D. Brandeis Papers, School of Law Library, University of Louisville, Louisville, Kentucky
CH I   Charles Hapgood, father of Norman, Hutchins, and William
CH II   Charles Hapgood, son of Hutchins and Neith Boyce Hapgood
CP   Columbia Conserve Company Papers, Lilly Library, Indiana University, Bloomington.
CW   *Collier's Weekly*
CY   Norman Hapgood, *The Changing Years* (New York: Farrar & Rinehart, 1930)
HH   Hutchins Hapgood
HI   *Hearst's International*
HM   *Harvard Monthly*
HP   Hutchins and Neith Boyce Hapgood Papers, Beinecke Rare Book and Manuscript Library, Yale University, New Haven, Connecticut
HW   *Harper's Weekly*
LB   Louis D. Brandeis
LC   Library of Congress, Washington, D.C.
NBH   Neith Boyce Hapgood (includes all references to her unmarried and pen name, Neith Boyce)
NH   Norman Hapgood
NYCA   *New York Commercial Advertiser*
NYG   *New York Globe*
VMW   Hutchins Hapgood, *A Victorian in the Modern World* (New York: Harcourt, Brace, 1939)
WPH   William P. Hapgood

Chapter 1, The Alton Years

1. CH I, "Reminiscences," MS, [*ca.* 1913], p. 140, copy, Miriam DeWitt Papers, in her possession, Washington, D.C.
2. *Ibid.*, p. 148; NH to Emma Hapgood, Apr. 21, 1882, HP.
3. Charles W. Marsh, *Recollections, 1837–1910*, p. 44.
4. NH to Emma Hapgood, May 25, 1878, HP; *ibid.*, Aug. 27, no year, HP; *VMW*, pp. 11, 46.
5. CH I, "Reminiscences," p. 145; *CY*, p. 40; CH I, "Reminiscences," p. 152; *CY*, p. 38.
6. *VMW*, p. 16.

7. Lewis Atherton, *Main Street on the Middle Border*, pp. 70, 73–74.
8. CH I, Diary, Feb, 22, 1913 (under May 14, 1859), p. 29, copy, DeWitt Papers; CH I to NBH and HH, no day, 1912, in NBH and HH, *The Story of an American Family*, p. 191.
9. *CY*, p. 22.
10. *Ibid.*, pp. 95, 14, 45.
11. *Ibid.*, p. 40; Page Smith, *As a City upon a Hill*, p. 213.
12. *VMW*, p. 10; CH I, "Reminiscences," p. 154.
13. *VMW*, pp. 54, 18–19; Walter E. Houghton, *The Victorian Frame of Mind, 1830–1870*, p. 353.
14. *VMW*, p. 54.
15. *Ibid.*, p. 20.
16. *Ibid.*, pp. 18–19.
17. *Ibid.*, p. 18.
18. *Ibid.*, pp. 16, 17.
19. *Ibid.*, pp. 47, 56.
20. HH, "[Autobiographical] Notes," MS, July 13, 1903, HP; *VMW*, p. 25.
21. *CY*, p. 30; *VMW*, p. 24; DeWitt, interview, Washington, D.C., Nov. 4, 1974; CH I, "Reminiscences," p. 142.
22. *VMW*, p. 39; *CY*, p. 32; WPH to Leslie Hopkinson, May 13, 1937, HP.
23. *CY*, p. 33.
24. *VMW*, pp. ix, 256.

Chapter 2, From Harvard to the *Commercial Advertiser*

1. *CY*, pp. 63, 71; Philip Littell, "Norman Hapgood," p. 13.
2. *CY*, p. 46.
3. Robert Morss Lovett, *All Our Years*, p. 46.
4. Editorial, *HM* 1 (1885):35.
5. *CY*, p. 76.
6. Editorial, *HM* 9 (1889):34; Thomas W. Lamont, *My Boyhood in a Parsonage*, p. 179; Leslie Hopkinson, "An Eager, Serviceable Citizen," *Christian Register*, June 10, 1937, p. 384; NH to Percy MacKaye, n.d., in Introduction, William Vaughn Moody, *Letters to Harriet*, pp. 20–21.
7. Editorial, *HM* 7 (1888):124, 125.
8. *VMW*, p. 76; editorial, *HM* 9 (1889):32.
9. Blake Nevius, *Robert Herrick*, p. 45.
10. NH, "Love as an Extra," pp. 178–79.
11. Barrett Wendell, "The Harvard Undergraduate," *HM* 8 (1889):6–9; NH, "Social Stages," pp. 73–79.
12. NH, "Mr. Santayana's Poems," p. 174; *CY*, p. 101; NH to Emma Hapgood, Oct. 6, 1894, HP; photograph, in *Harvard Portfolio* 4 (1893): opp. 29.
13. *VMW*, p. 92; HH to Emma Hapgood, Aug. 2, 1892, HP.
14. *VMW*, pp. 99–100.
15. HH, "The Student as Child," p. 11.
16. Charles Edward Russell, *These Shifting Scenes*, p. 34.
17. Frederic C. Howe, *The Confessions of a Reformer*, p. 42.

18. "New York Editors and Daily Papers, by an Insider," p. 63; Allan Nevins, *The Evening Post*, pp. 567, 545.

19. *CY*, p. 107; Lincoln Steffens to Harlow Gale, July 20, 1896, in *The Letters of Lincoln Steffens*, 1:123; Nevins, *Evening Post*, p. 552; Oswald Garrison Villard, *Fighting Years*, p. 118.

20. Robert Dunn, *World Alive*, p. 10; Villard, *Fighting Years*, p. 117; Lincoln Steffens, *The Autobiography of Lincoln Steffens*, p. 281.

21. As quoted in Steffens, *Autobiography*, p. 324.

Chapter 3, Literature and Journalism: The Drama

1. NH, *The Stage in America, 1897–1900*, pp. 112–15.
2. NH, *Literary Statesmen and Others*, p. 185.
3. NH, *Why Janet Should Read Shakspere*, p. 65.
4. NH, "The Upbuilding of the Theatre," p. 425.
5. NH, *Stage*, pp. 54, 44; NH, "Books and Plays," *CW*, Oct. 31, 1903, p. 19.
6. Edwin Osgood Grover, ed., *Annals of an Era*, p. 8.
7. NH, *Stage*, pp. 320, 318, 298–308, 224; NH, "The Problem Play," p. 85.
8. William Winter, *The Wallet of Time*, 2:591; NH, *Stage*, pp. 213, 255; *Oxford Companion to the Theatre*, s.v. "Ibsen, Henrik Johan"; James Gibbons Huneker, *Steeplejack*, 2:159, 146–47.
9. Villard, *Fighting Years*, p. 167; *CY*, p. 164; Franklin Fyles, *The Theatre and Its People*, p. 190.
10. NH, "Drama of the Month," *Bookman* 13 (1901):162; *NYCA*, Jan. 17, 1898.
11. NH, *Stage*, pp. 6–7, 134.
12. NH, "The Actor of To-Day," p. 126; NH, *Stage*, p. 51; Allardyce Nicoll, *A History of Late Nineteenth Century Drama, 1850–1900*, 1:7–27.
13. *NYCA*, May 30, 1899; NH, *Stage*, p. 46.
14. NH, *Stage*, p. 134; NH, "Heinrich Conried and What He Stands For," p. 83.
15. NH, "Upbuilding of the Theatre," p. 420; NH, "Heinrich Conried," p. 81.
16. *NYCA*, May 2, 1899; NH, "Heinrich Conried," p. 81.
17. *NYCA*, Jan. 28, 1898; NH, "Drama of the Month," *Bookman* 9 (1899):207–8.
18. William Winter, *Other Days*, pp. 306–7; idem, *Wallet*, 1:xix, 2:290; "Chronicle and Comment," *Bookman* 19 (1904):550.
19. John Ranken Towse, *Sixty Years of the Theater*, p. x; Winter, *Wallet*, 1:30–31; *New York Evening Post*, Jan. 12, 1901.
20. Winter, *Wallet*, 1:4-5, xviii-xix; Towse, *Sixty Years*, pp. 6–7.
21. NH, "Drama of the Month," *Bookman* 8 (1899):428; *NYCA*, Dec. 13, 1898.
22. Robert Harlow Bradley, "Proposals for Reform in the Art of the Theatre as Expressed in General American Periodicals, 1885–1915," Diss. Illinois 1964, p. 141.
23. "Shall New York Have an Endowed Theatre?" p. 16; George Henry Lewes, *On Actors and the Art of Acting*, pp. 182–87, 194–95.
24. Fyles, *Theatre*, pp. 103, 69–72, 102, 104–8; "The Lounger," *Critic* 41 (1902): 13–14.
25. "The Theater and the Critic," p. 528; Grace Isabel Colbron, review of NH's *The Stage in America, 1897–1900*, *Bookman* 13 (1901):241; W. Archer to C. Archer, Mar. 19, 1899, in Charles Archer, *William Archer*, pp. 244–45.
26. "Chronicle and Comment," *Bookman* 8 (1898):94; Moody, *Letters to Harriet*, p. 57.

27. Mrs. Patrick Campbell, *My Life and Some Letters*, p. 178; Fitch to John Corbin, Jan. 14, 1903, in *Clyde Fitch and His Letters*, pp. 227–28; Archie Binns, *Mrs. Fiske and the American Theatre*, p. 294.
28. "Theater and the Critic," p. 528; W. T. Price, "Critics and Criticism," p. 14; "The Great Theatrical Syndicate: How Six Dictators Control Our Amusements—III," p. 208.
29. S. R. Littlewood, *Dramatic Criticism*, p. 264; Fyles, *Theatre*, p. 187.
30. Alfred L. Bernheim, *The Business of the Theatre*, pp. 32, 40, 46.
31. NH, *Stage*, pp. 32–35; Monroe Lippman, "The Effect of the Theatrical Syndicate on Theatrical Art in America," pp. 275–82; *NYCA*, Feb. 1, 1898.
32. NH, *Stage*, p. 29; NH, "The Theatrical Syndicate," p. 115. Interestingly, in *Stage*, p. 29, Hapgood deleted "and the *Times*" from the last quotation.
33. NH, *Stage*, p. 29; NH, "Drama of the Month," *Bookman* 9 (1899): 207–8.
34. Terry to Shaw, Jan. 28, 1900, in *Ellen Terry and Bernard Shaw*, p. 269; *CY*, p. 133; "Theater and the Critic," p. 528; editorial, *New York Dramatic Mirror*, Oct. 26, 1901, p. 14; "A Plan to Dictate 'Criticism,'" *ibid.*, Feb. 23, 1901, p. 8.
35. *CY*, pp. 133, 167; CH I to NH, Aug. 13, 1902, HP.
36. "Great Theatrical Syndicate—III," p. 208.
37. The *Chicago Post* article was reprinted in "Trust Arrogance Rebuked," in *New York Dramatic Mirror*, Nov. 16, 1901, p. 2.
38. *NYCA*, Jan. 10 and 28, Mar. 11, 1898.
39. Winter, *Wallet*, 1:7–8; "The Newspaper and the Theater," p. 12; Henry Austin Clapp, *Reminiscences of a Dramatic Critic, with an Essay on the Art of Henry Irving*, pp. 23–24.
40. NH, "Readings and Reflections," *CW*, Dec. 31, 1904, p. 18.

Chapter 4, Journalism: Immigrants, Toughs, and Criminals

1. Steffens, *Autobiography*, p. 313.
2. *Ibid.*, p. 339.
3. Larzer Ziff, *The American 1890s*, p. 157.
4. Steffens, *Autobiography*, pp. 311–12; Richard Hofstadter, *The Age of Reform*, p. 189; Blanche Houseman Gelfant, *The American City Novel*, p. 17.
5. NBH, [Autobiography], MS, n.d., p. 137, HP.
6. HH to Leslie Hopkinson, Aug. 8, 1895, in NBH and HH, *American Family*, p. 185.
7. Steffens, *Autobiography*, pp. 244, 318; Henry F. May, *The End of American Innocence*, p. 283.
8. HH, *The Spirit of the Ghetto*, p. 244 (unless noted otherwise, all subsequent references to this book are to this edition); HH to NBH, n.d., HP; Moses Rischin, Introduction, HH, *The Spirit of the Ghetto*, John Harvard Library Edition (Cambridge, Mass., 1967), p. vii; Irving Howe, "The Subculture of *Yiddishkeit*," *New York Times Book Review*, Mar. 19, 1967, HP; Ronald Sanders, *The Downtown Jews*, p. 220; Rischin, Introduction, HH, *Ghetto*, p. vii.
9. Rischin, Introduction, HH, *Ghetto*, pp. xxxi, x; idem, "Abraham Cahan and the New York *Commercial Advertiser*," p. 315.
10. HH, *Ghetto*, p. 5.
11. HH to Leslie Hopkinson, July 3, 1894, in NBH and HH, *American Family*, p. 169; Charles Edward Russell, *Bare Hands and Stone Walls*, p. 79.
12. HH, *Ghetto*, p. 110; HH, "The Picturesque Ghetto," *Century*, n.s. 94 (1917):472.
13. HH, *Ghetto*, p. 60.

14. *Ibid.*, pp. 269–70.
15. HH, Preface, *The Spirit of the Ghetto*, rev. ed., n.p.; HH, "Ghetto since Gordin Died," newspaper clipping, n.d., HP.
16. *VMW*, p. 221.
17. Van Wyck Brooks, *The Confident Years, 1885–1915*, p. 132.
18. *VMW*, p. 164.
19. HH, "A Civilized Wanderer;" NBH, [Autobiography], pp. 145, 144; Melville E. Stone, *Fifty Years a Journalist*, p. 61.
20. HH, "Civilized Wanderer;" Josiah Flynt Willard, *Tramping with Tramps*, p. ix; Alfred Hodder, "Josiah Flynt—An Appreciation," in Willard, *My Life*, p. 346.
21. *VMW*, p. 163; Willard, *Tramping with Tramps*, pp. 90, 165.
22. Louis Filler, *Crusaders for American Liberalism*, p. 67; Willard, *The World of Graft*, p. 85.
23. Willard, *The Little Brother*, p. 191; Alfred Hodder, *A Fight for the City*, p. 79.
24. Hodder, *Fight for the City*, p. 135; Steffens, *Autobiography*, p. 325.
25. Mabel Dodge Luhan, *Intimate Memories*, vol. 3, *Movers and Shakers*, p. 45; NBH, [Autobiography], p. 136; NH to NBH, Nov. 24, 1930, HP.
26. *NYCA*, Nov. 17, 1900; HH, *Types from City Streets*, pp. 16–17, 18.
27. Ellery Sedgwick, *The Happy Profession*, p. 135; HH to Arthur F. Bentley, June 1, 1894, HP; *NYG*, May 13, 1913, clipping, HP; HH, *Ghetto*, p. 37.
28. HH, *Types*, p. 50; *VMW*, p. 153; HH, *Types*, p. 19.
29. Shorty, as quoted in Willard, *Tramping with Tramps*, pp. 145–46; Sharkey, as quoted in HH, *Types*, p. 347.
30. *VMW*, p. 115; Connors, as quoted in HH, *Types*, p. 34.
31. HH, "Civilized Wanderer;" HH, *Types*, p. 164; HH, "Poetry and Everyman," *NYG*, n.d., clipping, HP.
32. Stephen Crane, "An Experiment in Misery," in *The University of Virginia Edition of the Works of Stephen Crane*, 8:283–93; NBH, *The Bond*, pp. 178–88.
33. Jacob Riis, *How the Other Half Lives*, p. 207; David M. Fine, "Abraham Cahan, Stephen Crane, and the Romantic Tenement Tale of the Nineties," p. 99.
34. HH to Mabel Dodge, n.d., Mabel Dodge Luhan Papers, Beinecke Rare Book and Manuscript Library, Yale University, New Haven, Conn.; *NYG*, Oct. 14, 1911, clipping, HP; HH, "True Democracy, a Spirit," newspaper clipping, n.d., HP.
35. *VMW*, pp. 33, 326–27.
36. *Ibid.*, p. 126; *NYCA*, Aug. 20, 1898 (emphasis added).
37. Carl Van Vechten, *Peter Whiffle* (New York: Alfred A. Knopf, 1922), p. 116; Christopher Lasch, *The New Radicalism in America, 1889–1963*, pp. xv, 62–64; Harold H. Kolb, Jr., *The Illusion of Life*, p. 136.
38. HH, *Types*, pp. 99, 107, 110–11; HH to NBH, n.d., HP; NBH to Fanny Hapgood, Apr. 1, 1900, HP.
39. NBH, [Diary] (handwritten), June 29, 1903, p. 41, HP.
40. *VMW*, p. 186; HH to Robert Herrick, Aug. 22, 1905, HP.
41. The Butler manuscript, "David," and "Cristine," are in HP.
42. HH, *Thief*, p. 348.
43. *Ibid.*, p. 244; HH, "A New Form of Literature," p. 424.
44. HH, "New Form of Literature," p. 427; HH, *Types*, p. 23; *NYG*, May 13, 1913, clipping, HP.
45. Ray Stannard Baker, *American Chronicle*, p. 179.
46. *VMW*, p. 395.

Chapter 5, *Collier's:* The Early Years

1. NH, "Off Stage," p. 19; *CY*, p. 167.
2. NH, "Books and Plays," *CW*, Nov. 28, 1903, p. 28.
3. HH to Steffens, July 27, 1906, Lincoln Steffens Papers, Columbia University, New York, N.Y.
4. NH, "Books and Plays," *CW*, Dec. 26, 1903, p. 22.
5. *CY*, pp. 174–75; Robert J. Collier, "1879–1909," *CW*, Jan. 2, 1909, p. 13.
6. R. Collier to Theodore Roosevelt, Dec. 31, 1903, Theodore Roosevelt Papers, LC; *In Memoriam*, pp. 17, 19.
7. NH, "Robert J. Collier," p. 331; R. Collier to Peter F. Collier, Oct. 10, 1904, T. Roosevelt Papers; "Advertising Bulletin," *CW*, Jan. 8, 1910, p. 3; Gilson Willets, "The New Home of Collier's Weekly," *CW*, Feb. 22, 1902, p. 7.
8. Cecil Carnes, *Jimmy Hare, News Photographer*, p. 4; Willets, "New Home of Collier's," p. 7.
9. Collier's Weekly, Memorandum Book, 1905–10, LC.
10. *CY*, p. 168; Mark Sullivan, *The Education of an American*, p. 229.
11. As quoted in Zona Gale, "Editors of the Younger Generation," p. 325; Charles Hanson Towne, *Adventures in Editing*, p. 78.
12. *CY*, p. 167; R. Collier to Finley Peter Dunne, n.d., Finley Peter Dunne Papers, LC; T. Roosevelt to R. Collier, Dec. 31, 1903, T. Roosevelt Papers; Elmer Ellis, *Mr. Dooley's America*, p. 187.
13. *CY*, p. 167.
14. Heading to editorials, *HI* 46 (Oct. 1924), 8–9.
15. Arthur H. Gleason, "Norman Hapgood," p. 460.
16. NH to Emma Hapgood, Sept. 27, 1891, HP; NH, "I've Made Up My Mind," *HI* 46 (Oct. 1924), 102; HH to Fanny Hapgood, Nov. 8, 1888, HP; NH to Emma Hapgood, Oct. 15, 1892, HP; George E. Mowry, *The Era of Theodore Roosevelt*, p. 87.
17. Editorial, *CW*, Nov. 14, 1903, p. 4.
18. NH, "Mr. Gladstone," pp. 48, 46; Hofstadter, *Age of Reform*, pp. 167–68; Robert Morss Lovett, "Two Intellectuals," p. 350; NH, "Readings and Reflections," *CW*, Dec. 31, 1904, p. 18.
19. Review of NH's *Abraham Lincoln*, p. 779.
20. NH, "Books and Plays," *CW*, June 25, 1904, p. 18.
21. NH to Leslie Hopkinson, Jan. 11, 1898, HP; *VMW*, pp. 128, 146. The chaise longue in the Hapgoods' second-floor living room was placed at such an angle as to imply receiving an audience. See *Architectural Record* 18 (1905): frontispiece.
22. "The Week," p. 56; *Oxford Companion to the Theatre*, s.v. "Negro in the American Theatre"; HH to CH I, Aug. 26, 1915, HP.
23. *Springfield* (Mass.) *Republican*, June 21, 1908; "House of Mr. Norman Hapgood," pp. 8–13.
24. T. Roosevelt to P. Collier, Sept. 28 and Oct. 1, 1904; R. Collier to P. Collier, Oct. 10, 1904; T. Roosevelt to P. Collier, Oct. 13, 1904. All are in T. Roosevelt Papers.
25. Editorial, *CW*, Oct. 1, 1904, p. 8; T. Roosevelt to Eugene A. Philbin, Sept. 30, 1904, T. Roosevelt Papers.
26. T. Roosevelt to Lodge, Sept. 12, 1906, in Henry Cabot Lodge, ed., *Selections from the Correspondence of Theodore Roosevelt and Henry Cabot Lodge*, 2:231; NH to Sullivan, Oct. 23, 1906, as quoted in Edward LaRue Weldon, "Mark Sullivan's Progressive Journalism, 1874–1925: An Ironic Persuasion," Diss. Emory 1970, p. 52.

Chapter 6, The Journalism of Controversy

1. NH, "Editorial Talks," *CW*, Apr. 22, 1905, p. 25; Russell, *Bare Hands*, pp. 143-44.
2. *Indianapolis Star*, as quoted in editorial, *CW*, Oct. 5, 1907, p. 10; Finley Peter Dunne, "Mr. Dooley on National Housecleaning," *CW*, Dec. 16, 1905, p. 12; Upton Sinclair, *The Brass Check*, p. 29.
3. L. L. Seaman and Upton Sinclair, "Is Chicago Meat Clean?" *CW*, Apr. 22, 1905, p. 14; editorial, *CW*, Apr. 22, 1905, p. 9; Sinclair, *Brass Check*, pp. 24-25.
4. Sinclair, *Brass Check*, p. 30.
5. T. Roosevelt to Charles F. Stokes, Sept. 4, 1906, T. Roosevelt Papers.
6. Filler, *Crusaders for Liberalism*, p. 165; *CY*, pp. 170-71.
7. Robert R. Rowe, "Mann of Town Topics," p. 276; Burgess Johnson, *As Much as I Dare*, pp. 82-83.
8. Editorial, *CW*, Nov. 5, 1904, p. 9; *New York Times*, Jan. 26, 1906, p. 1.
9. Editorial, *CW*, Aug. 5, 1905, p. 6.
10. As quoted in *New York Times*, Jan. 26, 1906, p. 2.
11. *New York American*, Jan. 27, 1906.
12. Ibid., Jan. 25, 1906; *New York Times*, Jan. 27, 1906, p. 2; Samuel Clemens to NH, Sept. 15, 1905, Elizabeth Backman Papers, in her possession, Royalston, Mass.
13. Editorial, *CW*, Dec. 17, 1910, p. 7; Sullivan to T. Roosevelt, Dec. 30, 1910, T. Roosevelt Papers; *New York Times*, Feb. 24, 1906, p. 16, and Jan. 4, 1914, p. 11.
14. "Chronicle and Comment," *Bookman* 23 (1906):122.
15. Andy Logan, *The Man Who Robbed the Robber Barons*, p. 239; editorial, *CW*, Dec. 28, 1907, p. 5.
16. *New York American*, Jan. 27, 1906.
17. *New York Times*, Jan. 28, 1906, p. 2; Rowe, "Mann of Town Topics," p. 278; Hamilton Holt, *Commercialism and Journalism*, pp. 76-77; Logan, *Robber Barons*, p. 238; Sinclair, *Brass Check*, pp. 250, 252.
18. Jerome, as quoted in *New York American*, Jan. 29, 1906.
19. Editorial, *CW*, Jan. 4, 1908, p. 5.
20. Bok, *The Americanization of Edward Bok*, p. 344; Sullivan, *Education*, p. 191; Weldon, "Mark Sullivan's Progressive Journalism," p. 45n.
21. Filler, *Crusaders for Liberalism*, p. 152; "Aftermath," *CW*, Jan. 5, 1907, p. 11.
22. James Harvey Young, *The Medical Messiahs*, pp. 25, 28-30.
23. NH, "Criminal Newspaper Alliances with Fraud and Poison," *CW*, July 8, 1905, p. 22; editorial, *CW*, Apr. 22, 1905, p. 9.
24. Young, *Medical Messiahs*, p. 34; editorial, *CW*, June 17, 1911, p. 7; Young, *Medical Messiahs*, pp. 45-47, 55-57.
25. "Aftermath," p. 11; Judson Grenier, "Upton Sinclair and the Press," p. 430; Oscar E. Anderson, Jr., *The Health of a Nation*, p. 173; Filler, *Crusaders for Liberalism*, pp. 153-55.
26. "Editorial Bulletin," *CW*, Nov. 4, 1905, p. 26; John Adams Thayer, *Astir*, pp. 88-89; "The Idea Back of Collier's," *CW*, Jan. 2, 1909, p. 15.
27. Editorial, *CW*, June 30, 1906, p. 7; Sullivan to T. Roosevelt, Jan. 7, 1911, T. Roosevelt Papers; James Playsted Wood, *The Story of Advertising*, pp. 325-44; "Freedom of Advertising," pp. 951-52; "Idea Back of Collier's," p. 15.
28. Editorial, *CW*, Apr. 28, 1906, p. 10; T. Roosevelt to William Howard Taft, Mar. 15, 1906, in *The Letters of Theodore Roosevelt*, 5:183-84.

29. Gale, "Editors of the Younger Generation," p. 331.
30. *VMW*, p. 13; Harold S. Wilson, *McClure's Magazine and the Muckrakers*, p. 200; Russell, *Bare Hands*, opp. p. 140.
31. Sullivan to T. Roosevelt, Sept. 11, 1908, Mark Sullivan Papers, LC; editorial, *CW*, Oct. 31, 1908, p. 9; Donald F. Anderson, *William Howard Taft*, pp. 54–56.
32. Sullivan to Dunne, n.d., Dunne Papers; Taft to R. Collier, Mar. 13, 1909, William Howard Taft Papers, LC.
33. James R. Garfield, Diary, Sept. 21, 1909, James R. Garfield Papers, LC; editorial, *CW*, Aug. 28, 1909, p. 7.
34. NH, as quoted in U.S., Congress, Senate, Committee on the Judiciary, *The Nomination of Louis D. Brandeis to Be an Associate Justice of the Supreme Court of the United States, Hearings*, p. 455; George E. Mowry, *Theodore Roosevelt and the Progressive Movement*, p. 78.
35. James Penick, Jr., *Progressive Politics and Conservation*, pp. 139–40; *Columbus* (Ohio) *State Journal*, Mar. 8, 1911, clipping, Gifford Pinchot Papers, LC; Committee on Judiciary, *Nomination of Brandeis*, pp. 459, 455.
36. Editorial, *CW*, Feb. 5, 1910, p. 9; *ibid.*, Apr. 2, 1910, p. 9; *ibid.*, May 7, 1910, p. 7; Sullivan to LB, June 6, 1910, BP.
37. Alpheus Thomas Mason, *Brandeis*, p. 280; Mowry, *Era of Theodore Roosevelt*, p. 258.
38. Holt, *Commercialism and Journalism*, p. 97; Melvin I. Urofsky, *A Mind of One Piece*, pp. 166–67.
39. R. Collier to T. Roosevelt, Nov. 27, 1908, T. Roosevelt Papers; Sullivan to LB, Sept. 25, 1909, BP.
40. R. Collier to LB, Jan. 27, 1910, BP; "Editorial Bulletin," *CW*, Nov. 6, 1909, p. 7 (emphasis added); NH to Philip P. Wells, Apr. 6, 1910, BP; editorial, *CW*, Aug. 20, 1910, p. 9.
41. Frank Luther Mott, *A History of American Magazines*, 4:59; Katharine Buell Wilder, "Symbol for All That Is Tolerant," *Christian Register*, June 10, 1937, p. 383; William Kittle, "Is Your Magazine Progressive?" p. 7; McKelway to W. B. Blake, Oct. 9, 1916, A. J. McKelway Papers, LC; Sullivan, *Education*, p. 219; Will Irwin, *The Making of a Reporter*, p. 156; C. C. Regier, *The Era of the Muckrakers*, p. 115.
42. NH to Leslie Hopkinson, Sept. 3, 1914, BP; "Idea Back of Collier's," p. 15; editorial, *CW*, Sept. 26, 1908, p. 9.
43. Editorial, *CW*, May 13, 1911, p. 13.
44. T. Roosevelt to R. Collier, July 14, 1908, T. Roosevelt Papers; editorial, *CW*, June 22, 1912, p. 8; Arthur S. Link, *Wilson*, vol. 1, *The Road to the White House*, p. 401.
45. George Rublee to LB, July 18, 1912, BP; *CY*, pp. 214–15; LB to NH, July 3, 1912, BP; LB to Alfred Brandeis, July 14, 1912, BP.
46. NH to CH I, July 22, 1912, HP; editorial, *CW*, Aug. 24, 1912, p. 8; *ibid.* (a second editorial); NH to Baker, Sept. 4, 1912, Ray Stannard Baker Papers, LC.
47. As quoted in *New York Evening Post*, Oct. 19, 1912, p. 2.
48. R. Collier to LB, Mar. 2, 1910, BP; Irwin, "Synopsis of the Making of a Reporter," MS, n.d., Will Irwin Papers, Hoover Institution on War, Revolution and Peace, Stanford University, Stanford, Calif.; Sullivan, *Education*, pp. 295–97; Dunne to Robert Hamill, Sept. 17, 1919, in Ellis, *Mr. Dooley's America*, pp. 254–55; Frederick L. Collins to NH, Apr. 9, 1913, BP; [C. J. Post] to Sinclair, n.d., in Sinclair, *Brass Check*, p. 44. The *Weekly's* apparent failure to pursue a suit against the Postum Cereal Company might also have indicated financial stringency.
49. NH to LB, Oct. 30, 1912, BP.
50. Sullivan, *Education*, p. 236.

51. *Ibid.*, p. 304; Sullivan to T. Roosevelt, Oct. 25, 1912, T. Roosevelt Papers.
52. *New York Times*, Oct. 20, 1912, p. 15.
53. Editorial, *Springfield* (Mass.) *Republican*, Oct. 20, 1912; J. Russell Smith to LB, Jan. 6, 1914, BP.
54. R. Collier to LB, Nov. 12, 1912, BP; LB to NH, Nov. 14, 1912, BP.

Chapter 7, Wilson Partisan

1. *NYCA*, Aug. 20, 1898.
2. Edwin R. Lewinson, *John Purroy Mitchel*, p. 235.
3. As quoted in *New York American*, Oct. 20, 1912; NH to LB, Oct. 27, 1912, BP.
4. NH to LB, Oct. 27 and 23, 1912, BP; C. M. Francis, "The Fighting Magazines," p. 474; NH to LB, Oct. 23, 1912, BP.
5. NH to LB, Oct. 27 and Nov. 7, 1912, Mar. 12 and Apr. 16, 1913. All are in BP.
6. *Ibid.*, Nov. 7, 1912, BP; "To the Stockholders of the Harper's Weekly Corporation," Sept. 1, 1914, Charles R. Crane Papers, Archive of Russian and East European History and Culture, Columbia University, New York, N.Y.
7. Editorial, *HW*, Aug. 16, 1913, p. 3.
8. *Ibid.*, Sept. 20, 1913, p. 5.
9. Arthur S. Link, *Woodrow Wilson and the Progressive Era*, p. 289.
10. Editorial, *HW*, July 11, 1914, p. 25; NH to McKelway, Dec. 22, 1913, McKelway Papers; Littell, "Norman Hapgood," p. 15; NH to Howard D. Wheeler, Jan. 6, 1915, McKelway Papers; McKelway to Wilson, Feb. 5, 1914, McKelway Papers; Alvin Johnson, *Pioneer's Progress*, pp. 232–33.
11. *CY*, p. 225; Crane to Wilson, May 23, 1913, Woodrow Wilson Papers, LC; Mason, *Brandeis*, p. 527.
12. NH, *Norman Hapgood's Weekly Letter*, Oct. 30, 1928, n.p.; NH to Wilson, Apr. 7, 1915, Wilson Papers.
13. Editorial, *HW*, Aug. 16, 1913, p. 3.
14. NH, "Juggling Consciences," p. 187.
15. NH to E. W. Scripps, Dec. 11, 1913, BP.
16. LB to Walter S. Rogers, Dec. 8, [1913], BP; *New York Times*, May 19, 1913, p. 9; NH to White, Feb. 2, 1914, William Allen White Papers, LC.
17. NH to Cleveland Dodge, Jan. 12, 1914, BP; NH to Crane, Jan. 15, 1914, BP; William Kent to NH, June 16, 1914, William Kent Family Papers, Sterling Memorial Library, Yale University.
18. NH to Scripps, July 12, 1914, BP; H. W. Paine to NH, Sept. 23, 1913, BP.
19. NH to C. Dodge, Jan. 23, 1914, BP; Crane to Joseph Tumulty, Sept. 17, 1914, Wilson Papers; Robert C. Bannister, Jr., *Ray Stannard Baker*, pp. 147, 168–69, 173.
20. NH to C. Dodge, Jan. 12, 1914; Harper's Weekly Corporation, Statement for Twelve Months Ending Aug. 31, 1915; E. F. Chase to Rogers, Sept. 2, 1915. All are in BP.
21. NH to Scripps, Dec. 11, 1913, BP; Chase to Rogers, Jan. 12, 1915, BP.
22. Wheeler to McKelway, May 25, 1915, McKelway Papers; NH to LB, July 7, 1915, BP; McKelway to Wheeler, Sept. 3, 1914, McKelway Papers.
23. [NH] to McKelway, Nov. 5, 1914, McKelway Papers; NH to Hopkinson, Sept. 13, 1914, BP; NH to LB, Dec. 13, 1913, BP.

24. Emory R. Buckner to LB, Oct. 23 and Nov. 12, 1915, July 15, 1916. All are in BP.
25. NH to LB, May 12, 1916, BP.
26. *Ibid.*, Apr. 7, 1916, BP; NH to House, Nov. 9, [1915], Edward M. House Papers, Sterling Memorial Library, Yale University; Chase to Rogers, Feb. 1, 1916, BP.
27. Sinclair, *Brass Check*, pp. 290, 229–31, 291; Dunne to Hamill, Sept. 17, 1919, in Ellis, *Mr. Dooley's America*, pp. 254–55.
28. Sinclair, *Brass Check*, p. 230; Filler, *Crusaders for Liberalism*, p. 363; NH to LB, Oct. 27, 1912, and May 12, 1913, BP; Sinclair, *Brass Check*, p. 290.
29. Robert S. Maxwell, "A Note on the Muckrakers," pp. 55–60.
30. Emilie Hapgood to LB, [Apr.] 23, 1916, BP.
31. NH to Wilson, Nov. 6, 1916, Wilson Papers; *CY*, p. 242.
32. DeWitt, interview.
33. Editorial, *CW*, Oct. 24, 1908, p. 5.
34. Editorial, *HW*, Aug. 15, 1914, p. 145; cover, *ibid.*, Oct. 3. 1914; editorials, *ibid.*, Sept. 5, 1914, p. 217.
35. Robert H. Wiebe, *The Search for Order, 1877–1920*, p. 237; NH, "The Prussian Menace," *HW*, Sept. 19, 1914, p. 274; editorial, *ibid.*, Sept. 5, 1914, p. 218; Christopher Lasch, *The American Liberals and the Russian Revolution*, p. 213.
36. House, Diary, Feb. 7, 1919, House Papers; NH to House, Nov. 19, 1916, June 4, 1918, House Papers; Frank Polk to Robert Lansing, Mar. 7, 1919, Robert Lansing Papers, LC; Wilson to Lansing, Mar. 22, 1919, Lansing Papers.
37. Lasch, *American Liberals*, p. 147.
38. NH to Wilson, Aug. 9, 1919, Wilson Papers; Lasch, *American Liberals*, p. 127.
39. Breckinridge Long, Diary, Aug. 11, 1919, Breckinridge Long Papers, LC; NH to Lansing, Aug. 21, 1919, General Records of the Department of State, Record Group 59, National Archives and Records Service, Washington, D.C.; Long, Diary, Aug. 23, 1919, Long Papers; Long to Lansing, memorandum, Aug. 25, 1919, Long Papers.
40. Alvey A. Adee to Long, Aug. 28, 1919, RG 59, National Archives; NH to Wilson, Sept. 2, 1919, Wilson Papers; William Phillips to Lansing, Sept. 10, 1919, Lansing Papers; Lansing to Lodge, Sept. 28, 1919, Long Papers; Lodge to Lansing, Sept. 30, 1919, Long Papers.
41. "Minister Hapgood Returns," p. 6; "Hapgood," pp. 2–5; *New York Times*, Dec. 30, 1919, p. 12.
42. NH to LB, Apr. 9, 1919, BP; NH to Willis Booth, Apr. 9, 1919, Long Papers.
43. NH, "More Brains, Good Lord," p. 19; editorial, *HI* 46 (July 1924), 8.
44. Editorial, *HI* 44 (July 1923), 10; John M. Thompson, *Russia, Bolshevism, and the Versailles Peace*, pp. 361–62.
45. NH, "Foreign Issues in the Presidential Campaign," p. 418.

Chapter 8, From Labor to Emotional Crisis

1. *NYG*, May 7, 1912.
2. HH to NBH, [1904 or 1905], HP.
3. HH, *An Anarchist Woman*, p. 297.
4. HH, "A Marionette," p. 10.
5. *VMW*, p. 581.

Notes to Pages 144 to 160   235

6. William Stott, *Documentary Expression in Thirties America*, pp. 190–210; HH to Terry Carlin, Mar. 31, 1914, HP; Arthur and Barbara Gelb, *O'Neill*, p. 287; W. A. Swanberg, *Dreiser*, p. 200; HH to P. Hapgood, Feb. 4, 1929, Powers Hapgood Papers, Lilly Library, Indiana University.

7. HH, "David," pp. 11, 48, 89, 119, 196–97, MS, HP; *VMW*, pp. 215–17; David Edstrom, *The Testament of Caliban*, pp. 227–32, 234, 242–43; James R. Mellow, *Charmed Circle*, pp. 134–36; Gertrude Stein, "Men," in *Two*, pp. 310–15.

8. NBH to HH, [1905], HP.

9. Robert P. Falk, "The Literary Criticism of the Genteel Decades, 1870–1900," in Floyd Stovall, ed., *The Development of American Literary Criticism*, pp. 152–53; Kolb, *Illusion of Life*, pp. 40, 42–43, 143.

10. HH to Emma Hapgood, Dec. 25, [1907], HP.

11. HH to NBH, May 1, 1909, HP; *ibid.*, n.d., HP; HH to Lovett, [Jan. 15, 1909], HP.

12. *VMW*, p. 285.

13. Jane Addams, "Ethical Survivals in Municipal Corruption," p. 277; Sloan, Diary, Apr. 15, 1909, in Bruce St. John, *John Sloan*, p. 37.

14. *NYG*, Mar. 5, 1912; HH, "Motion Picture Censorship," *NYG*, n.d., clipping, HP; [HH], "Love at First Sight," newspaper editorial, n.d., clipping, HP.

15. HH, *Labor*, p. 369; HH to Steffens, Nov. 4, 1908, Steffens Papers; *NYG*, Apr. 26, 1912; Walter Lippmann, *A Preface to Politics*, pp. 4–8.

16. Editorial, *NYG*, [Nov. 11, 1912], clipping, HP; *NYG*, Oct. 3, 1912; [HH], editorial, *ibid.*, [1912], clipping, HP; *NYG*, Oct. 3, 1912; Lasch, *American Liberals*, p. 167.

17. *NYG*, July 5 and Sept. 27, 1912.

18. HH, "Why Tammany Hall Remains," *NYG*, n.d., clipping, HP; HH, *Types*, pp. 56–59, 62.

19. *NYG*, July 18, 1912.

20. HH, letter to editor, *New York Times*, Aug. 27, 1913, HP.

21. *NYG*, July 13 and Nov. 6, 1912.

22. HH, "The M'Namaras and the News," newspaper clipping, n.d., HP; *NYG*, Feb. 21, 1913.

23. *NYG*, Jan. 27, 1913.

24. Whitlock to Octavia Roberts, Mar. 5, 1910, in Brand Whitlock, *The Letters and Journal of Brand Whitlock*, 1:132; Luhan, *Intimate Memories*, 3:45; NBH to CH II, Jan. 4, no year, HP; Robert Morss Lovett, "The Victorian Set Free," p. 307; Luhan, *Intimate Memories*, 3:47; Beatrix Faust, interview, Richmond, N.H., Nov. 18, 1974.

25. Baker, Diary, Dec. 5, 1913, Baker Papers.

26. *VMW*, p. 348; HH, *Labor*, pp. 394–95.

27. [HH], *Lover*, p. 54; HH to M. Dodge, Mar. 14, 1914, Luhan Papers; HH, "The Trend of the Time," *NYG*, n.d., clipping, HP; *VMW*, p. 394.

28. NBH, [Autobiography], p. 151; Baker, Diary, Dec. 5, 1913, Baker Papers; L. Stein to Mabel Weeks, Aug. 12, 1910, in Leo Stein, *Journey into the Self*, p. 40.

29. Max Eastman, *Enjoyment of Living*, p. 525; Luhan, *Intimate Memories*, 3:48.

30. NBH, *Harry*, p. 44; HH to NBH, Mar. 25, 1917, HP.

31. NBH, [Autobiography], pp. 51a, 10; NBH to HH, June 19, 1898, HP; DeWitt, interview.

32. NBH, [Diary], June 20, 1903, HP.

33. *Ibid.*, June 22, 1903, HP.

34. HH, *Labor*, p. 396; [HH], *Lover*, p. 107.

35. NBH to HH, May 16, [1916], HP; Faust, interview; NBH to M. Dodge, Oct. 8, no year, HP; CH II, interview, Richmond, N.H., Nov. 18, 1974; NBH to M. Dodge, [Jan. 1916], Luhan Papers.
36. *VMW*, p. 117; HH, *Anarchist Woman*, p. 224; DeWitt, interview.
37. HH to Steffens, Feb. 22, 1909, Steffens Papers; *VMW*, p. 259; HH to Alfred Stieglitz, Aug. 30, 1912, Alfred Stieglitz Papers, Beinecke Rare Book and Manuscript Library, Yale University.
38. *VMW*, p. 407.
39. *Ibid.*, p. 400; HH, "Cristine," p. 157; *VMW*, p. 392; NBH to CH I, Oct. 20, 1913, HP.
40. HH to M. Dodge, Oct. 31, 1915, Luhan Papers; HH to Stieglitz, Nov. 7, 1920, Stieglitz Papers; *VMW*, p. 434; NBH to Steffens, Jan. 8, [1919], Steffens Papers.
41. HH to Luhan, Oct. 12, [1936], Luhan Papers; *VMW*, p. 410; [HH], *Lover*, pp. 16, 130.
42. NBH and HH, *Enemies*, p. 130.
43. See Alfred Kreymborg, *Troubadour*, p. 307.

Chapter 9, The Columbia Conserve Company

1. WPH, *An Experiment in Industrial Democracy* (1930), p. 3; HH to Leslie Hopkinson, Aug. 8, 1895, in NBH and HH, *American Family*, p. 185; NH, "Norman Hapgood's Page," *Leslie's Weekly*, Apr. 20, 1918, p. 539.
2. WPH to Emma Hapgood, Apr. 28, [1895], P. Hapgood Papers.
3. WPH to HH, Jan. 27, 1924, HP; CH I to NH, Jan. 18, 1911, HP.
4. WPH, *Experiment* (1930), p. 5; Russell E. Vance, Jr., "An Unsuccessful Experiment in Industrial Democracy: The Columbia Conserve Company," Diss. Indiana 1956, pp. 34, 38.
5. WPH, *Experiment* (1930), p. 3; Vance, "Unsuccessful Experiment," p. 42.
6. WPH, *Experiment* (1930), p. 4.
7. *VMW*, p. 259; NH to LB, Apr. 10, 1913, BP; Luhan, *Intimate Memories*, 3:56.
8. Vance, "Unsuccessful Experiment," p. 44.
9. WPH, "The High Adventure of a Cannery," p. 682; Vance, "Unsuccessful Experiment," p. 58.
10. Paul H. Douglas, *The Columbia Conserve Company*, pp. 21, 22; WPH, "High Adventure," p. 657.
11. WPH, *Experiment* (1930), p. 28.
12. Council Minutes, Jan. 21 and Feb. 1, 1935, CP.
13. WPH, "Canning," p. 44; WPH, *Experiment* (1930), p. 19.
14. Vance, "Unsuccessful Experiment," p. 69; United States, Department of Labor, Women's Bureau, *Application of Labor Legislation to the Fruit and Vegetable Canning and Preserving Industries*, pp. 112, 46.
15. WPH, *An Experiment in Industrial Democracy* (1931), p. 36.
16. Douglas, *Columbia*, p. 6; Council Minutes, Dec. 18, 1925, CP; Scrapbooks, CP; WPH, *Experiment* (1931), p. 43.
17. Report of Secretary, National Canners Association, *Fourteenth Annual Convention*, p. 3; Annual Stockholders' Meeting, Jan. 6, 1920, CP.
18. Common Council Minutes, May 15, 1931, CP; "Summary of Important Factors

in the Progress of the Columbia Conserve Company Since January 1934, and to March 1939," MS, Mar. 1, 1939, CP.

19. WPH to LB, Aug. 27, 1931, BP.
20. Council Minutes, Feb. 3, 1932, CP.
21. Annual Council Meeting, July 15, 1932, CP.
22. Council Minutes, July 15, 1932, CP; NH to LB, Aug. 17, 1931, BP; *CY,* p. 290.
23. P. Hapgood to Eleanor Hapgood, Nov. 18, [1917], P. Hapgood Papers.
24. Label, in WPH, *An Experiment in Industrial Democracy* (1932), n.p.
25. Council Minutes, Dec. 29, 1932, CP.
26. *Ibid.,* Jan. 4, 1933, CP.
27. *Ibid.,* Jan. 6, 1933, CP.
28. NH to LB, Apr. 11 and June 9, 1933, BP.
29. WPH, *The Columbia Conserve Company,* p. 93; Council Minutes, May 8, 1933, CP.
30. WPH, *Columbia Conserve,* p. iii.
31. WPH, "Supplementary Chapter to the Booklet 'The Columbia Conserve Company—An Experiment in Workers' Management and Ownership,' " MS, Mar. 1, 1941, CP.
32. Vance, "Unsuccessful Experiment," p. 295.
33. Douglas, *Columbia,* p. 53; W. Jett Lauck, *Political and Industrial Democracy, 1776–1926,* p. 286; C. Canby Balderston, *Executive Guidance of Industrial Relations,* p. 308; Emma Bellamy to NH, Feb. 7, 1934, Backman Papers.
34. Council Minutes, Dec. 1, 1939, CP.
35. WPH, *Experiment* (1930), pp. 13, 12.
36. On the antitrusters see Ellis W. Hawley, *The New Deal and the Problem of Monopoly,* pp. 201–3.
37. Douglas, *Columbia,* p. 56; Common Council Minutes, Dec. 23, 1929, CP; NH to LB, Sept. 5, 1932, BP.
38. Lauck, *Political and Industrial Democracy,* p. 344; WPH to LB, Nov. 24, 1930, HP.
39. HH to WPH, Nov. 28, 1933, in WPH, *Columbia Conserve,* p. 184.

Chapter 10, Final Years

1. NH to LB, Jan. 8, [1920], BP; NH, "Readings and Reflections," *CW,* Jan. 28, 1905, p. 18; editorial, *ibid.,* June 22, 1912, p. 9; *ibid.,* Apr. 9, 1904, p. 4; editorial, *HW,* May 2, 1914, p. 3.
2. Oswald Garrison Villard, "William Randolph Hearst and His Moral Press," p. 360; *CY,* p. 260.
3. NH to House, July 14, 1918, House Papers; NH to LB, June 22, 1920, BP.
4. NH to White, Apr. 5, 1922, White Papers; NH to Baker, June 20, 1922, Baker Papers.
5. Editorial, *HI* 45 (May 1924), 8; *CY,* pp. 181-82; Paul de Kruif, *The Sweeping Wind,* p. 53.
6. *CY,* p. 280.
7. NH and Henry Moskowitz, *Up from the City Streets* (1927); NH to Franklin D. Roosevelt, Feb. 20, 1936, President's Personal File, Franklin D. Roosevelt Library, Hyde Park, N.Y.; Hawley, *New Deal and Monopoly,* p. 290.
8. NH to "Bob," Dec. 3, 1927, HP; Hopkinson, "An Eager, Serviceable Citizen," p. 384; Elizabeth Backman, interview, Royalston, Mass., Nov. 29, 1974.

9. Elizabeth, Norman's widow, died in 1974.
10. Henry Himmell [?] to HH, Dec. 20, 1932, HP; HH, "Is Dreiser Anti-Semitic?" p. 436.
11. HH to Stieglitz, Sept. 19, 1921, Stieglitz Papers; HH to Luhan, Jan. 8, 1937, Luhan Papers.
12. HH to M. Dodge, Nov. 9, no year, Luhan Papers; Luhan, *Intimate Memories*, 3: 367–68.
13. HH to Luhan, Oct. 12, [1926], Luhan Papers; HH to Stieglitz, Apr. 19, [1925?], Stieglitz Papers; HH, as quoted in Luhan, *Intimate Memories*, 3:273.
14. HH to Stieglitz, June 17, 1937 (copy), HP.
15. HH to Luhan, Apr. 15, 1940, Luhan Papers; *VMW*, pp. 469–70, 503–4.
16. HH, fragment, [Diary], Jan. 11, 1927; HH, [Diary], Feb. 2 and 19, 1927. All are in HP.
17. HH, fragment, [Diary], Jan. 11, 1927, HP; HH to NBH, Apr. 3, 1927, HP.
18. *VMW*, p. 524 (emphasis added); Editors of *Consumer Reports*, *The Medicine Show*, p. 52.
19. HH to CH II, Dec. 12, 1929; HH to NBH, Apr. 27, 1930; HH to CH II, Dec. 12, 1929. All are in HP.
20. HH to Steffens, June 11, 1925, Steffens Papers; Theodore Dreiser, "Esther Norn," in Dreiser, *A Gallery of Women*, 2 vols. (New York: Horace Liveright, 1929), 2:759.
21. Cowles to Bentley, July 1954, DeWitt Papers; CH I to NBH and HH, Mar. 12, 1912, HP; DeWitt, interview.
22. HH to WPH, July 20, no year, HP.
23. HH to Frances Perkins, Jan. 4, 1934, HP.
24. HH to Luhan, Nov. 8, 1938, Luhan Papers.
25. Luhan, *Intimate Memories*, 3:51; NH to HH, Dec. 27, 1930, HP. Earlier autobiographical efforts, all in HP, included: "[Autobiographical] Notes," MS, July 3, 1903; "A Homeric Effort in Illinois," MS, n.d.; "Sydney West," MS, n.d.
26. L. Stein to Maurice Sterne, [1939?], in Stein, *Journey into the Self*, p. 176; Luhan to HH, n.d., HP; NBH and HH, "The Primrose Path," MS, n.d., HP; [F. Howe] to HH, Nov. 8, 1938, HP.
27. HH to Luhan, Nov. 10, 1938, Luhan Papers; Ridgely Torrence to HH, Mar. 31, 1940, HP.
28. L. Stein to HH, n.d., HP.
29. John P. Marquand, *The Late George Apley* (Boston: Little, Brown, 1937), p. 1.
30. HH to Luhan, Mar. 16, [1937], Luhan Papers.
31. Lovett, "Victorian Set Free," p. 307; Wright Houghland to HH, Dec. 6, 1939, HP.
32. Van Vechten to HH, Dec. 13, 1939, Carl Van Vechten Papers, Beinecke Rare Book and Manuscript Library, Yale University; Berenson to HH, Dec. 25, 1939, HP; Lasch, *New Radicalism*, p. 107; Mitchell Kennerley to HH, Nov. 17, 1939, HP; HH to Mowry Saben, Sept. 17, 1940, HP; Albert Parry, *Garrets and Pretenders*, pp. xi–xiv.
33. WPH to NH, Dec. 19, 1936, HP.
34. WPH to HH, May 25, 1940, HP; Annual Stockholders' Meeting, July 18, 1941, CP.
35. Annual Council Meeting, July 24, 1942, CP; WPH to Elizabeth Hapgood, Sept. 8, 1942, HP.
36. WPH, "To Our Stockholders," MS, Mar. 29, 1943, CP.

Notes to Pages 206 to 221   239

37. WPH, "To the Stockholders of the Columbia Conserve Company," MS, Sept. 30, 1943, CP; Vance, "Unsuccessful Experiment," p. 345.
38. HH to WPH, July 20, 1942, HP; Vance, "Unsuccessful Experiment," p. 363; *Alton (Ill.) Evening Telegraph*, Aug. 22, 1960, clipping, DeWitt Papers.

Chapter 11, Conclusion

1. HH to NBH, [1905], (emphasis added), Aug. 2, 1913, Jan. 29, 1918, HP; NH to HH, Jan. 29, 1931, HP.
2. NBH to HH, [1905?], HP; HH, "On Respectability," MS, n.d., HP; HH to CH II, Nov. 8, 1929, HP; *VMW*, p. 128.
3. HH, "My Forty Years of Drink," p. 2.
4. NBH to HH, n.d., HP; WPH, as quoted in P. Hapgood to Eleanor Hapgood, Nov. 12, [1927], P. Hapgood Papers; WPH to DeWitt, Dec. 9, 1954, DeWitt Papers.
5. HH to Stieglitz, Sept. 21, 1921, Stieglitz Papers; HH to NBH, Mar. 10, 1927, HP; [Mary Hapgood] to HH, Jan. 29, 1935, HP; P. Hapgood to NH, Feb. 4, 1929, HP.
6. HH to P. Hapgood, Mar. 28, 1944, P. Hapgood Papers; WPH to HH, Oct. 26, 1943, P. Hapgood Papers; WPH to NBH, Nov. 28, 1944, HP; NBH to WPH, Mar. 27, 1945, HP.
7. DeWitt, Faust, CH II, interviews.
8. Sedgwick, *Happy Profession*, p. 126; Luhan, *Intimate Memories*, 3:56; NBH to HH, n.d., HP; NH, as quoted in Luhan, *Intimate Memories*, 3:57.
9. HH to Luhan, May 21, 1937, Luhan Papers.
10. HH to NBH, n.d., HP; Lasch, *New Radicalism*, pp. xiv–xv; May, *End of American Innocence*, p. 296; *New York Times*, Feb. 23, 1920, p. 12.
11. Editorial, *Christian Register*, May 27, 1937, p. 350; HH to F. Roosevelt, Dec. 2, 1940 (copy), HP; HH to [Lovett?], Oct. 1, 1940, HP; NBH to "Katrina," Aug. 18, [1940], HP.
12. CH I to CH II, Sept. 6, 1916, HP; HH to NBH, [1899], HP. Charles Hapgood's advice to his grandson was probably wise; he became a historian.
13. CH I, "Reminiscences," pp. 157–58.
14. Editorial, *HW*, Sept. 5, 1914, p. 223; *New York American*, Sept. 28, 1921.
15. HH, "My Forty Years of Drink," p. 2; NBH to CH I, Mar. 10, 1912, HP; editorial, *Christian Register*, Jan. 7, 1937, p. 2; *VMW*, p. 541; Faust, interview.
16. Houghton, *Victorian Frame of Mind*, pp. 220–21.
17. HH to Luhan, May 21, 1937, Luhan Papers.
18. WPH, *Experiment* (1930), pp. 10, 18.
19. P. Hapgood to Eleanor Hapgood and WPH, Jan. 27, 1918, P. Hapgood Papers.
20. HH, "What 291 Is to Me," *Camera Work*, no. 47 (1914), p. 11; L. Stein to M. Dodge, n.d., in Stein, *Journey into the Self*, p. 119; *NYG*, [Jan. 29, 1913], clipping, HP; Berenson to NBH, Mar. 19, 1946, HP.
21. NBH, as quoted in DeWitt, interview; HH to DeWitt, Dec. 2, [1943?], DeWitt Papers; HH, "Husbands and Wives," newspaper clipping, [1911], HP; HH, "Cristine," p. 56.
22. HH, "Sydney West"; *VMW*, p. 408; HH to Luhan, Dec. 28, 1940, Luhan Papers.
23. *VMW*, pp. 3–5; [HH], *Lover*, pp. 18–19, 52, 89.
24. CH I to NBH and HH, Mar. 12, no year, HP; WPH to HH, Jan. 7, 1924, HP.

Selected Bibliography

Manuscript Collections

The Hutchins and Neith Boyce Hapgood Papers in the Beinecke Rare Book and Manuscript Library, Yale University, New Haven, Connecticut, were the single most important manuscript collection for this study. Besides the correspondence of Hutchins and Neith, it includes manuscripts of unpublished books and articles and a nice assortment of material about Norman and William Hapgood. While working on a book of family letters, Hutchins and Neith fattened their own holdings by recruiting Hapgood papers in the possession of friends. The Miriam DeWitt Papers, in her possession in Washington, D.C., and the Charles Hapgood Papers, in his possession in Richmond, New Hampshire, were quite useful. Beatrix Faust of Richmond, New Hampshire, has a copy of her grandfather's diary and reminiscences. The Mabel Dodge Luhan and Alfred Stieglitz papers were very good on Hutchins's emotional state, especially after his lapse from regular writing. The Carl Van Vechten Papers had some serviceable items. The Luhan, Stieglitz, and Van Vechten papers are all in the Beinecke Library. The Lincoln Steffens Papers, Columbia University Library, New York, New York, had a few valuable letters as did the Max Eastman Papers, Lilly Library, Indiana University, Bloomington.

Norman Hapgood left no real collection of papers. His daughter, Elizabeth Backman, has in her possession in Royalston, Massachusetts, some of his youthful letters and some incoming correspondence. The Louis D. Brandeis Papers in the School of Law Library, University of Louisville, Louisville, Kentucky, were excellent on Hapgood's leaving *Collier's* and the *Harper's* venture. The A. J. McKelway Papers in the Library of Congress, Washington, D.C., and the Charles R. Crane Papers in the Archive of Russian and East European History and Culture, Columbia University, also contained revealing information about the *Harper's* years. The Theodore Roosevelt Papers and the Woodrow Wilson Papers, both in the Library of Congress, were valuable for

Hapgood's relations with those presidents. The papers of Ray Stannard Baker, Finley Peter Dunne, Mark Sullivan, and William Allen White were of general use. The papers of James R. Garfield, Amos Pinchot, Gifford Pinchot, William Howard Taft, Henry L. Stimson, and the William Kent Family included material on the Ballinger-Pinchot affair. The papers of R. S. Baker, Dunne, Sullivan, White, Garfield, the Pinchots, and Taft are in the Library of Congress; those of Stimson and the Kent Family are in the Sterling Memorial Library, Yale University. The Collier's Weekly Memorandum Book, a separate item in the Library of Congress, was worth examining. The Robert Lansing Papers and the Breckinridge Long Papers in the Library of Congress, the Edward M. House Papers and the Frank L. Polk Papers in the Sterling Library, and the General Records of the Department of State, in the National Archives and Record Service, Washington, D.C., were indispensable to an understanding of Hapgood's diplomatic service in Denmark. The House Papers were also informative about Hapgood in the 1920s and 1930s. The President's Personal File and the Harry Hopkins Papers, in the Franklin D. Roosevelt Library, Hyde Park, New York, included some material about Hapgood's later years.

The papers of S. S. McClure, Samuel M. Ralston, and Upton Sinclair, in the Lilly Library, the George Pierce Baker Papers in the Sterling Library, the papers of Richard Watson Gilder, the Macmillan Company, H. L. Mencken, and Annie Russell, in the New York Public Library, the papers of Minnie Maddern Fiske, Felix Frankfurter, John Purroy Mitchel, and Brand Whitlock, in the Library of Congress, the Ida M. Tarbell Papers in the Reis Memorial Library, Allegheny College, Meadville, Pennsylvania, and the Mark Twain Papers in the General Library, University of California, Berkeley, contained items of interest. The Will Irwin Papers and the Mark Sullivan Papers in the Hoover Institution on War, Revolution and Peace, Stanford University, Stanford, California, contained little relating to Norman Hapgood.

William Hapgood did not leave a separate collection of papers. The Columbia Conserve Company Papers were invaluable for tracing his activities at Columbia. The Powers Hapgood Papers include some items on William Hapgood as well as material relating to the Hapgood family in general. The Arthur F. Bentley Papers contain some of William Hapgood's letters from his later years. The Columbia Conserve Company, Powers Hapgood, and Bentley papers are all in the Lilly Library.

Interviews

Elizabeth Backman, Royalston, Massachusetts, Nov. 29, 1974.
Miriam DeWitt, Washington, D.C., Nov. 4, 1974.
Beatrix Faust, Richmond, New Hampshire, Nov. 18, 1974.
Charles Hapgood, Richmond, New Hampshire, Nov. 18, 1974.

Other Unpublished Material

Roten, Paul. "The Contributions of Harrison Grey Fiske to the American Theater as Editor of the New York Dramatic Mirror." Ph.D. dissertation, University of Michigan, 1962.
Woodbury, Robert Louis. "William Kent: Progressive Gadfly, 1864–1928." Ph.D. dissertation, Yale University, 1967.

Newspapers and Periodicals

Christian Register, 1936–37.
Collier's Weekly, 1900–1913.
Harper's Weekly, 1913–16.
Harvard Monthly, 1888–92.
Hearst's International, 1922–25.
New York American, 1921.
New York Commercial Advertiser, 1897–1902.
New York Globe, 1911–13.

Books and Pamphlets

Addams, Jane. *Newer Ideals of Peace.* New York: Macmillan Co., 1907.
Anderson, Donald F. *William Howard Taft: A Conservative's Conception of the Presidency.* Ithaca: Cornell University Press, 1973.
Anderson, Oscar E., Jr. *The Health of a Nation: Harvey W. Wiley and the Fight for Pure Food.* Chicago: University of Chicago Press for University of Cincinnati Press, 1958.
Archer, Charles. *William Archer: Life, Work, and Friendships.* London: George Allen & Unwin, 1931.
Atherton, Lewis. *Main Street on the Middle Border.* Bloomington: Indiana University Press, 1954.

Selected Bibliography

Baker, Ray Stannard. *American Chronicle: The Autobiography of Ray Stannard Baker.* New York: Charles Scribner's Sons, 1945.

Balderston, C. Canby. *Executive Guidance of Industrial Relations: An Analysis of the Experience of Twenty-Five Companies.* Philadelphia: University of Pennsylvania Press, 1935.

Bannister, Robert C., Jr. *Ray Stannard Baker: The Mind and Thought of a Progressive.* New Haven: Yale University Press, 1966.

Bernheim, Alfred L. *The Business of the Theatre: An Economic History of the American Theatre, 1750–1932.* New York: Benjamin Blom, 1964.

Berthoff, Warner. *The Ferment of Realism: American Literature, 1884–1919.* New York: Free Press, 1965.

Binns, Archie. *Mrs. Fiske and the American Theatre.* New York: Crown Publishers, 1955.

Bogart, Ernest Ludlow, and Charles Manfred Thompson, *The Industrial State, 1870–1893.* The Centennial History of Illinois, edited by Clarence Walworth Alvord, vol. 4. Springfield: Illinois Centennial Commission, 1920.

Bok, Edward. *The Americanization of Edward Bok.* New York: Charles Scribner's Sons, 1920.

Brandeis, Louis D. *Letters of Louis D. Brandeis.* Edited by Melvin I. Urofsky and David W. Levy. 3 vols. Albany: State University of New York Press, 1971–.

———. *Other People's Money and How the Bankers Use It.* New York: Frederick A. Stokes Co., 1914.

Bronson, Walter C. *The History of Brown University, 1764–1914.* Providence: Brown University, 1914.

Brooks, Van Wyck. *The Confident Years, 1885–1914.* New York: E. P. Dutton & Co., 1952.

Brophy, John. *A Miner's Life.* Edited by John O. P. Hall. Madison: University of Wisconsin Press, 1964.

Campbell, Mrs. Patrick. *My Life and Some Letters.* New York: Dodd, Mead & Co., 1922.

Carnes, Cecil. *Jimmy Hare, News Photographer.* New York: Macmillan Co., 1940.

Clapp, Henry Austin. *Reminiscences of a Dramatic Critic, with an Essay on the Art of Henry Irving.* Boston: Houghton Mifflin & Co., 1902.

Crane, Stephen. *The University of Virginia Edition of the Works of Stephen Crane.* Edited by Fredson Bowers. 10 vols. Charlottesville: University Press of Virginia, 1969–75.

Croly, Herbert. *The Promise of American Life.* 1909. Reprint. New York: E. P. Dutton & Co., 1963.

de Kruif, Paul. *The Sweeping Wind: A Memoir.* New York: Harcourt, Brace & World, 1962.

Douglas, Paul H. *The Columbia Conserve Company: A Unique Experiment in Industrial Democracy.* Chicago: University of Chicago Press, 1925.

Dunn, Robert. *World Alive: A Personal Story.* New York: Crown Publishers, 1956.

Eastman, Max. *Enjoyment of Living.* New York: Harper & Brothers, 1948.

Editors of Consumer Reports. *The Medicine Show: Some Plain Truths about Popular Remedies for Common Ailments.* Rev. ed. Mount Vernon, N.Y.: Consumers Union, 1970.

Edstrom, David. *The Testament of Caliban.* New York: Funk & Wagnalls Co., 1937.

Ellis, Elmer. *Mr. Dooley's America: A Life of Finley Peter Dunne.* New York: Alfred A. Knopf, 1941.

Felheim, Marvin. *The Theater of Augustin Daly: An Account of the Late Nineteenth Century American Stage.* Cambridge: Harvard University Press, 1956.

Filler, Louis. *Crusaders for American Liberalism.* New York: Harcourt, Brace & Co., 1939.

Fitch, Clyde. *Clyde Fitch and His Letters.* Edited by Montrose J. Moses and Virginia Gerson. Boston: Little, Brown & Co., 1924.

Frye, Northrop. *A Study of English Romanticism.* New York: Random House, 1968.

Fyles, Franklin. *The Theatre and Its People.* New York: Doubleday, Page & Co., 1900.

Gelb, Arthur and Barbara. *O'Neill.* New York: Harper & Brothers, 1962.

Gelfant, Blanche Houseman. *The American City Novel.* Norman: University of Oklahoma Press, 1954.

Godkin, Edwin Lawrence. *Life and Letters of Edwin Lawrence Godkin.* Edited by Rollo Ogden. 2 vols. New York: Macmillan Co., 1907.

Grover, Edwin Osgood, ed. *Annals of an Era: Percy MacKaye and the MacKaye Family, 1826–1932.* Washington, D.C.: Pioneer Press for Dartmouth College, 1932.

Halpern, Martin. *William Vaughn Moody.* New York: Twayne, 1964.

Hapgood, Hutchins. *An Anarchist Woman.* New York: Duffield & Co., 1909.

———. *The Autobiography of a Thief.* New York: Fox, Duffield & Co., 1903.

———. *Paul Jones.* Boston: Houghton Mifflin & Co., 1901.

Selected Bibliography

———. *The Spirit of Labor.* New York: Duffield & Co., 1907.
———. *The Spirit of the Ghetto: Studies of the Jewish Quarter in New York.* New York: Funk & Wagnalls Co., 1902.
———. *The Spirit of the Ghetto: Studies of the Jewish Quarter in New York.* Rev. ed. New York: Funk & Wagnalls Co., 1909.
[———]. *The Story of a Lover.* New York: Boni & Liveright, 1919.
———. *Types from City Streets.* New York: Funk & Wagnalls, 1910.
———. *A Victorian in the Modern World.* New York: Harcourt, Brace & Co., 1939.
Hapgood, Neith Boyce. *The Bond.* New York: Duffield & Co., 1908.
———. *The Eternal Spring: A Novel.* New York: Fox, Duffield & Co., 1906.
———. *The Forerunner.* New York: Fox, Duffield & Co., 1903.
———. *Harry.* New York: Thomas Seltzer, 1923.
———. *Proud Lady.* New York: Alfred A. Knopf, 1923.
———, and Hutchins Hapgood. *Enemies: A Play.* In *The Provincetown Plays,* edited by George Cram Cook and Frank Shay. Cincinnati: Stewart Kidd Co., 1921.
———, and Hutchins Hapgood. *The Story of an American Family.* N.p., n.d.
Hapgood, Norman. *Abraham Lincoln: The Man of the People.* New York: Macmillan Co., 1899.
———. *The Advancing Hour.* New York: Boni & Liveright, 1920.
———. *The Changing Years: Reminiscences of Norman Hapgood.* New York: Farrar & Rinehart, 1930.
———. *The Columbia Conserve Company and the Committee of Four.* N.p., 1934.
———. *Daniel Webster.* Boston: Small, Maynard & Co., 1899.
———. *George Washington.* New York: Macmillan Co., 1901.
———. *Industry and Progress.* New Haven: Yale University Press, 1911.
———. *The Jewish Commonwealth.* New York: Zionist Organization of America, 1919.
———. *Literary Statesmen and Others: Essays on Men Seen from a Distance.* Chicago: Herbert S. Stone & Co., 1897.
———. *The Stage in America, 1897–1900.* New York: Macmillan Co., 1901.
———. *Why Janet Should Read Shakspere.* New York: Century Co., 1929.
———, and Henry Moskowitz. *Up from the City Streets: Alfred E. Smith, a Biographical Study in Contemporary Politics.* New York: Harcourt, Brace & Co., 1927.
———, ed. *Professional Patriots.* New York: Albert & Charles Boni, 1927.

Hapgood, Warren. *The Hapgood Family: Descendants of Shadrach, 1656–1898*. 2d ed. Boston: By the Author, 1898.
Hapgood, William P. *The Columbia Conserve Company: An Experiment in Workers' Management and Ownership*. N.p., [1934].
———. *An Experiment in Industrial Democracy: The Results of Fifteen Years of Self-Government*. 2d rev. ed. Yellow Springs, Ohio: Antioch Press, 1932.
———. *An Experiment in Industrial Democracy: The Results of Fourteen Years of Self-Government*. N.p., [1931].
———. *An Experiment in Industrial Democracy: The Results of Thirteen Years of Self-Government*. New York: Kirby Page, [1930].
Harrison, John M., and Harry Stein, eds. *Muckraking: Past, Present, and Future*. University Park: Pennsylvania State University Press, 1973.
Hartnoll, Phyllis, ed. *The Oxford Companion to the Theatre*. 3d ed. London: Oxford University Press, 1967.
Hawley, Ellis W. *The New Deal and the Problem of Monopoly: A Study in Economic Ambivalence*. Princeton: Princeton University Press, 1966.
Historical Catalogue of Brown University, 1764–1894. Providence: P. S. Remington & Co., 1895.
History of Madison County, Illinois, Illustrated with Biographical Sketches of Many Prominent Men and Pioneers. Edwardsville, Ill.: W. R. Brink & Co., 1882.
Hodder, Alfred. *A Fight for the City*. New York: Macmillan Co., 1903.
Hofstadter, Richard. *The Age of Reform: From Bryan to F. D. R.* New York: Alfred A. Knopf, 1955.
Holt, Hamilton. *Commercialism and Journalism*. Boston: Houghton Mifflin Co., 1909.
Houghton, Walter E. *The Victorian Frame of Mind, 1830–1870*. New Haven: Yale University Press, 1957.
Howe, Frederic C. *The Confessions of a Reformer*. New York: Charles Scribner's Sons, 1925.
Howe, Mark A. De Wolfe. *A Venture in Remembrance*. Boston: Little, Brown & Co., 1941.
Huneker, James Gibbons. *Steeplejack*. 2 vols. New York: Charles Scribner's Sons, 1920.
In Memoriam: Peter Fenelon Collier. New York: n.p., 1910.
Irwin, Will. *The Making of a Reporter*. New York: G. P. Putnam's Sons, 1942.

———. *Propaganda and the News, or What Makes You Think So?* New York: Whittlesey House, 1936.
Johnson, Alvin. *Pioneer's Progress: An Autobiography.* New York: Viking Press, 1952.
Johnson, Burgess. *As Much as I Dare: A Personal Recollection.* New York: Ives Washburn, 1944.
Jones, Howard Mumford. *Revolution and Romanticism.* Cambridge: Harvard University Press, Belknap Press, 1974.
Kinne, Wisner Payne. *George Pierce Baker and the American Theatre.* Cambridge: Harvard University Press, 1954.
Kolb, Harold H., Jr. *The Illusion of Life: American Realism as a Literary Form.* Charlottesville: University Press of Virginia, 1969.
Kreymborg, Alfred. *Troubadour: An Autobiography.* New York: Boni & Liveright, 1925.
Lamont, Thomas W. *My Boyhood in a Parsonage: Some Brief Sketches of American Life toward the Close of the Last Century.* New York: Harper & Brothers, 1946.
Lasch, Christopher. *The American Liberals and the Russian Revolution.* New York: Columbia University Press, 1962.
———. *The New Radicalism in America, 1889–1963: The Intellectual as a Social Type.* New York: Alfred A. Knopf, 1965.
Lauck, W. Jett. *Political and Industrial Democracy, 1776–1926.* New York: Funk & Wagnalls Co., 1926.
Lewes, George Henry. *On Actors and the Art of Acting.* 1875. Reprint. New York: Greenwood Press, 1968.
Lewinson, Edwin R. *John Purroy Mitchel: The Boy Mayor of New York.* New York: Astra Books, 1965.
Link, Arthur S. *Wilson.* Vol. 2, *The New Freedom.* Princeton: Princeton University Press, 1956.
———. *Wilson.* Vol. 1, *The Road to the White House.* Princeton: Princeton University Press, 1947.
———. *Woodrow Wilson and the Progressive Era, 1910–1917.* New York: Harper & Row, 1954.
Lippmann, Walter. *A Preface to Politics.* 1913. Reprint. New York: Macmillan Co., 1933.
Littlewood, S. R. *Dramatic Criticism.* London: Sir Isaac Pitman & Sons, 1939.
Lodge, Henry Cabot, ed. *Selections from the Correspondence of Theodore Roosevelt and Henry Cabot Lodge.* 2 vols. New York: Charles Scribner's Sons, 1925.

Logan, Andy. *The Man Who Robbed the Robber Barons.* New York: W. W. Norton, 1965.
Lovett, Robert Morss. *All Our Years: The Autobiography of Robert Morss Lovett.* New York: Viking Press, 1948.
Luhan, Mabel Dodge. *Intimate Memories.* Vol. 3, *Movers and Shakers.* New York: Harcourt, Brace & Co., 1936.
Lyon, Peter. *Success Story: The Life and Times of S. S. McClure.* New York: Charles Scribner's Sons, 1963.
McClure, S. S. *My Autobiography.* New York: Frederick Ungar Publishing Co., 1963.
Marsh, Charles W. *Recollections, 1837–1910.* Chicago: Farm Implement News Co., 1910.
Mason, Alpheus Thomas. *Brandeis: A Free Man's Life.* New York: Viking Press, 1946.
May, Henry F. *The End of American Innocence: The First Years of Our Own Time, 1912–1917.* Chicago: Quadrangle Books, 1964.
Mellow, James R. *Charmed Circle: Gertrude Stein and Company.* New York: Praeger Publishers, 1974.
Moody, William Vaughn. *Letters to Harriet.* Edited by Percy MacKaye. Boston: Houghton Mifflin Co., 1935.
———. *Some Letters of William Vaughn Moody.* Edited by Daniel Gregory Mason. New York: AMS Press, 1969.
Moses, Montrose J. *The Life of Heinrich Conried.* New York: Thomas Y. Crowell Co., 1916.
Mott, Frank Luther. *American Journalism: A History, 1690–1960.* 3d ed. New York: Macmillan Co., 1962.
———. *A History of American Magazines.* 4 vols. Cambridge: Harvard University Press, Belknap Press, 1930–38.
Mowry, George E. *The Era of Theodore Roosevelt.* New York: Harper & Brothers, 1958.
———. *Theodore Roosevelt and the Progressive Movement.* Madison: University of Wisconsin Press, 1946.
National Canners Association. *Fourteenth Annual Convention.* N.p., 1921.
Nevins, Allan. *The Evening Post: A Century of Journalism.* New York: Boni & Liveright, 1922.
Nevius, Blake. *Robert Herrick: The Development of a Novelist.* Berkeley and Los Angeles: University of California Press, 1962.
Nicoll, Allardyce. *A History of Late Nineteenth Century Drama, 1850–1900.* 2 vols. Cambridge: At the University Press, 1946.

Selected Bibliography

Norton, W. T., ed. and comp. *Centennial History of Madison County, Illinois, and Its People, 1812 to 1912.* 2 vols. Chicago: Lewis Publishing Co., 1912.
Parry, Albert. *Garrets and Pretenders: A History of Bohemianism in America.* Rev. ed. New York: Dover Publications, 1960.
Penick, James Jr. *Progressive Politics and Conservation: The Ballinger-Pinchot Affair.* Chicago: University of Chicago Press, 1968.
Price, Warren C. *The Literature of Journalism: An Annotated Bibliography.* Minneapolis: University of Minnesota Press, 1959.
Pringle, Henry F. *The Life and Times of William Howard Taft: A Biography.* 2 vols. New York: Farrar & Rinehart, 1939.
Quinn, Arthur Hobson. *A History of American Drama: From the Civil War to the Present Day.* 2 vols. Rev. ed. New York: F. S. Crofts & Co., 1936.
Regier, C. C. *The Era of the Muckrakers.* Chapel Hill: University of North Carolina Press, 1932.
Riis, Jacob. *How the Other Half Lives: Studies among the Tenements of New York.* 1898. Reprint. New York: Hill & Wang, 1957.
———. *Out of Mulberry Street: Stories of Tenement Life in New York City.* New York: Century Co., 1898.
Rischin, Moses. *The Promised City: New York's Jews, 1870–1914.* Rev. ed. New York: Harper & Row, 1970.
Roberts, Mark. *The Tradition of Romantic Morality.* New York: Harper & Row, 1973.
Roosevelt, Theodore. *The Letters of Theodore Roosevelt.* Edited by Elting E. Morison and John M. Blum. 8 vols. Cambridge: Harvard University Press, 1951–54.
———. *The Strenuous Life: Essays and Addresses.* New York: Century Co., 1900.
Russell, Charles Edward. *Bare Hands and Stone Walls: Some Recollections of a Side-Line Reformer.* New York: Charles Scribner's Sons, 1933.
———. *These Shifting Scenes.* New York: Hodder & Stoughton, George H. Doran Co., 1914.
St. John, Bruce. *John Sloan.* New York: Praeger Publishers, 1971.
Sanders, Ronald. *The Downtown Jews: Portraits of an Immigrant Generation.* New York: Harper & Row, 1969.
Sedgwick, Ellery. *The Happy Profession.* Boston: Little, Brown & Co., 1946.
Sheehan, Donald J. *This Was Publishing: A Chronicle of the Book Publishing*

Trade in the Gilded Age. Bloomington: Indiana University Press, 1952.
Sinclair, Upton. *The Brass Check: A Study in American Journalism.* 1919. Reprint. New York: Johnson Reprint, 1970.
Smith, Page. *As a City upon a Hill: The Town in American History.* New York: Alfred A. Knopf, 1966.
Sochen, June. *The New Woman: Feminism in Greenwich Village, 1910–1920.* New York: Quadrangle Books, 1972.
Steffens, Lincoln. *The Autobiography of Lincoln Steffens.* New York: Harcourt, Brace & Co., 1931.
——. *The Letters of Lincoln Steffens.* Edited by Ella Winter and Granville Hicks. 2 vols. New York: Harcourt, Brace & Co., 1938.
Stein, Leo. *Journey into the Self: Being the Letters, Papers, and Journals of Leo Stein.* Edited by Edmund Fuller. New York: Crown Publishers, 1950.
Stone, Melville E. *Fifty Years a Journalist.* Garden City, N.Y.: Doubleday, Page & Co., 1921.
Stott, William. *Documentary Expression and Thirties America.* New York: Oxford University Press, 1973.
Stovall, Floyd, ed. *The Development of American Literary Criticism.* Chapel Hill: University of North Carolina Press, 1955.
Sullivan, Mark. *The Education of an American.* New York: Doubleday, Doran & Co., 1938.
Swanberg, W. A. *Dreiser.* New York: Charles Scribner's Sons, 1965.
Terry, Ellen, and Bernard Shaw. *Ellen Terry and Bernard Shaw: A Correspondence.* Edited by Christopher St. John. New York: Fountain Press, 1931.
Thayer, John Adams. *Astir: A Publisher's Life-Story.* Boston: Small, Maynard & Co., 1910.
Thompson, John M. *Russia, Bolshevism, and the Versailles Peace.* Princeton: Princeton University Press, 1966.
Towne, Charles Hanson. *Adventures in Editing.* New York: D. Appleton & Co., 1926.
Towse, John Ranken. *Sixty Years of the Theater: An Old Critic's Memories.* New York: Funk & Wagnalls Co., 1916.
United States. Congress. Senate. Committee on the Judiciary. *The Nomination of Louis D. Brandeis to Be an Associate Justice of the Supreme Court of the United States. Hearings* before the subcommittee of the Committee on the Judiciary of the United States, 64th Cong., 1st sess., 1916.

———. Department of Labor. Women's Bureau. *Application of Labor Legislation to the Fruit and Vegetable Canning and Preserving Industries.* Bulletin no. 176. Washington, D.C.: Government Printing Office, 1940.

———. Federal Trade Commission. *Report of Federal Trade Commission on Canned Foods.* Washington, D.C.: Government Printing Office, 1918.

Urofsky, Melvin I. *A Mind of One Piece: Brandeis and American Reform.* New York: Charles Scribner's Sons, 1971.

Villard, Oswald Garrison. *Fighting Years: Memoirs of a Liberal Editor.* New York: Harcourt, Brace & Co., 1939.

Warren, Austin. *The New England Conscience.* Ann Arbor: University of Michigan Press, 1966.

Whitlock, Brand. *The Letters and Journal of Brand Whitlock.* Edited by Allan Nevins. 2 vols. New York: D. Appleton-Century Co., 1936.

Wiebe, Robert H. *The Search for Order, 1877–1920.* New York: Hill & Wang, 1967.

Willard, Josiah Flynt. *The Little Brother: A Story of Tramp Life.* New York: Century Co., 1902.

———. *My Life.* New York: Outing Publishing Co., 1908.

———. *Notes of an Itinerant Policeman.* Boston: L. C. Page & Co., 1900.

———. *Tramping with Tramps: Studies and Sketches of Vagabond Life.* New York: Century Co., 1900.

———. *The World of Graft.* New York: McClure, Phillips & Co., 1901.

———, and Alfred Hodder. *The Powers That Prey.* New York: McClure, Phillips & Co., 1900.

Wilson, Harold S. *McClure's Magazine and the Muckrakers.* Princeton: Princeton University Press, 1970.

Winter, William. *The Life of David Belasco.* 2 vols. New York: Moffat, Yard & Co., 1918.

———. *Other Days: Being Chronicles and Memories of the Stage.* New York: Moffat, Yard & Co., 1908.

———. *Vagrant Memories: Being Further Recollections of Other Days.* New York: George H. Doran Co., 1915.

———. *The Wallet of Time: Containing Personal, Biographical, and Critical Reminisence of the American Theatre.* 2 vols. New York: Moffat, Yard & Co., 1913.

Wood, James Playsted. *The Story of Advertising.* New York: Ronald Press Co., 1958.

Young, James Harvey. *The Medical Messiahs: A Social History of Health Quackery in Twentieth-Century America.* Princeton: Princeton University Press, 1967.

Ziff, Larzer. *The American 1890s: Life and Times of a Lost Generation.* New York: Viking Press, 1968.

Articles

Abbot, Willis J. "Chicago Papers and Their Makers." *Review of Reviews* 11 (1895):646–65.

Addams, Jane. "Ethical Survivals in Municipal Corruption." *International Journal of Ethics* 8 (1898):273–91.

Cassedy, James H. "Muckraking and Medicine: Samuel Hopkins Adams." *American Quarterly* 16 (1964):85–99.

"Chronicle and Comment." *Bookman* 7 (1898):273–87; 8 (1898): 89–109; 9 (1899):3–22; 12 (1900):313–33; 18 (1904):465–84; 19 (1904):537–57; 23 (1906):121–33; 25 (1907):113–30.

"A Different Employer: William P. Hapgood." In *Adventurous Americans,* edited by Devere Allen. New York: Farrar & Rinehart, 1932.

"The Dramatic Critic and the Trust." *Independent,* Sept. 30, 1909, pp. 770–71.

Fine, David M. "Abraham Cahan, Stephen Crane, and the Romantic Tenement Tale of the Nineties." *American Studies* 14 (1973):95–107.

Francis, C. M. "The Fighting Magazines." *Bookman* 31 (1910):474–77.

"Fredom of Advertising." *Independent,* Oct. 17, 1907, pp. 951–52.

Gale, Zona. "Editors of the Younger Generation." *Critic* 44 (1904): 318–31.

Gleason, Arthur H. "Norman Hapgood." *American Magazine* 70 (1910): 460–62.

"The Great Theatrical Syndicate: How Six Dictators Control Our Amusements—III." *Leslie's Monthly* 59 (1904):202–10.

Grenier, Judson. "Upton Sinclair and the Press: *The Brass Check* Reconsidered." *Journalism Quarterly* 49 (1972):427–36.

Handlin, Oscar. "American Views of the Jew at the Opening of the Twentieth Century." *Publications of the American Jewish Historical Society* 40 (1951):323–44.

"Hapgood." *Harvey's Weekly,* Jan. 10, 1920, pp. 2–5.

Hapgood, Hutchins. "The Earnestness That Wins Wealth." *World's Work* 6 (1903): 3458–65.

———. "Is Dreiser Anti-Semitic?" *Nation,* Apr. 17, 1935, pp. 436–48.

———. "The New Editor of Harper's Weekly." *Independent*, Nov. 13, 1913, pp. 310–11.
———. "A New Form of Literature." *Bookman* 21 (1905):424–27.
———. "The Reaction against Ibsen." *Harvard Monthly* 13 (1891): 51–57.
———. "The Student as Child." *Harvard Monthly* 15 (1892):11–13.
Hapgood, Norman. "The Actor of To-Day." *Atlantic Monthly* 83 (1899):119–27.
———. "Alfred E. Smith." *Forum* 80 (1928):133–34.
———. "The Drama of Ideas." *Contemporary Review* (London) (1898): 712–23.
———. "Employees See the Balance Sheet *Every Week.*" *Food Industries* 6 (1934):294–96.
———. "The Ethics of Realism." *Harvard Monthly* 8 (1889):102–7.
———. "Foreign Issues in the Presidential Campaign." *American Scholar* 1 (1932):418–22.
———. "Getting at the Truth about Russia." *Independent*, July 3, 1920, p. 12.
———. "Heinrich Conried and What He Stands For." *Outlook*, May 7, 1904, pp. 80–84.
———. "Is Wilson's Dream Coming True?" *Annals of the American Academy of Political and Social Science*, no. 126 (1926), pp. 151–53.
———. "Journalism." In *Every-Day Ethics*. New Haven: Yale University Press, 1910.
———. "Juggling Consciences." *Forum* 77 (1927):185–88.
———. "Love as an Extra." *Harvard Monthly* 11 (1891):176–85.
———. "More Brains, Good Lord." *New Republic*, Sept. 1, 1920, pp. 17–19.
———. "Mr. Gladstone." *Contemporary Review* (London) 74 (1898): 34–53.
———. "Mr. Mallock and the Positivists." *Harvard Monthly* 11 (1890): 59–71.
———. "Mr. Santayana's Poems." *Harvard Monthly* 14 (1894):168–77.
———. "Off Stage." *Delineator* 111 (Oct. 1927), 19.
———. "The Problem Play." In *Recent English Dramatists*. Philadelphia: Press of the Booklover's Library, 1901.
———. "A Programme of Reconstruction." *New Republic*, Nov. 16, 1918, pp. 70–73.
———. "The Reporter and Literature." *Bookman* 5 (1897):119–21.
———. "Robert J. Collier." *American Magazine* 69 (1910):331.
———. "Social Stages." *Harvard Monthly* 13 (1891):73–79.

———. "The Theatrical Syndicate." *International Monthly* 1 (1900): 99–122.
———. "An Unbeliever Goes to Church." *Forum* 90 (1933):285–88.
———. "The Upbuilding of the Theatre." *Atlantic Monthly* 83 (1899): 419–25.
———. "Why I Am a Zionist." *Forum* 78 (1927):71–76.
———. "Why I Shall Vote for La Follette." *New Republic*, Oct. 15, 1924, pp. 168–69.
Hapgood, William P. "Canning." *Survey*, Apr. 1, 1929, pp. 43–45.
———. "The High Adventure of a Cannery." *Survey*, Sept. 1, 1922, p. 655.
"House of Mr. Norman Hapgood." *Architectural Record* 18 (1905):8–13.
Hyde, George Merriam. "Literary Statesmen and Others." *Bookman* 7 (1898):339–41.
"The Independent Has Acquired Harper's Weekly." *Independent*, May 8, 1916, p. 195.
Kittle, William. "Is Your Magazine Progressive?" *La Follette's Weekly*, July 27, 1912, p. 7.
Lippman, Monroe. "The Effect of the Theatrical Syndicate on Theatrical Art in America." *Quarterly Journal of Speech* 26 (1940):275–82.
Littell, Philip. "Norman Hapgood." *New Republic*, Dec. 12, 1914, pp. 13–15.
Lovett, Robert Morss. "Two Intellectuals." *New Republic*, Feb. 11, 1931, pp. 349–52.
———. "The Victorian Set Free." *New Republic*, Oct. 18, 1939, pp. 307–8.
Mason, Daniel Gregory. "At Harvard in the Nineties." *New England Quarterly* 9 (1936):43–70.
Maxwell, Robert S. "A Note on the Muckrakers." *Mid-America* 43 (1961):55–60.
"Minister Hapgood Returns." *Harvey's Weekly*, Dec. 20, 1919, pp. 6–7.
"Mr. Norman Hapgood and 'Collier's Weekly.' " *Outlook*, Nov. 2, 1912, pp. 472–73.
"New York Editors and Daily Papers, by an Insider." *Chautauquan* 27 (1898):56–64.
"The Newspaper and the Theater." *Outlook*, Sept. 4, 1909, pp. 12–13.
Nichols, John E. "Publishers and Drug Advertising: 1933–1938." *Journalism Quarterly* 49 (1972):144–47.
Ogden, Rollo. "Some Aspects of Journalism." *Atlantic Monthly* 98 (1906):12–20.

Selected Bibliography

"Peter Fenelon Collier." *Outlook*, May 8, 1909, p. 56.
Price, W. T. "Critics and Criticism." *Theatre* 1 (Sept. 1901), 12–14.
"A Real Newspaper." *Outlook*, Nov. 23, 1901, pp. 765–66.
Review of Norman Hapgood's *The Stage in America, 1897–1900*. *Nation*, May 16, 1901, pp. 401–2.
Review of Norman Hapgood's *The Stage in America, 1897–1900*. *Theatre* 1 (July 1901):16.
Reviews of Norman Hapgood's *Abraham Lincoln: The Man of the People* and Ida M. Tarbell's *The Life of Abraham Lincoln*. *American Historical Review* 5 (1900):778–82.
Rischin, Moses. "Abraham Cahan and the New York *Commercial Advertiser*: A Study in Acculturation." *Publication of the American Jewish Historical Society* 43 (1953):10–36.
Rowe, Robert R. "Mann of Town Topics." *American Mercury* 8 (1926): 271–80.
"Saunterings." *Town Topics*, Oct. 20, 1904, pp. 3–15.
Saveth, Edward N. "The Problem of American Family History." *American Quarterly* 21 (1969):311–29.
Sedgwick, Ellery. "The Man with the Muck Rake." *American Magazine* 62 (1906):111–12.
"Shall New York Have an Endowed Theatre?" *Theatre* 2 (May 1902), 16–19.
"The Shape of Things." *Nation*, May 8, 1937, pp. 521–23.
Stein, Gertrude. "Men." In *Two: Gertrude Stein and Her Brother and Other Early Portraits*. New Haven: Yale University Press, 1951.
"The Theater and the Critic." *Outlook*, Nov. 2, 1901, pp. 528–29.
Towse, John Ranken. "A Critical Review of Daly's Theater." *Century* 56 (1898):261–64.
Villard, Oswald Garrison. "William Randolph Hearst and His Moral Press." *Nation*, Mar. 28, 1923, pp. 357–61.
"The Week." *New Republic*, Mar. 5, 1930, pp. 55–57.

Index

Adams, Samuel Hopkins, 79, 98, 100, 106
Addams, Jane, 81, 148, 152
Alton, Ill., 1-5, 12, 14, 15
Anarchist Woman, An (Hutchins Hapgood), 141
Archer, William, 41, 42
Arnold, Matthew, 23, 42, 64, 102
Atherton, Lewis, 6
Autobiography of a Thief, The (Hutchins Hapgood), 70, 71

Baker, Ray Stannard, 72, 80, 87, 110, 128, 155, 156
Ballinger-Pinchot affair, 102-5
Ballinger, Richard, 103, 104, 107
Bentley, Arthur F., 27, 159
Berenson, Bernard, 22, 158, 203, 212, 218
Bigelow, Emilie. *See* Hapgood, Emilie Bigelow
Bok, Edward, 78, 96
Booth, Willis, 138
Boyce, Neith. *See* Hapgood, Neith Boyce
Bradley, Robert Harlow, 41
Brandeis, Louis D., 104, 105, 109-10, 112, 115, 126, 130, 138, 150, 168, 171, 176, 186, 188, 192, 212
Brooks, Van Wyck, 57-58
Brophy, John, 177, 180
Bryan, William Jennings, 98, 103, 121
Buckner, Emory R., 130

Cahan, Abraham, 51, 53, 55, 56, 57, 58, 69
Campbell, Mrs. Patrick, 43
Cannon, Joseph, 103, 106
Carlin, Terry, 143
Carpenter, George Rice, 20, 29
Caulfield, Jim, 71
Chase, E. F., 127

Chicago Evening Post, 26, 28, 70, 142
Christensen, Ethyln, 178
Collier, Lucy, 159
Collier, Peter F., 74-75, 85, 88
Collier, Robert J., 73, 75-78, 85, 88, 91, 103, 106, 107, 109, 111-15, 117, 131, 212
Collier's Weekly, 73-81, 83-115, 119
Columbia Conserve Company, 146, 167-80, 182-88
Connors, Chuck, 64, 66
Conried, Heinrich, 37-38
Cowles, John, 199
Crane, Charles R., 103, 125, 128, 130, 131, 133, 193, 212
Crane, Stephen, 66, 145, 150
"Cristine," 164
Croly, Herbert, 81, 152

Dale, Alan, 92
Daly, Augustin, 40, 45
de Kruif, Paul, 191
Deuel, Judge Joseph, 90, 91
Dodge, Cleveland, 125, 126
Dodge, Mabel. *See* Luhan, Mabel Dodge
Donovan, Dan, 178
Donovan, Mary. *See* Hapgood, Mary Donovan
Douglas, Paul, 170, 180, 184
Dreiser, Theodore, 52, 64, 144, 162, 194, 198
Dunne, Finley Peter, 31, 70, 78, 79, 103

Eastman, Max, 157, 201
Edstrom, David, 144-45
Eliot, Charles W., 18, 19, 30, 119
Enemies (Neith Boyce and Hutchins Hapgood), 72, 160, 163-64
Epstein, Jacob, 56

Index

Fads and Fancies, 92
Ferguson, Miss (tutor of Hapgood brothers), 12
Filler, Louis, 60, 89, 97, 131
Fiske, Mrs. *See* Fiske, Minnie Maddern
Fiske, Harrison Grey, 44-45
Fiske, Minnie Maddern, 35, 43, 44, 119
Fitch, Clyde, 43
Flynt, Josiah. *See* Willard, Josiah Flynt
Folk, Joseph, 81, 85
Fyles, Franklin, 41, 45

Gale, Zona, 101
Gaynor, William J., 153
Glavis, Louis, 103, 105
Gleason, Arthur H., 80, 106, 189, 191
Godkin, Edwin L., 29, 30
Griffou Push, 58

Hapgood, Beatrix (daughter of Hutchins and Neith), 155, 198
Hapgood, Boyce (son of Hutchins and Neith), 69, 162
Hapgood, Charles (father of Norman, Hutchins, and William), 1-2, 4-7, 14, 18, 20, 80, 166, 168, 214-15, 216, 221
Hapgood, Charles (son of Hutchins and Neith), 198, 210
Hapgood, Eleanor Page (wife of William), 167, 206, 210
Hapgood, Elizabeth (daughter of Norman and Elizabeth R.), 193
Hapgood, Elizabeth R. (Norman's second wife), 133, 134, 135, 206
Hapgood, Emilie Bigelow (Norman's first wife), 83-84, 93, 132-33, 193, 201, 209
Hapgood, Fanny (mother of Norman, Hutchins, and William), 2, 15, 20, 210
Hapgood, Hutchins: and Bowery, 62-69; and brothers, 208-11; and Columbia Conserve Company, 168, 188; emotional problems of, 8-10, 26, 160-62, 194-98, 218-21; and Griffou Push, 58-62; at Harvard, 18-19, 23-24, 27; and "human documents," 70-72, 144-46; and labor, 141-43; and Neith Boyce Hapgood, 157-60; and *New York Commercial Advertiser,* 28, 50-53, 55; and *New York Globe,* 147-48, 149-55; political views of, 148, 149-53, 214; and *The Spirit of the Ghetto,* 55-58; and *A Victorian in the Modern World,* 200-204.
Hapgood, Mary Donovan (wife of Powers), 177
Hapgood, Miriam (daughter of Hutchins and Neith), 198
Hapgood, Neith Boyce (wife of Hutchins), 31, 53, 69, 72, 74, 155, 157, 162, 196, 204, 210, 218, 220
Hapgood, Norman: and brothers, 10-11, 209-10; and Columbia Conserve Company, 168, 175-76, 179, 188; and *Collier's Weekly,* 73, 78-80, 84-115; and *Harper's Weekly,* 118-32; at Harvard, 18-26; and *Hearst's International,* 190-91; as minister to Denmark, 135-40; and mugwumpery, 80-83; and theater, 32-49; youth of, 2, 7, 10, 11-12, 14
Hapgood, Norman, Jr. (son of Norman and Elizabeth R.), 193
Hapgood, Powers (son of William and Eleanor), 172, 177, 179, 180, 209, 218
Hapgood, Ruth (daughter of Charles and Fanny), 4, 12, 15
Hapgood, Ruth (daughter of Norman and Emilie), 84, 116, 193, 211
Hapgood, Ten Eyck (David) (son of Norman and Elizabeth R.), 62
Hapgood, William Powers: and brothers, 12; early career of, 165-66; and Columbia Conserve Company, 166-80; 182-88, 204-6, 221; at Harvard, 24; political views of, 206, 214; youth of, 4, 7, 11
Harvard Monthly, 21-23, 50, 73
Harvard University, 18-31
Harvey, Col. George, 118, 138
Hearst, William Randolph, 69, 189, 191
Hodder, Alfred, 58-61
Hofstadter, Richard, 52, 81
Holt, Hamilton, 105, 131
Houghton, Walter E., 217
House, Col. Edward, 133

Index

Howe, Frederic C., 29, 80, 152, 199, 200, 201, 203

Ibsen, Henrik, 35
Irving Place Theater, 37-38
Irwin, Will, 189, 191

James, William, 18, 19, 24, 30
Jerome, William Travers, 59, 61, 81, 95
Johannsen, Anton, 142
Johnson, Alvin, 121

Kent, William, 126

Lamont, Thomas W., 22, 118, 131, 155

Lansing, Robert, 130, 136
Laodicean Club, 20-21
Lasch, Christopher, 68, 134, 151, 203-4, 212
Lauck, W. Jett, 184
Lawson, Thomas W., 87, 129
Leslie's Weekly, 118, 134, 138
Link, Arthur S., 109, 119
Lippmann, Walter, 67, 150, 155
Literary Statesmen and Others (Norman Hapgood), 32, 43
Littell, Philip, 19, 20, 121
Little Brother, The (Willard), 60
Littlewood, S. R., 43-44
Lodge, Henry Cabot, 86, 136
Long, Breckinridge, 136
Lovett, Robert Morss, 20, 21, 22, 23, 82, 147, 155, 203
Luhan, Mabel Dodge, 147, 155, 156, 157-60, 169, 194-95, 200, 201, 202, 204, 211, 212, 218, 220

McClure, S. S., 77, 78, 79
MacKaye, Percy, 22, 34, 43
McKelway, A. J., 107, 121, 129
Mann, William d'Alton, 90, 91, 94
Marie (subject of *An Anarchist Woman*), 143
Marquand, John P., 202
Maxwell, Robert S., 132
Mellow, James R., 145
Mermaid Club, 20
Milwaukee Sentinel, 28
Mitchel, John Purroy, 116
Moody, William Vaughn, 20, 22, 43

Moskowitz, Henry, 192, 193
Mott, Frank Luther, 107
Mugwumpery, 24, 81
Myers, Arlie, 178

Nevius, Blake, 24
New York American, 95, 162, 190
New York Commercial Advertiser, 28, 30, 46, 47, 50-51, 61, 69, 74, 212
New York Dramatic Mirror, 45, 46-47
New York Evening Post, 29-30, 147, 161, 189
New York Globe, 162

Ogden, Rollo, 147

Page, Eleanor. *See* Hapgood, Eleanor Page
Patterson, E. C., 111, 112
Pinchot, Gifford, 103
Polk, Frank, 133, 135
Post, C. W., 132
Powers, Fanny Louise. *See* Hapgood, Fanny

Reynolds, Elizabeth Kempley. *See* Hapgood, Elizabeth R.
Riis, Jacob, 57, 66
Rischin, Moses, 56
Rogers, Walter S., 126
Roosevelt, Franklin D., 192, 217
Roosevelt, Theodore, 53, 78, 84-86, 88, 93, 101, 108, 109, 110, 111, 113, 151
Rosenwald, Julius, 125
Rublee, George, 28
Russell, Charles Edward, 29, 56

Sanders, Ronald, 55
Scripps, E. W., 127, 128
Seaman, Major L. L., 88-89
Sedgwick, Ellery, 64, 211
Shaw, George Bernard, 34, 42, 46
Sinclair, Upton, 87-89, 98, 101, 131, 132
Sloan, John, 119, 148
Smith, Alfred E., 121, 192
Spirit of Labor, The (Hutchins Hapgood), 141
Spirit of the Ghetto, The (Hutchins Hapgood), 55-58, 64-65, 70, 146
Stage in America, 1897-1900, The (Norman Hapgood), 33
Steffens, Lincoln, 30, 50, 51, 52, 53, 55,

Index

Steffens, Lincoln *(cont.)*
  57, 61-62, 74, 80, 87, 150, 152, 160, 197, 201, 203, 204, 210, 212
Stein, Gertrude, 145, 201
Stein, Leo, 27, 156, 200, 201, 212, 218
Sterne, Maurice, 145, 200
Stieglitz, Alfred, 194, 195
Story of a Lover, The (Hutchins Hapgood), 156, 160, 162-63, 213
Stott, William, 144
Sullivan, Mark, 77, 79, 93, 96, 99, 100, 103, 105, 106, 109, 111, 113, 128, 211, 212
Syndicate, 39, 44-49

Taft, William Howard, 102-3, 104, 109
Terry, Ellen, 46
Theatrical Trust. *See* Syndicate
Torrence, Ridgely, 84, 200
Townsend, Edward, 66
Town Topics, 86, 89-96
Towse, J. Ranken, 35, 39-40, 41
Twain, Mark, 92

Types from City Streets (Hutchins Hapgood), 63, 69, 141, 144

Vance, Russell E., Jr., 171, 183
Van Vechten, Carl, 68, 155, 203
Victorian in the Modern World, A (Hutchins Hapgood), 8-9, 160, 200-204, 211
Villard, Oswald Garrison, 30, 35, 85, 151, 189

Wheeler, Howard D., 127
White, William Allen, 190
Whitlock, Brand, 154
Why Janet Should Read Shakspere (Norman Hapgood), 50
Wiebe, Robert H., 134
Willard, Josiah Flynt, 58-62, 65, 67, 71, 74, 212
Wilson, Harold, 102
Wilson, Woodrow, 108, 109, 111, 122, 130, 133, 150, 190, 212
Winter, William, 35, 39-40, 41, 46
Wright, H. J., 30, 47, 53

Ziff, Larzer, 51